READING DISABILITY
Developmental Dyslexia

SAMUEL TORREY ORTON, A.M., M.D., D.Sc. (Hon.)
(1879-1948)

READING DISABILITY

Developmental Dyslexia

By

LLOYD J. THOMPSON, A.B., M.D.

Clinical Professor Emeritus of Psychiatry
University of North Carolina
Chapel Hill, North Carolina

With a Foreword by

Richard L. Masland, M.D.

Director, National Institute of Neurological Diseases and Blindness
National Institutes of Health, Public Health Service
U.S. Department of Health, Education, and Welfare
Bethesda, Maryland

CHARLES C THOMAS • PUBLISHER
Springfield · Illinois · U. S. A.

Published and Distributed Throughout the World by
CHARLES C THOMAS · PUBLISHER
BANNERSTONE HOUSE
301-327 East Lawrence Avenue, Springfield, Illinois, U.S.A.
NATCHEZ PLANTATION HOUSE
735 North Atlantic Boulevard, Fort Lauderdale, Florida, U.S.A.

© *1966, by* CHARLES C THOMAS · PUBLISHER
Library of Congress Catalog Card Number: 66-16823

*With THOMAS BOOKS careful attention is given to all details of
manufacturing and design. It is the Publisher's desire to present books
that are satisfactory as to their physical qualities and artistic possibilities
and appropriate for their particular use. THOMAS BOOKS will be true
to those laws of quality that assure a good name and good will.*

Printed in the United States of America
H-2

FOREWORD

IT IS A FUNDAMENTAL TENET in this country that all men are created equal. It is an unfortunate fact that in some quarters this principle is being misconstrued to mean, also, that all children are created identical. Nowhere is the lack of identical endowment of children more clearly evident than in the varied capabilities which they demonstrate when faced with the defined academic requirements of our educational system.

The increasing necessity for the mastery of academic skills for the achievement of an effective role in our present complex society is throwing into prominence the serious difficulties in learning experienced by a disturbingly large proportion of children. Whereas previously it was assumed that all such problems merely reflected a lack of overall intelligence—that is "mental deficiency," or "mental retardation," it is now recognized that in many instances, impairment of learning ability reflects some limited deviation of the intellectual processes. Under these circumstances, an individual whose overall intelligence may be normal or superior may at the same time experience difficulties in the mastery of intellectual tasks apparently requiring the use of some specific perceptual skill or intellectual process. Such an individual may fail to learn when taught according to techniques suitable for the average child, yet learn quite well when given special instruction which bypasses the intellectual block, or builds upon other perceptual or intellectual skills not ordinarily required for the mastery of the task.

A group recently selected to review this problem has suggested the term "minimal brain dysfunction" for this overall group of disorders. They are also referred to as "specific learning disabilities" or less correctly as "brain injured." The developmental dyslexias are an important facet of this overall problem, which also includes other deviations of language, intellect and behavior.

The variety of terms which have been coined for these conditions reflects our lack of knowledge regarding their nature. Some consider

[v]

them manifestations of inherited traits. Others attribute them to subtle defects or injury of brain structure. Still others find psychological factors in home or school to impair or inhibit the learning process. It is not adequately recognized that none of the above-mentioned factors can ever operate in isolation. The individual's performance today reflects the totality of his life experience. It depends upon the inherent genetic endowment of his brain, upon modifications of brain growth by illness or injury, and by the way in which his system has interacted with the emotional and perceptual stimuli to which he has been subjected.

In this book, Dr. Thompson has carefully and impartially reviewed the history of our understanding of developmental dyslexia and the several concepts regarding its causation. He concludes that although in this condition emotional and socioeconomic influences are of importance in learning, and although brain damage may account for difficulties in various aspects of language learning, in the majority of children with reading, spelling and writing disabilities there exists an innate or constitutional predisposition based on hereditary factors.

An acceptance of this thesis is essential if we are to accomplish the next step, namely a precise understanding of the nature of these innate deviations of intellectual performance, and of the instructional techniques which will obviate them. The cause will not be helped by those who are fighting to defend this or that old or new system of reading instruction. It will be helped only by those who recognize and appreciate the vast diversity of intellects, and who will seek to provide for each child the teaching experience which is appropriate to his way of learning.

In this comprehensive review, there is assembled a wealth of knowledge to provide a clear picture of the problem. For parents who have faced the frustration of dealing with such a child, a recognition that such knowledge exists opens up new avenues for effective action. For those who carry the responsibility for the guidance and counseling of children and parents, there is no longer any excuse for failure to recognize and understand the nature of this disability. For those who must plan for the future education of our children, this knowledge provides an essential foundation for the vast and difficult task of providing adequately for the needs of those with developmental dyslexia.

RICHARD L. MASLAND, M.D.

PREFACE

Half the World Can't Read
UNESCO Pamphlet (1958)

THE TERM "READING DISABILITY," as used in the title of this book, pertains to the inability of an individual to acquire skill in reading and spelling that is commensurate with his general level of intelligence. This short definition will be enlarged upon in later discussion, and the more recently adopted scientific term "developmental dyslexia" will be explained.

Reading ability and reading disability are topics of tremendous importance today. Education, the keynote and theme in plans for progress, demands an ability to read. Inability to read is directly related in a causal manner to school dropouts, unemployment, poverty, voting disqualification, juvenile delinquency and crime.

Yet, the problem of reading disability goes unrecognized for what it really is by many specialists in education and even by psychiatrists and psychologists. Unfortunately, quite a few children who have a reading disability are considered to be mental retardates who cannot learn or recalcitrants who will not. Even today—in the midst of our considerable knowledge about language disorders—many "dyslexic" children are treated as they were over half a century ago, when Hinshelwood, a pioneer in this field, said that they were dealt with as imbeciles or "harshly flogged for not trying."

Under the original name "congenital word-blindness," this defect in acquiring skill in reading, spelling and writing was first recognized in 1896. Since then, extensive literature on the topic has been produced, often utilizing other names for the same condition. Authorities now agree that at least one child in ten has, in some degree, a specific language disability in the field of reading, spelling and writing. This estimate does not include children with speech disorders or blindness or those with mental retardation. In other words, one child out of ten who has the intelligence to read does not have the ability to read at a level proportionate to his intelligence.

A large number of excellent studies that concern reading disability have been carried out and books on this topic have been published in several languages—Danish, German, French, Spanish, and English. Many of these publications—excellent though they are for professional personnel—are not readily understood by the layman. For this reason, the writer has undertaken the dual task of presenting the subject in terms that will be helpful to the professional worker and at the same time be within scope of interested laymen.

This book is intended as an "overview" or general summary of our knowledge about specific language disabilities. Speech disorders are definitely a related part of language disturbances, but to include them would carry beyond the intent of this volume. The expression "overview" may be open to challenge because reading disability is a multidisciplinary problem, and one person cannot be a specialist in every facet of its ramifications.

The book starts with an historical review of the literature on language disorders which are the result of brain damage (the story of "aphasia"). Following this is the summary of concepts concerning innate or constitutional factors in reading disability. Because Dr. Samuel T. Orton made outstanding contributions in this field, his story is summarized and the work of his followers is reviewed. The contrasting approach with emphasis on emotional and environmental influences in learning to read, as found in the psychoanalytic literature, is reviewed in considerable detail. Other environmental influences related to social and economic status and to educational methods are discussed.

A chapter giving case histories illustrates the various characteristics of reading disability, especially with reference to clinical findings. This chapter is followed by one which discusses the more recent neurological and neurophysiological studies of cerebral dominance and of genetics as they relate to reading disability. Finally, after summarizing the problem of reading disability, the writer presents his own interpretations, some of which, quite naturally, stem from his viewpoint: that innate or constitutional factors as manifested in a developmental lag are more frequent, more important, but less well recognized, than factors such as brain damage or emotional and environmental influences. He goes on to suggest methods for recognizing those persons with reading disability and to make recommendations for remedying their handicap.

INTRODUCTION

Reading is man's most potent skill. Without reading his world is circumscribed by his neighbors. All he learns is what he picks up in conversation, information garbled in its transmission, delayed by the slow seepage of news through word of mouth.

W. W. CHARTERS (1941)

THE WORLD-WIDE population explosion and the rapidly accelerating technological advances of the last quarter of a century have caused an upheaval in our socioeconomic concepts. There are more and more people to be educated; there are fewer and fewer jobs for the poorly educated. Only those who have an education can hope to survive in our changing world. Those who do not take advantage of the educational opportunities offered to them, or those who are not *able* to, will be left out of the mainstream of human progress.

In the United States it is taken for granted that everyone can read. With education not only available but compulsory for all children, the assumption that everyone who has attended school can read is taken for fact. Yet, there are indications at all levels of our society that this fact, which we accept so readily, may be far from the truth. The truth is that about 11 per cent of the adult population of this country has not learned to read up to the fourth-grade level.

Education depends primarily on communication through spoken or written words. Early in history, education depended largely on verbal communication, but since the invention of the printing press the written word has become a requisite to practically all phases of education. Also, reading the printed or written word enables us to enjoy many of the good things of life, to communicate with each other, and to share the experiences of others through recorded history, scientific records, stories, plays and poetry. Written words may be a source of joy and inspiration just as a painted picture or the score of a symphony may be.

The process of reading involves the capacity to perceive, to recognize symbols, and to integrate them into meaningful sequence. It also

[ix]

involves some capacity for abstract reasoning. Any person who has some dysfunction or developmental lag in reading, emotional block in learning, or is "just a slow reader" is handicapped regardless of his endowment of general intelligence or his abilities in other fields. Reading is so fundamental that it cannot be bypassed without tremendous loss.

Specific Reading Disability (Developmental Dyslexia)[1]

Although the term "specific reading disability" is used, it should be pointed out that disabilities in other fields of language, such as spelling or writing or speech, are usually found along with the reading disturbance. Sometimes speech disorders, sometimes poor spelling, sometimes awkwardness will be the presenting problem rather than an inability to read; but varying constellations of more than one of these specific handicaps will be found if searched for. Very often recognition of any one or any group of these disturbances comes only after a child has manifested behavior, adjustment, or emotional problems. It is possible, too, that he may have been considered a mentally retarded child.

The majority of published studies concerning speech, reading, and other aspects of language dysfunction point out that the poor reader

---

[1] As noted in the Preface, the short and simple expression "reading disability" has been used in the title of this book. In more exact terminology, the word "specific" is placed before "reading disability" to indicate a differentiation from lack of reading that is due to absence of education. Furthermore, it implies that the learning problem is specific to the language area and does not extend into other fields such as science and mathematics. A broader and perhaps better designation— namely, "specific language disability"—often referred to as "S. L. D.," is gaining in favor, but the short expression "reading disability" remains as a convenient term in common usage.

Concerning developmental dyslexia, the word "dyslexia" comes from Greek *dys* + *lexis*. *Dys* means hard, bad or difficult; *lexis* pertains to words or to the vocabulary of a language as distinguished from its grammar. "Dyslexia," then, is the ideal word to describe specific reading disability, but it was used in the earlier descriptions of language disturbances to apply to reading disturbances due to organic brain pathology. However, when the qualifying word "developmental" is used, we rule out brain injury and bring in the concept of developmental lag. Therefore, "developmental dyslexia" is the best term for the language disability dealt with in this book. In the text, "specific reading disability," "innate dyslexia," "strephosymbolia," and even "word-blindness" will appear in context with the immediate topic under discussion but as synonyms for "developmental dyslexia."

is usually a poor speller, is often an atrocious handwriter (unless he prints), is inclined to be awkward, shows some evidence of confused or unestablished dominance, and may have some form of speech disorder. Various combinations of these dysfunctions are found too often to be considered mere happenstance.

Practically all persons with any combination of the above-mentioned disabilities will have emotional problems which seem to be related to the handicap. Many of these emotional problems may be the direct result of the disability, but some may be caused by extraneous factors which, in turn, augment the language dysfunction. It seems evident that the specific reading disability may become the focus for anxiety and hostility that arise from other sources. At the same time, the disability itself is creating discouragement, feelings of inferiority, loss of motivation, anxiety and hostility.

In fact, some well-trained professional people in the field of education are prone to recognize only environmental causation. Even some psychiatrists specializing in child psychiatry say, "Yes, we see reading disability frequently, but it is all emotional." Some professional people maintain that reading disability is entirely a matter of motivation, stimulation from the outside, or the result of faulty teaching methods. Others claim that reading difficulty has no relation to spelling, writing, or speech deficiencies and certainly not to lateral dominance. To still others it is an all or none proposition with no shades of gray between the extremes—you read or you don't read; you spell or you don't spell; you are right-handed or you are left-handed.

On numerous occasions, the writer has mentioned the problem of reading disability in the presence of well-educated people only to be met with negative statements such as, "Why, anyone can learn to read if he only tries," or "Only the feebleminded can't read." When the analogy of reading disability to color-blindness, tone-deafness, or physical awkwardness is brought up, these same people shrug their shoulders and say, "Well, that's different."

Except for language disturbances caused by brain damage, it appears from the writer's studies and experience that there are innate or constitutional factors underlying a majority of language disabilities, and that only infrequently can emotional and environmental factors be considered the one and only primary or fundamental cause. In this simple statement, the writer reveals his stand—bias, if such it is—and admits that one of the main purposes in writing this book is to call attention to the often-overlooked or denied existence of original endowment, which manifests itself as a developmental lag in language facilities.

The writer also believes that this is not a defeatist or nihilistic point of view. On the contrary, with early recognition of the problem and with specialized help, the lag can be corrected in large measure in the majority of instances. The writer is also optimistic because some children—even without specialized help—as they grow older and more mature in other ways, find avenues that circumvent their specific disability and become fairly adequate in reading.[2] In fact, the developmental or maturational lag in language may catch up appreciably with other abilities as the individual grows older, but there is ample evidence that rarely does it catch up entirely.

Prevalence of Reading Disability

Numerous estimates have been made of the prevalence of language disabilities. Obviously, estimates depend on the criteria that are used. One investigator, for example, will classify dyslexia with illiteracy, although it is obvious that all illiterates do not have a specific reading disability. Some illiteracy is due simply to lack of education. Another investigator may state that a child two or more years retarded in reading has a reading disability without mentioning his I. Q. and other factors. The dyslexic child may be illiterate because he did not go to school, or he may be two or more years retarded in his reading; but he should show additional earmarks of dyslexia before he is classified as a dyslexic. He should manifest the other characteristics that accompany specific reading disability: the hesitant, stilted and stum-

---

[2]Anna Gillingham (1952), an expert in the field of remedial reading and spelling, said: "Acute students of biography have told us that great men often make their greatest contribution to human affairs, to art, to scholarship, along the line of some great handicap of their own early life. More than one of my difficult readers has later manifested a real flair for English expression."

The writer has collected evidence which shows that men of eminence, such as Thomas Edison, Harvey Cushing, Auguste Rodin, Woodrow Wilson, and others, had some degree of language disability in their earlier years of life.

bling manner of reading orally, reversal of letters and words, peculiarities of spelling, and familial incidence of language disturbance.

Before turning to the incidence of reading disability, it must be noted that about 3 per cent of all school children are mentally retarded and, consequently, are retarded in reading as in all other school subjects. However, a few mentally retarded children have, in addition to their general backwardness, a special disability in reading. Using the Durrell Analysis of Reading Difficulty, Daly and Lee (1960) studied seventy-seven mentally retarded subjects with mental ages ranging from 6 years-1 month to 12 years-7 months but with chronoligical ages ranging from 10 years-2 months to 18 years-6 months. They found that 48 per cent of the boys and 30 per cent of the girls were reading at a level below their general capacity.

In the estimates of specific reading disability that follow, the majority of investigators have excluded the mentally retarded children. Their figures refer to children with average or above-average general ability.

Orton (1926) originally estimated that 4 per cent of school children have specific reading disability, but later he raised this figure to about 10 per cent.

Marion Monroe (1932), a pioneer in remedial reading, in her book, *Children Who Cannot Read,* stated categorically that 12 per cent of the total school population have reading retardation.

Gray (1939) said: "Records of the achievements of pupils show that 20 to 30 per cent of the pupils who enter either junior or senior high school read so poorly that they can engage in required reading activities only with great difficulty."

Hallgren (1950), reporting his studies in Sweden, calculated that 10 per cent of the population have a definite degree of reading disability. Hermann (1955), reporting his studies in Denmark, likewise estimated the incidence at about 10 per cent.

Fabian (1955) defined reading disability as more than 25 per cent deviation from the norm and found such in 10 per cent of the children in several second grades. Ninety-five per cent of these children with reading disability were boys.[3]

---

[3]With reading, as with speech disturbances, the males outnumber the females to a startling degree. Orton said four to one; Rabinovitch said ten to one; Cole said seven or eight boys out of ten children. Other investigators substantiate the marked prevalence among males.

Witty (1956) recorded that "a study of 7,380 graduates from the eighth grade in one large city showed that 2,169 were reading at or below the sixth grade level." These figures indicate that almost one-third of these graduates were retarded in reading.

Rabinovitch (1959) said: "Probably 10 per cent of children of average intelligence in our American schools are reading so inadequately for their grade placement that their total adjustment is impaired."

Walcutt (1961) stated: "In the official jargon, this 'congenital' inadequacy is known as 'specific reading disability,' and it is suffered by anywhere from 20 to 35 per cent of our young people."

Lippman (1962), in his book on child psychiatry, started the chapter on reading disability with this statement: "The problem of reading disability is so frequent (affecting 10 to 15 per cent of school children) . . ."

Saunders (1962) stated: "The present president of the Orton Society, Mrs. Sally B. Childs, in a personal communication, estimated

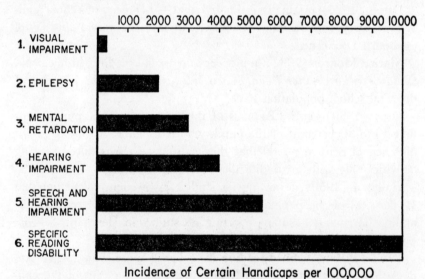

Incidence of Certain Handicaps per 100,000
School Age Children (5-17 Years of Age).

FIGURE 1.

FIGURE 1. Sources of Information. 1. *Visual Impairment.* The National Society for the Prevention of Blindness, Inc. estimated that in 1963 there were 107,000 partially-seeing children in the 5-19 age group. In 1962, their estimate for the number of blind children in the same age group was 36,230. The total figure,

142,230 is almost exactly 0.3 per cent of the number of school-age children (5-17) according to the Bureau of the Census figures for 1963. Account must be taken of the fact that very few blind children are enrolled in public schools. (This estimate and those that follow have been corroborated by the National Institute for Neurological Diseases and Blindness.)

2. *Epilepsy.* The Epilepsy Foundation (1964), with reference to incidence stated, "One out of every 100. Among children, the estimate is one out of 50." This is 2 per cent for all children, including those of preschool age where the incidence of convulsive disorders is high.

3. *Mental Retardation.* At the American Medical Association Conference on Mental Retardation held in April 1964, it was agreed that 3 per cent prevalence of mental retardation might hold for school-age children, but that the over-all prevalence would be lower. This estimate of 3 per cent was adhered to in their *Mental Retardation Handbook.* (See *JAMA,* Vol. 191, No. 3, Jan. 18, 1965). The 3 per cent figure closely matches the estimate of the President's Committee on Mental Retardation. (Attention is called to the fact that not infrequently children with specific language disability are erroneously classified among the mentally retarded.)

4. *Hearing Impairment.* The American Hearing Society (National Federation of Hearing and Speech Services), in a personal letter dated March 24, 1965, stated, "In general the number of hard of hearing school children is calculated to be 1-½ million." This figure is 3 per cent of school-age children, and it does not include the totally deaf who would not be enrolled in public schools. According to the NINDB this figure seems too low, and they refer to an unpublished report which "suggests that a closer approximation of the number of hard of hearing school-age children would be 5 per cent." A middle ground estimate of 4 per cent has been used in the figure.

5. *Speech and Hearing Impairment.* The American Speech and Hearing Association in a statement issued in October 1964 said, "More than 2½ million school children have speech and hearing problems." This number is 5 per cent of the school-age population according to the Bureau of the Census figures for 1964. In answer to a request for individual figures on the two impairments, the NINDB replied, "Because the two defects 'hard of hearing,' and 'speech and hearing' frequently occur in combination, it is difficult, statistically, to separate these categories of impairments. However, the figure 5.4 per cent is considered a conservative estimate. . . ."

6. *Specific Reading Disability.* The majority of authorities in the field of specific reading disability (developmental dyslexia) agree that about 10 per cent of school children have this handicap in some degree. The NINDB, after mentioning that reading disability may be related to a number of factors affecting large numbers of children, stated, "On the basis of various estimates from information in this country and abroad, the prevalence of all forms of reading disability has been placed at 150 per 1,000 or 15 per cent. However, with respect to the category commonly called specific dyslexia, 10 per cent is probably a reasonable estimate."

that, irrespective of etiology, 20 to 30 per cent of today's school population is retarded in reading."

Newbrough and Kelly (1962) reported on sixth-grade reading scores of 3,946 students as follows: 14 per cent were low, i.e., at or below grade 4.I; 78 per cent were at-grade, i.e., 4.I to 8.I; and 5 per cent were high, 8.I or above.

In the Report of the Regents Conference on Improving Reading at the University of the State of New York in 1962, it was recorded that 35 per cent of all American youths are seriously retarded in reading.

Critchley (1964) said: "Although Hermann's figure of 10% of dyslexics among Danish school-children tallies exactly with Sinclair's survey of primary schools in Edinburgh, I should judge this figure as almost certainly too high for England." However, he went on to say: "At the same time the problem is grave enough and sufficiently important to justify official recognition. Facilities should be made for the early recognition of dyslexics, followed by opportunities for these children to receive individual, sympathetic, and intensive tuition, either in special classes or in special schools, residential or otherwise."

The increase in the estimated incidence of specific reading disability from the low of 4 per cent, as given by Orton in 1926, to the several recent estimates of over 10 per cent is probably due to an increased awareness of the problem rather than to any decline in children's ability, or methods of teaching, or other alleged causes. The apparent increase in the incidence of reading disability parallels the apparent increase in the incidence of other ailments, such as mental disorders, which have been brought to light by better diagnostic methods and acumen.

On the basis of accumulated studies, it appears that approximately 10 per cent of school children in the United States have developmental dyslexia in some degree. The incidence of developmental dyslexia, as compared with other childhood handicaps, is shown in Figure 1.

Classification of Reading Disability

There can be no doubt that disturbances in speech, reading, writing and other language functions are produced directly by organic brain pathology. The various forms of aphasia that follow a cerebral accident (a stroke), a head injury, an infection of the brain, or a brain tumor are examples of acquired language defects. Nor can there be any doubt that in certain instances emotional blocking or inhibition can cause language disturbances. In addition, there is well-documented evidence which shows that language disability can be attributed to innate or constitutional factors.

Thus, we come to a causal classification of language disturbances that has been formulated by other writers. The causes fall into three categories:

1. Acquired organic damage in the central nervous system;
2. Emotional, environmental, or psychological disturbances;
3. Innate or constitutional factors.[4]

The expression "specific reading disability" or "developmental dyslexia" refers to the third category. Not infrequently, of course, there may be an overlapping or blending of all three of these causal groupings. In addition, there remains a "no man's land" within the area of normal physiological variation, where it is suspected that one or more of these causative fields may be contributory. As Winston Churchill once said, "Nature seldom draws a line without smudging it."

Unrecognized Problem

In spite of the high incidence of specific reading disability, both laymen and those in profesional fields—such as medicine, education, social work and psychology—have a "blind spot" in recognizing the condition in children. Many parents who have a dyslexic child realize that something is wrong with the child, but often they are unaware of the existence of developmental dyslexia. As for the professionals who should be fully informed, many of them seem to resist recognizing dyslexia when they are confronted with dyslexic children in doctors' offices, in classrooms, in clinics.

---

[4] The word "innate" means inborn, natural, not acquired. Innate qualities or characteristics are part of one's constitution and implicate heredity. Hereditary factors have been shown to exist in developmental dyslexia. Early writers used the word "congenital." Congenital means born with, existing or dating from birth. In common usage, congenital has come to mean a defect acquired during development of the fetus in the womb as distinguished from an heredity defect or one transmitted by the germ plasm.

In textbooks and monographs that deal with problem or exceptional children, the attention and approach to developmental dyslexia are extremely variable. Some authors of recent books do not mention such a handicap but write extensively on exceptionalities such as mental retardation, speech defects, birth injuries, impaired hearing or vision, the emotionally disturbed child and even the gifted child. Certain community surveys concerned with problem children have discussed in detail all the conditions mentioned above without one word about reading disability.

The standard textbook on psychiatry by Noyes, which has been used in the majority of medical schools over the past three decades, did not discuss developmental dyslexia until the last two editions. The sixth edition in 1963 gives a short but succinct statement about developmental dyslexia:

> Another type of conduct [sic] disturbance occurs in children who have learning disturbances at school. As Levy has recently pointed out, the motivational explanation for the conduct disturbances is inappropriate in such instances. The motivational problem is secondary; the primary issue is the capacity of the child to learn. At the present time approximately 12% of all children in the United States fail to learn as well as the average. Although these children have better than normal intelligence and their social and vocabulary development is excellent, as well as their vision, they suffer from dyslexia, occasionally, but not always, associated with left-handedness and with difficulty in converting to right-handed writing. . . . Many conduct disabilities founded on such a basis disappear rapidly with improvement in the reading. Here, the use of a remedial teacher is often the effective technique to bring about a satisfactory modification of the behavior disturbance.

ACKNOWLEDGMENTS

THE AUTHOR'S FRIENDSHIP with Dr. and Mrs. Samuel T. Orton, which dates back to 1920, inspired the writing of this book. Clinical work with Mrs. Orton since 1950 has enhanced the writer's interest in the field of language disturbances. The author acknowledges his debt to Roger Saunders and Lucia Karnes for their sustained encouragement in this undertaking.

The author also acknowledges an indirect debt to other colleagues. Several of them have steadfastly insisted that reading disability is entirely an emotional problem or a product of the environment unless outspoken brain damage can be demonstrated. The stand they have taken—which excludes innate and constitutional factors in reading disability—prompts him to present other sides of the topic.

Finally, the author records his appreciation of the excellent editorial assistance given by Mrs. Geraldine Foster. She has acted as the "touchstone" between scientific phraseology and the expression of ideas in good, readable English. In fact, she has become an expert not only in the "remedial reading" of this manuscript but in her total understanding of language disorders.

COPYRIGHT PERMISSIONS

Permission has been obtained from both the publishers and the authors (if alive) to use the exact quotations from copy-righted publications where the reproduction has been at all detailed. Rather than cite each instance in the text, the acknowledgments of permission have been grouped as follows:

W. B. Saunders Company, Philadelphia, Pennsylvania:
> NOYES, A. P., AND KOLB, L. C.: *Modern Clinical Psychiatry*. 6th Edition, 1963, p. 492.

American Medical Association, Chicago, Illinois:
> ORTON, S. T.: Neuropathology I. *Archives of Neurology and Psychiatry*, *15*:763-775, 1925.
> ORTON, S. T.: Neuropathology II. *Archives of Neurology and Psychiatry*, *16*:451-470, 1925.

KINSBOURNE, M., AND WARRINGTON, E. K.: The developmental Gerstmann syndrome. *Archives of Neurology*, 8:490-502, 1963.

School and Society, New York, New York:

ORTON, S. T.: An impediment to learning to read—a neurological explanation of the reading disability. Vol. XXVIII, No. 715. September 1928.

Association for Research in Nervous and Mental Disease, Inc., New York, New York:

ORTON, S. T.: Some studies in language function. In: *Localization of .Function in the Cerebral Cortex.* Baltimore, The Williams & Wilkins Co., 1934, pp. 614-633.

International Universities Press, New York, New York:

FREUD, SIGMUND: *On Aphasia*, 1891. Translation by E. Stengel, 1953.

KLEIN, E.: Psychoanalytic aspects of school problems. In: *The Psychoanalytic Study of the Child*, Vol. III-IV, 1949, pp. 369-390.

ROSEN, V. H.: Strephosymbolia: an intrasystemic disturbance of the synthetic function of the ego. In: *The Psychoanalytic Study of the Child*, Vol. X, 1955, pp. 83-99.

JARVIS, V.: Clinical observations of the visual problem in reading disability. In: *The Psychoanalytic Study of the Child*, Vol. XIII, 1958, pp. 451-470.

DORIS, J., AND SOLNIT, A. J.: Treatment of children with brain damage and associated school problems. *Journal of American Academy of Child Psychiatry*, 2:618-635, 1963.

W. W. Norton & Company, Inc., New York, New York:

ORTON, S. T.: *Reading, Writing and Speech Problems in Children.* 1937. (Renewal of copyright by June L. Orton in 1964.)

PEARSON, G. H. J., AND ENGLISH, O. S.: *Common Neuroses of Children and Adults.* 1937.

PEARSON, G. H. J.: *Psychoanalysis and the Education of the Child.* 1954.

Grune & Stratton, Inc., New York, New York:

BENDER, LAURETTA: Problems in conceptualization and communication in children with developmental dyslexia. In: *Psychopathology of Communication*, edited by Hoch and Zubin. 1958, pp. 155-167.

Appleton-Century-Crofts, New York, New York:

GALLAGHER, J. R.: *Medical Care of the Adolescent*, Second Edition, 1966, pp. 122-123.

The Psychoanalytic Quarterly, New York, New York:

MAHLER, M. S.: Pseudoimbecility: A magic cap of invisibility. *11*:149-164, 1942.

The American Orthopsychiatric Association, Inc., New York, New York (as published in the *American Journal of Orthopsychiatry*):

SILVERMAN, J. S., FITE, M. W., AND MOSHER, M. M.: Learning problems 1. Clinical findings in reading disability children—special cases of intellectual inhibition. *29*:298-314, 1959.

RUBENSTEIN, B. O., FALICK, M. L., AND LEVITT, M.: Learning problems 2. Learning impotence: A suggested diagnostic category. *29*:315-323, 1959.

ACKNOWLEDGMENTS

SPERRY, B. M., STAVER, N., REINER, B. S., AND ULRICH, D.: Renunciation and denial in learning difficulties. 28:98-111, 1958.

PRENTICE, N. M., AND SPERRY, B. M.: Therapeutically oriented tutoring of children with primary neurotic learning inhibitions. 35:521-531, 1965.

GRUNEBAUM, M. G., HURWITZ, I., PRENTICE, N. M., AND SPERRY, B. M.: Fathers of sons with primary neurotic learning inhibitions. 32:462-472, 1962.

Harvard University Press as Publisher for the Harvard University Graduate School of Education, Cambridge, Massachusetts:

AUSTIN, M. C.: *The Torchlighters: Tomorrow's Teachers of Reading.* 1961.

Hoeber Medical Division, Harper & Row, Publishers, Inc., New York, New York:

NIELSEN, J. M.: *Agnosia, Apraxia, Aphasia. Their Value in Cerebral Localization.* 1946.

British Medical Journal, London, England:

X (Anonymous): Experiences of a sufferer from word-blindness. *British Journal of Ophthalmology.* 20:73-76, 1936.

Bulletin of the Menninger Clinic, Topeka, Kansas:

MURPHY, L. B.: Psychoanalysis and child development. 21:177-188, 1957.

Cambridge University Press, American Branch, New York, New York:

WILLMER, E. N.: *Retinal Structural and Colour Vision.* 1946.

Little, Brown and Company, Boston, Massachusetts:

From *Cradles of Eminence* by Victor and Mildred G. Goertzel. Copyright © 1962 by Victor and Mildred Goerttzel. Reprinted by permission of Little, Brown and Company, publishers.

Hogarth Press, Ltd., London, England:

To Sigmund Freud Copyrights Ltd., Mr. James Strachey and The Hogarth Press Ltd. to quote from "Three Essays on Sexuality" and "The Psychoanalytic View of Psychogenic Disturbances of Vision" from Volumes VII (1901-1905) and XI (1910) of the Standard Edition of the *Complete Psychological Works of Sigmund Freud.*

Basic Books, Inc., Publishers, New York, New York:

From "Reading and Learning Disabilities," by Ralph D. Rabinovitch, Chapter 43 of *American Handbook of Psychiatry,* edited by Silvano Arieti, © 1959 by Basic Books, Inc., Publishers, New York.

From *Three Essays on the Theory of Sexuality* by Sigmund Freud, Basic Books, Inc., Publishers, New York, 1962.

From the *Collected Papers of Sigmund Freud,* Basic Books, Inc., Publishers, New York, 1959. (Title of Chapter IX of the *Collected Papers,* "Psychogenic Visual Disturbance according to Psycho-Analytic Conceptions.")

Butterworths, Washington, D.C., and London, England:

Brain, W. R.: *Speech Disorders,* Second Edition. 1965.

Charles C Thomas, Publisher, Springfield, Illinois:

HERMANN, K.: *Reading Disability.* 1959.

CRITCHLEY, M.: *Developmental Dyslexia.* 1964.

L.J.T.

CONTENTS

READING DISABILITY
Developmental Dyslexia

Chapter I

APHASIA: HISTORICAL BACKGROUND

Aphasia simply reproduces a state which existed in the course of the normal process of learning to speak and read.

SIGMUND FREUD (1891)

As a background for the understanding of all language disturbances, it is necessary to review the literature on aphasia. Literally, the word "aphasia" refers only to the speech aspects of language. It comes from the Greek word *phanai,* which means "to speak." The prefix "a" means "not;" therefore, the entire word means "not to speak." However, the term "aphasia" has come to be used quite loosely to denote almost any kind of language disorder but with the implication that the disturbance is due to some acquired brain damage.

Among the numerous subdivisions or types of aphasia, we find the words "alexia" (not to read) and "dyslexia" (difficult reading). Again, the use of these words as a type or symptom of aphasia usually implies brain damage. However, as stated in the Introduction, when the qualifying word "developmental" is used, we rule out brain injury and bring in the concept of developmental lag.

Critchley (1964) in his monograph *Developmental Dyslexia* said: "The current neurological conception of a specific and constitutional type of difficulty in learning to interpret printed symbols, took origin from a background of acquired brain disease, out of a process of analogy." By analogy Critchley meant that the symptoms in developmental dyslexia parallel to a large extent those found in cases of acquired brain damage. It was also on the basis of neuropathology that Orton, an outstanding authority, derived by analogy his valuable concepts concerning specific reading disability or "strephosymbolia," as he called the condition.

Historically, too, the greater part of the literature on language dysfunctions from the earliest recordings to the end of the nineteenth century was concerned almost entirely with brain pathology. The

[3]

emphasis was on speech disturbances with little consideration given to reading disturbances.[1]

Early Sporadic Reports

Case reports on aphasia were recorded before the time of Hippocrates (400 B.C.). Critchley (1959) stated that reports on traumatic aphasia were recorded some 2500 to 3000 years before Christ. Hippocrates, maintaining that the brain was the organ of the body with which men thought, pointed out that injury to one side of the brain produced paralysis in the opposite side of the body. He found that loss of speech sometimes accompanied such paralysis. Aristotle also wrote about what we would now call dysphasia (disturbed speech).

Benton and Joynt (1960), who reviewed the literature on aphasia from the time of Hippocrates to 1800, said that most of the clinical forms of motor aphasia (speech disorders) had been described before 1800, but that *sensory* aphasia (reading and hearing disorders) had not been recognized as a specific entity. Until the nineteenth century aphasia was attributed to brain injury or disease, but there was little speculation about the exact locus in the brain. The disorder was roughly assigned to one side of the brain or the other. There was some speculation, however, that the basic psychopathology of aphasic disorders was an interruption in the connections between images or ideas and their linguistic signs. For example, Benton and Joynt cited Trousseau's *Clinique Médicale* in which a quotation from Pliney (A.D. 23-79) was given to illustrate that the "physiological conditions of aphasia" were not unknown in antiquity:

> And yet there is not a thing in man so fraile and brittle againe as it [memory], whether it be occasioned by disease, by casual injuries and occurrents, or by feare, through which it faileth sometime in part, and otherwhiles decaieth generally and is cleane lost. One with the stroke of a stone, fell presently to forget his letters onely, and could read no more; otherwise his memory served him well enough.

---

[1]Comprehensive and critical reviews of the literature on aphasia have been published recently by Critchley, Benton and Joynt, Penfield and Roberts, and other students of the topic. Much of the historical material that follows has been drawn from these sources with special emphasis on or attention to reading rather than speaking.

According to Critchley, "The writings of St. Teresa (1515-1583) here and there show traces of an inability to comprehend written and printed symbols, or what we would nowadays be tempted to regard as dyslexia." Also, according to Critchley, in 1673 Patrick Blair described the case of a man who, suffering from apoplexy, lost the power of reading though not of writing.

Critchley and others called attention to a case report by Johann Schmidt published in 1676 under the title, "Loss of Reading Ability following Apoplexy with Preservation of Writing." In describing the afflictions of a sixty-five-year-old man with apoplexy and epilepsy, Schmidt said:

> A final evil remained to be overcome. He could not read written characters, much less combine them in any way. He did not know a single letter nor could he distinguish one from another. But it is remarkable that, if some name were given to him to be written, he could write it readily spelling it correctly. However, he could not read what he had written even though it was in his own hand. Nor could he distinguish or identify the characters.

In the early literature the writings of a French physician, Jacques Lordat (1773-1870), were important. In 1843, he described his own inability to read after he had suffered what he called a "cerebral accident." He was an eminent teacher of medicine at the Medical School of Montpellier and about fifty-two years of age when his illness occurred. He first noticed his inability to express his thoughts in speech. When he turned to reading for solace, he found that his reading ability had also disappeared. In describing his condition, he wrote: "Syntax had disappeared along with words: the alphabet alone remained, but the junction of letters to form words was a study I would have to undertake." He could not read what he himself had written. It is quite clear that he recognized and recorded the symptoms of sensory aphasia and reading disability, although he did not use such terms. Instead he said, "To this disease I have given the name verbal amnesia." Lordat's ability to read (and write) returned to him before the speaking difficulty disappeared. Apparently, there was good recovery of all language faculties because Lordat continued to teach for many years and lived to his ninety-eighth birthday.

Because his medical knowledge enhanced his ability to describe objectively his own experience of aphasic disorder, Lordat made a significant contribution to the understanding of aphasia. This is borne out by the fact that many subsequent writers have used the term *amnésie verbale* of Lordat when referring to reading disturbances.

From the time of the earliest recordings through the first half of the nineteenth century, studies and case reports concerning aphasia had been sporadic and intermittent; they seemed to elicit no steady attention from the medical profession.

Broca's Era

It was not until a little over a hundred years ago, in 1861, that Paul Broca started his investigations which were to form the ground-work for the modern study of language disorders in their various manifestations.[2] Broca, a French surgeon and anatomist, focused his attention on speech disorders, and reading disturbances were not re-ferred to in his first two reports. He seemed to be interested mainly in establishing proof of a center for articulate speech in the left third frontal convolution of the brain. Penfield and Roberts (1959) in their book *Speech and Brain-Mechanisms* stated that after Hippo-crates there was no serious consideration of subdivisions of functional areas within the brain until 1861, when Broca pointed out that there was an area in the brain especially devoted to speech.

Broca wrote about a patient who had lost the power of speech without other serious defect. At autopsy, a restricted lesion in the region of the left third frontal convolution of the brain was found. Broca claimed that this area is the speech center of the brain. Ac-cording to Penfield and Roberts, Broca used the term *alogie* to denote loss of ideas, while he used *amnésie verbale* of Lordat to apply to loss of conventional connections between idea and word. Patients who suffered from this disorder used words which had no connection with the objects seen. These patients still had memory as they recognized objects, places and persons by gesturing or pointing, but they had forgotten the special memory of the spoken and written words that

---

[2]Attention is called to a paper written in 1836 by Marc Dax of France; in this paper Dax claimed that speech dominance was in the left hemisphere. This paper was not published until 1865, when Dax's son brought it out after Broca had stim-ulated interest in the topic.

applied to these objects and places. Broca used the term *aphémie* for the condition in which a patient was unable to speak the word appropriate to a given object.[3]

Broca's publications attracted the interest and attention of physicians in France and other countries. Almost immediately several investigators—Bastian, Kussmaul, Charcot, Pierre Marie, Wernicke, Jackson, Trousseau and others—began to study language disorders and to publish the results of their findings.

Bastian began writing on aphasia in 1869. According to Penfield and Roberts, Bastian was the first to describe word-deafness and word-blindness. Although he did not use the term word-deafness, he pointed out that a person suffering from this disorder could hear well, but could not recognize spoken words correctly. Neither did he use the term word-blindness in describing a person who had normal vision, but was unable to recognize written words. Bastian maintained that these defects were localized in Broca's area of the brain. In his first writings on aphasia he foretold the discovery of a sensory type of aphasia.

It was not until 1877 that Kussmaul introduced the actual terms "word-deafness" and "word-blindness." Kussmaul was one of the great men in German medicine in the nineteenth century. He was an internist, but his monograph on speech disturbances—first published in 1877—went through several editions and translations. Kussmaul maintained that word-deafness and word-blindness were entities separate from aphasia:

> We have discovered cases in the literature, which were known as aphasia, but should not be designated as such, inasmuch as the patients were able to express themselves in speaking and writing. They were neither inarticulate (incapable of speech) nor illiterate (incapable of writing); but despite an acute sense of hearing they could no longer comprehend words they heard or, despite good vision, they could no longer read words they saw. For the sake of

---

[3]*Aphémie*, as used by Broca, meant an inability to speak due to a lesion in the central nervous system. Other investigators quickly adopted the term "aphasia" as a more appropriate synonym. Broca objected, saying that aphasia meant without phases of the moon and, therefore, without brightness or ideas. Trousseau, on the other hand, learned from a Greek that *aphémie* meant infamy. Trousseau preferred the term aphasia.

brevity these pathological disabilities are named: word deafness and word blindness (*caecitas et surditas verbalis*).

In 1874, Wernicke, a German neurophatholgist, published a monograph on aphasia when he was only twenty-eight years of age. In this treatise he concentrated on sensory aphasia, which was the counterpart of Broca's motor aphasia. Sensory aphasia, from Wernicke's point of view, pertained to loss of visual and auditory recognition or understanding with preservation of the ability to use articulate speech. He attributed the disorder to a lesion in the first temporal convolution of the brain, but he also called attention to the role of the sensory pathways leading into the brain. Wernicke thought that the anterior part of the brain was concerned with movement (motor) and the posterior (including the temporal lobe) with sensory impressions. He thought, too, that the nerve cells in the brain cortex were neither motor nor sensory but depended on their connections to determine their function. Moreover, he separated the general auditory area from the auditory speech area and located the latter in the first temporal convolution. According to Wernicke, a lesion in the auditory speech area would produce loss of understanding of speech (word-deafness) and, in addition, inability to read and write because the distorted hearing of words would interfere with the learning process (word-blindness).

Although there were many other investigators who contributed valuable information to the understanding of aphasia, it appears that Broca (motor aphasia) and Wernicke (sensory aphasia) were the real pioneers. Broca pursued his investigations, concentrating on speech disorders, while Wernicke concentrated on visual and auditory disturbances.

Hughlings Jackson, an English neurologist, attempted to synthesize the work of Broca and Wernicke. His first studies on aphasia were published in 1864 and 1868, and he continued to publish significant observations through the next several decades.

One of Jackson's greatest contributions was his conception of a "hierarchy of levels" in the nervous system for both motor and sensory functions. He thought that the highest level represents an integration of function for both sides of the body, whereas a center in the middle level represents only one-half or one side of the body. (For Orton's explanation of sensory levels, see footnote, page 28.)

Jackson considered that the verbalizing process occurs in two stages. He tried to demonstrate that the first stage rests in the revival of images symbolized; that "perception is the termination of a stage beginning by the unconscious or subconscious revival of images which are in effect 'image-symbols;' that we think not only by aid of those symbols, ordinarily so-called (words), but by aid of symbol-images." The second stage of the process is speech itself. Jackson went on to say, "It is, I think, because speech and perception are preceded by an unconscious or subconscious reproduction of words and images, that we seem to have 'faculties' of speech and of perception, as it were, above and independent of the rest of ourselves."

At another time Jackson wrote: "I think that the left is the side for the automatic revival of images and the right the side for their voluntary revival—for recognition." He believed that a specific lesion did not produce a specific symptom, but that activity of a lower level, released from the control of a higher level, produced various manifestations. These included inability to speak, to write and to read. Among other manifestations of a brain lesion, he described what he called "partial imperceptions" in a patient who at times did not recognize objects, places or persons, and who put her clothes on backwards.

Freud's Contribution

In 1891, Sigmund Freud, then a neurologist and later a psychoanalyst, published a monograph entitled *On Aphasia*. In this monograph Freud criticized the theories advanced by most of the authorities on aphasia and in particular many of Wernicke's interpretations, but he seemed to accept the concepts formulated by Hughlings Jackson.

At that time and even later, speech disturbances continued to be the focus of attention, but Freud brought in definite references to reading, writing and spelling. He discussed the various psychological and physiological elements involved in learning to read, write and spell. He said: "The idea, or concept, of the object is itself another complex of associations composed of the most varied visual, auditory, tactile, kinaesthetic and other impressions."

About reading and writing, Freud was more specific:

> In writing as well as in speaking we receive kinaesthetic impressions from the movements carried out by the muscles involved. However, the impressions from the hand are more distinct and intensive than those coming from the speech muscles, either because we are used to attributing great value to the perceptions of the hand also in relation to functions other than writing, or because they are associated with visual impressions: we can see ourselves writing but not speaking. . . .

> In some cases of subcortical alexia reading is aided by writing: the letter images incapable of direct association with the acoustic element, are nevertheless associated with it by means of the kinaesthetic impressions aroused in the process of "drawing from a model," and in this way they are recognized. . . . Impairment in the recognition of letters naturally implies inability to read. However, it is possible for a reading disorder to be present without loss of the ability to recognize letters. This may result from a variety of lesions and conditions such as can be readily understood from earlier remarks about the intricate processes of associations which enter into the act of reading.

To the above observations, Freud added a footnote:

> I believe that some physiological and individual peculiarities of memory can be explained by the changing role of its individual elements. One may have a good memory yet be unable to retain proper names and numbers. Individuals who excel in remembering names and numbers belong to the visual type, i.e., they have a predilection for recalling visual images of objects even if they think in sound images.

Although focusing his attention on speech disorders, Freud broadened his perspective to include all language disturbances. In the same monograph he said:

> In assessing the functions of the speech apparatus under pathological conditions we are adopting as a guiding principle Hughlings Jackson's doctrine that all these modes of reaction represent instances of functional retrogression (dis-involution) of a highly organized apparatus, and therefore correspond to previous states of its functional development. This means that under all circum-

stances an arrangement of associations which, having been acquired later, belongs to a higher level of functioning, will be lost, while an earlier and simpler one will be preserved.

When Freud wrote these words, he was referring to organic pathology. He made no mention of innate endowment, nor did he attribute "language inhibition" to psychogenetic origins. However, he did say:

> There were cases of aphasia in which no localized lesion needed to be assumed and the symptoms could be attributed to an alteration of a physiological constant in the speech apparatus. Aphasia simply reproduces a state which existed in the course of the normal process of learning to speak and read.

This is the first time in medical literature that we find such a definite statement that language dysfunction may be due to innate and developmental factors.

Freud's monograph on aphasia was a milestone, but it received little recognition at the time it was written in spite of the fact that it summed up and gave a critical analysis of practically all of the important theories and findings in the field of language disorders from the neuropathological viewpoint. Included, too, were many transient but succinct references to philosophical and psychological concepts. A present-day reader can pick up the threads of some basic elements in psychoanalytic principles which Freud formulated within the next few years.

Stengel, who translated this forgotten monograph into English in 1953, said in his introduction:

> The idea that disturbances of function similar to those caused by brain lesions occur in the healthy person under conditions of fatigue and lack of attention was implicit in the theory of evolution and dissolution. It is therefore not surprising to find observations in this book which foreshadowed important psychopathological discoveries. What Freud said about paraphasia, i.e., the mistaken use of words, reads like a prelude to the chapter on errors and slips of the tongue in *Psychopathology of Everyday Life*. Freud's observations on paraphasia are still up-to-date.

It should be emphasized again that Freud and the other writers on aphasia were drawing conclusions based on the study of adults who had acquired some organic lesion in the brain; moreover, speech, rather than reading, was the focus of attention and investigation. Thus far, there had been only mild and fleeting suggestions hidden in a mass of scientific formulations that some people might be born with a predisposition toward language disability. Very little is found in the early literature to indicate that language dysfunction in reading, writing, or spelling might be caused by emotional disturbances and even less that it might be innate or hereditary.

Consideration of further studies and observations in the field of organic pathology related to dyslexia will be set aside for the present and taken up in a later chapter because the end of the nineteenth century signalled a new approach. At that time, several investigators suddenly recognized the possibility that congenital anomalies or innate endowment might be the fundamental cause of dyslexia. For this reason, attention will now be given to the historical background of developmental dyslexia.

Chapter II

SPECIFIC READING DISABILITY (DEVELOPMENTAL DYSLEXIA): HISTORICAL BACKGROUND

The schoolmaster who taught him for some years says that he would be the smartest lad in school if instruction were entirely oral.

W. PRINGLE MORGAN (1896)

Wﾍ THE GREAT CONCENTRATION on the study of language disorders by many outstanding scientists during the last half of the nineteenth century, it seems incredible that no one advanced the idea that some people with language disturbances might just "grow up that way," without organic insult to the brain or without emotional bases for the disability.[1]

Certainly, handicaps such as color-blindness, tone-deafness and even general awkwardness had been known to occur without brain damage or psychogenetic etiology. Also, very special abilities in mathematics, music, memory, fluency of speech, poetry and writing had long been recognized as special "gifts" which were not attributed to any anomaly of the brain. These special aptitudes were looked upon as endowments bestowed by nature. Often these "gifts" became manifest with-

[1]In July, 1867, H. B. Wilbur published a paper on aphasia in the *American Journal of Insanity*. Wilbur was superintendent of an institution for feebleminded children in New York State. He was conversant with the reports of Broca and the other European writers on aphasia. His article, written with a colorful choice of words and phrases, pertained to the study of aphasia in several of the retarded children under his care. He discussed language disturbances that appeared to be due to some cause other than mental retardation. In a few instances, his case descriptions strongly suggested word-blindness or word-deafness—leaving the impression that these particular children were not really feebleminded. However, Wilbur only suggested that these children were aphasic without further clarification.

Orton (1928) referred to an article published in 1885 by Oswald Berkan of Germany on reading disability as related to mental deficiency. Berkan called such cases partial imbeciles (halbidiote), but apparently his observation went unnoticed.

[13]

out any associated emotional problems, and sometimes in spite of
emotional difficulties or because of them.

If special gifts could be the result of nature's largess, why did no
investigator at least postulate the theory that special disabilities might
be the result of nature's lack of bounty? It was not until around the
year 1896—and from several quarters almost simultaneously—that
investigators began to call attention to the fact that some people do
"just grow up" with certain deficiencies or disabilities in language
functions, particularly reading.

Original Studies

W. Pringle Morgan, an English ophthalmologist, is credited with
being the first to give a definitive description of specific reading disability. Hidden in a few paragraphs in the *British Medical Journal,*
Morgan's article remains as a classic and precise delineation of reading disability accompanied by spelling errors. Morgan recorded the
case of a fourteen-year-old boy who was unable to learn to read in
spite of normal vision and otherwise normal status. He found no
evidence of brain injury in this boy, who seemed to have good intelligence. Morgan said: "He knows his letters and can read and write
them. His eyes are normal, there is no hemianopsia and his eyesight
is good. The schoolmaster who taught him for some years says that
he would be the smartest lad in school if instruction were entirely oral."

The boy's spelling showed certain singular characteristics. His name
was Percy, but he wrote it "Precy." He displayed other spelling disparities; for example, he wrote:

> "scone" for song
> "Englis" for English
> "seasow" for seashore
> "wichout" for without

Thus, we see that "Precy" reveals the typical picture of reading and
spelling disability in a person who has a lack of facility in the perception and visual memory of words. Typical, too, is the spelling "by
ear" rather than by sight and the reversal in the order of letters, although Morgan did not call attention to either of these characteristics.

Morgan called this kind of disturbance "congenital word-blindness"
and said that it was "evidently congenital and due most probably to

defective development of that region of the brain, disease of which in adults produces practically the same symptoms, that is, the left angular gyrus."

Morgan's case report appeared in the November 7, 1896 issue of the *British Medical Journal*. It is interesting that James Kerr, an English school physician, in his Howard Medal Prize Essay, dated June, 1896, mentioned that reading disabilities occur in children of normal intelligence. However, his essay was not published until 1897, and it is very probable that neither writer knew about the contribution of the other until later on. It is known that Morgan's interest was stimulated by Hinshelwood's report on acquired word-blindness in adults, which was made a year earlier.

James Hinshelwood, an ophthalmologist of Glasgow, made a great contribution to the study of reading disability. He studied the condition over a long period of time and published a series of articles of great benefit to subsequent investigators. He remained the "torch-lighter" in the field of reading disability for over two decades.

In the *Lancet* (December 21, 1895), Hinshelwood wrote about word-blindness and visual memory in a case of organic brain damage. He made no mention of "congenital word-blindness," but he explained in some detail the process of learning to read. He discussed the singular mathematical abilities that some people have, and he also cited instances of people with good memory for figures, but not for words, who revealed no evidence of brain injury.

Hinshelwood's next article in the *Lancet* (November 21, 1896) was entitled "A Case of Dyslexia: A Peculiar Form of Word-blindness." This paper was based on a case of organic injury. In 1898, Hinshelwood reported on an organically acquired case of word- without letter-blindness. In the following year, he reported on another case of letter- without word-blindness. Here he noted "mistakes in spelling, changing the place of some of the letters and even suppressing a letter." He expressed the view that "the visual memory of numbers, of letters and of words are stored in perfectly distinct though adjacent cerebral areas."

It was not until May, 1900 that Hinshelwood published an article entitled "Congenital Word-blindness." He gave a detailed description of two cases from his own practice, summarized Morgan's case, and reviewed one reported by Bastian. Once more he localized the defect in the angular and supramarginal gyri in the left side of the brain in right-handed people. He said that the condition could be due to disease, injury at birth, or *defective development.* He thought that the cases due to defective development were not so rare, but that they went unrecognized. He said that children with this kind of special disability were often treated as imbeciles or harshly flogged for not trying. Hinshelwood took an optimistic view that the disability could be overcome by patient and persistent training.

In 1900, Hinshelwood published a book with the interesting title, *Letter-, Word- and Mind-blindness.* He continued to publish and present the findings of his research at medical conferences. Then, in 1917, he wrote his monograph on *Congenital Word-blindness,* which many later writers referred to as a landmark in the history of reading disability. He gave a detailed and systematic description of the symptoms of congenital word-blindness and noted again how closely these symptoms paralled those found in cases where the defect was caused by drain damage. He reiterated his view that the condition could be due to some developmental defect (agenesis), starting during early embryonic growth in the gyrus angularis of the dominant hemisphere of the brain. Hinshelwood wanted to restrict the term "congenital word-blindness" to the more severe cases where, without doubt or exaggeration, the condition could be regarded as abnormal or pathological, yet without evidence of acquired brain disease or injury. He did not make a clear distinction, however, between the normal variations in reading ability and the "pathological" cases.

Turning back to the time just after 1896, we find that other English ophthalmologists published similar observations: E. Nettleship (1901), Sydney Stephenson (1904), C. J. Thomas (1905), and J. H. Fisher (1908). In addition to giving clear-cut descriptions of reading disability, they emphasized certain hereditary aspects of the condition as well as its prevalence in boys.

In 1908, A. Peters published an article in Germany "Ueber Kongenitale Wortblindheit," which discussed reading, writing, and spelling disabilities. Other similar articles in German followed. The writings in German would indicate that reading disability is not confined to persons whose native language is English. Peters and the other German writers gave credit to Morgan and the other English investigators for their pioneer work in reading disability.

Early Studies in the United States

It is evident that English investigators were the first to recognize the problem of specific reading disability, although they called it congenital word-blindness. The first recorded observations on the condition came almost entirely from ophthalmologists. It is difficult to date the recognition of the existence of such a problem in the United States, but it was not until after the turn of the century. Although researchers in this country had shown great interest in all aspects of "organic aphasia" and other speech disturbances, no articles were published until a few years after Morgan's seminal work. Bakwin and Bakwin (1960) stated in their textbook that "the problem of the nonreader and the poor reader is an old one. References to it were made by Horace Mann as long ago as 1838, and it was subject for comment in the New York City School reports back in 1904."

J. H. Claiborne, an ophthalmologist in New York City, might properly be called the pioneer in this field in the United States.[2] In the *Journal of the American Medical Association* dated December 1, 1906, he published a paper entitled "Types of Congenital Symbol Amblyopia," in which he stated that "the first American observer who has recorded any observations on this subject is A. Schapringer who read a paper on the subject before the Section of Ophthalmology of the New York Academy of Medicine, February 19, 1906. His paper was followed by one by myself in which I referred to two cases." Claiborne's paper was based on the two cases he referred to at the medical

---

[2]An isolated reference to reading disability, however, was found in a paper by Edward Jackson of Denver, Colorado. It was published in March of 1906 under the title "Developmental Alexia (Congenital Word-Blindness)." Jackson had read the paper before the Colorado Medical Society in 1905. He gave details about two cases which he had studied for some time. One of these had shown marked improvement over a span of five years; therefore, the original diagnosis must have been made about 1900. Jackson summarized eighteen cases from the reports made in England. He said that Nettleship (1901) reported on five cases, going back to 1882, but they were not fully recognized at that time. He mentioned the use of phonic and kinaesthetic approaches as a way of overcoming the handicap. He said: "In many cases it is probably only a question of delayed development," but he considered the possibility of a specific defect in brain development. No further references to articles by Jackson could be found.

meeting in February of 1906, but he added several interesting observations and suggestions. Not satisfied with the term "blindness," he
suggested the use of "amblyopia" which means blunt or dim vision,
not complete blindness. "Symbol amblyopia," as used in the title of
his paper, meant amblyopia for letters, words and figures. One of
his cases, a boy aged nine, had difficulty with letters and words, but
not with figures. Concerning figures, he "knew them all and did additions and subtractions as well as any boy his age." This, then, was
a case of word-amblyopia, not figure-amblyopia.

On the other hand, Claiborne pointed out that many persons
who read well are unable to learn mathematics, and such persons
may have figure-amblyopia. He confessed that he, himself, had always had trouble with figures and he admitted that he had figure-
amblyopia. There is abundant evidence that he was a great reader
and a prolific writer. Claiborne went on to say that many persons
have imperfect appreciation of or memory for musical sounds. For
this disability, he used the term "amblymusia." Claiborne's attempt to
get away from the implication of blindness or deafness was a laudable
one, but few subsequent writers followed his terminology.

Claiborne adhered to the general concept prevalent at that time in
attributing the condition to brain damage. He said: "The lesion is
doubtless a congenital one, and it probably consists in imperfect development and tardy reaction of the word and letter memory-cells."
He made the interesting suggestion that children so afflicted should
be changed over to be left-handed writers on the basis that the other
side of the brain (without the lesion) might pick up and carry on
or reinforce the lagging side. He stated, "It is improbable that the
corresponding cells on the right side are similarly affected, and thus
the speech center and the centers for symbols and sounds may be
transferred to that side." Apparently, Claiborne was not aware of
the fact that the nondominant side does not take over such functions
after the first two or three years of life; neither was he aware of the
confused dominance which exists in so many cases.

Claiborne was optimistic that the handicap could be ameliorated.
As treatment, he advocated "methods of teaching to waken the torpid
cells into activity." He also said, "I believe the basis of instruction
should be repetition."

The contributions of E. B. McCready parallel, in some degree, those of Claiborne. McCready's first article on "Congenital Word-blindness as a Cause of Backwardness in School Children" was published in January, 1910. Later in the same year he wrote a paper entitled, "Biological Variation in the Higher Cerebral Centers Causing Retardation." In 1926, he published in the *American Journal of Psychiatry* an article on "Defects in the Zone of Language (Word-deafness and Word-blindness)."

McCready reported on cases where there was no evidence of aphasia produced by organic disease but where there was reason to suspect hereditary influence—hence, his terminology, "biological variation." He was also interested in delayed acquisition of speech which might be due to word-deafness. He referred to Bastian's article on "Aphasia and Other Speech Defects" (1898) and quoted Bastian as follows:

> Some curious cases of congenital speech defect were described
> by Hadden, to which the term "idioglossia" has been applied.
> These children have, to a certain extent, a language of their own,
> so that when asked to repeat phrases they make use of different,
> though definite, sounds instead of those proper to the words that
> should be employed.

Concerning both word-blindness and word-deafness, McCready pointed out that children with such handicaps are often considered to be feebleminded. He went on to say that "these children may eventually become feeble-minded by deprivation unless their condition is exactly recognized and the proper treatment instituted." This is an interesting statement in the light of present-day studies of sensory deprivation.

It should be pointed out that the many eminent ophthalmologists—both in this country and abroad—who first recognized word-blindness for what it was were unanimous in pointing out that the cause of this disorder was not to be found in any dysfunction or disease of the eyes.[3] Present-day ophthalmologists concur with this stand taken by their earlier colleagues. It is only natural that ophthalmology was the med-

---

[3]Several writers have referred to a recent pronouncement of the Ophthalmological Section of the Los Angeles Medical Society which stated that it took 50 per cent or more reduced visual acuity to disturb reading; that farsightedness and astig-

ical specialty to which parents and teachers turned in seeking the cause of reading disability.

Early Contributions of Psychologists and Educators

Before the twentieth century, some of the classic studies of experimental psychologists were concerned with the process of reading without giving consideration to reading disability *per se*. For example, Wundt, Cattell, Javal, Erdmann and Dodge carried on fundamental studies pertaining to the eye and to mechanics of reading. But it was not until the turn of the century that psychologists—especially those concerned with education—became interested in reading disability.

Many specialists look upon W. F. Dearborn as the pioneer American educational psychologist in the field of reading because of his treatise, "The Psychology of Reading" (1906). His subsequent studies over a period of years, his intense interest in reading problems, and his flair for teaching stimulated several of his colleagues to concentrate on reading and reading problems.

It is interesting to note that E. B. Huey, independent of Dearborn, published a book on *The Psychology and Pedagogy of Reading* (1908). This classic should be read today as background material, although it contained nothing about specific reading disability and no reference to the medical literature in existence at that time.

The many contributions of individual psychologists in the first two decades of this century will not be reviewed here because the Research Committee of the Commonwealth Fund made a study of the work and writings of these educators and psychologists. The committee's report was published in 1925 under the title of "Summary of Investigations Related to Reading." William S. Gray of the University of Chicago was chairman of the committee and author of the report (the other members of the committee were not named). The bibliography, which made up a large part of this report, contained 436 references to articles and books published prior to July, 1924. A chronological tabulation of the references in this report shows that there was an accelerated investigation of reading problems from 1896

---

matism had to be very marked; and that cross-eyedness with normal vision in one eye had little or no effect on reading ability.

This information will be referred to later in the discussion of the list of causes proposed by educators, psychologists, and others who often start the list with "visual defects."

through 1924. Prior to 1896 there were only four articles; from 1896 through 1900 there were ten; in the next decade (1901-1910) there were twenty; in the next five years (1911-1915) there were forty-nine. Then in the next five years (1916-1920), 151 appeared. Finally, from 1921 through 1924, the count was 201.

Practically all the references in Gray's report dealt with publications by American psychologists and educators. There was one reference to Hinshelwood, the English ophthalmologist, but Morgan and the other English and American ophthalmologists were not mentioned. The subject matter, as indicated by the titles of the references, pertained almost entirely to reading tests, methods of teaching, eye movements and the "psychology" of reading. Except for the reference to Hinshelwood, the only other titles that mentioned congenital word-blindness or a similar term were by Clara Schmitt (1918) and J. E. Wallace Wallin (1920). Although Gray devoted 214 pages to a discussion of the literature, no reference was made in the index to such topics as "word-blindness," "aphasia," "dyslexia," "heredity," "dominance," "reversals," etc.

Many of the references in the bibliography pertain to reading tests compiled by well-known psychologists and educators: W. S. Gray, Courtis, Gates, C. T. Gray, Judd, Monroe, Otis, Pintner, Schmitt, Starch and Thorndike. Most of these psychologists were interested in establishing tests for reading ability on an empirical basis or through "scientific theory" related to learning processes. Most of them, too, were interested in teaching methods, motivation, and environmental factors. While they occasionally referred to the investigations and explanations from clinical medicine and neuropathology, very few of these contributors carried on studies which were based on medical findings.

Gray listed fifteen of his own contributions in his report; among them was an article entitled "Diagnostic and Remedial Steps in Reading" published in 1921. In this study he listed the following causes of poor reading: irregular attendance at school, poor health, malnutrition, nervous disorders, nationality, inappropriate methods of instruction, inadequate reading, visual defects, vocal defects, breathing irregularities, auditory defects and defects in the brain tissue. In addition, he listed another group of causes which he called psychological in character. They included general mental incapacity, inadequate attention to meaning, failure to associate proper meaning with words, limited eye-voice span, limited span of recognition, inability to remember new words easily, capacity to learn words only very slowly, forgetting words quickly and easily, and inability to analyze and pronounce words effectively. This latter group of causes has many of the "earmarks" of specific reading disability (dyslexia), but Gray did not spell this out.

After publication of the first edition of the Commonwealth report (1925), Gray continued to publish summaries of investigations in the field of reading. The last one came out in 1959, the year of his death.[4] During his lifetime Gray was recognized internationally as an authority in the field of reading. Because of his competence, he was asked to prepare the United Nations report on this topic.

Studies by Augusta Bronner and Leta Hollingworth merit special attention. Bronner was the psychologist in the *first* child guidance clinic, which was established in Chicago in 1909 by Dr. William A. Healy. In 1917 she published *The Psychology of Special Abilities and Disabilities*. Among the several disabilities dealt with, Bronner discussed special defects in number work, special defects in language ability and special defects in separate mental processes. She gave considerable attention to reading, spelling and spoken language with an inclusive review of the pertinent literature.

Bronner reported in considerable detail her study of seven cases of defect in language. All were boys: five were fifteen years of age or over, two were eleven. They presented the symptoms characteristic of reading and spelling disabilities and, in some cases, a variety of other language deficits such as poor auditory memory, etc. There was no mention of handedness or dominance. In her illustrations of reproduced writings, several instances of reversals in spelling occurred, but she made no note of these errors. The case histories revealed no suggestion of acquired brain damage.

By way of summary, Bronner stated:

It may be said that analysis of the reading process shows that there are involved (a) perception of form and sound, and dis-

---

[4]In addition to books, Gray always published a yearly summary of reading investigations in the *Journal of Educational Research*. Since his death, Helen Robinson has continued this service in *The Reading Teacher*.

crimination of forms and sounds; (b) association of sounds with visually perceived letters, of names with groups of symbols, and of meanings with groups of words; (c) memory, motor, visual and auditory factors; and (d) the motor processes as used in inner speech and in reading aloud. Reviewing the whole process, we see that in the actual performance of reading there must be finally some synthetic process uniting all the separate elements. This is a point that has been little emphasized by students of the psychology of reading, but its validity and importance seem clearly established through our analysis of cases of special difficulty in reading. Analysis of the mental processes involved in reading has never been applied to individual cases of inability to learn to read, so far as we know. The fact that some individuals have a pronounced disability in this field has been observed, it is true. It is exceedingly interesting to find that neurologists and even ophthalmologists have dealt with this question far more than psychologists.

In 1918, Leta Hollingworth, an educational psychologist, published a paper, "The Psychology of Special Disability in Spelling." She came to the conclusion that infrequent cases are found of children who cannot learn to spell or whose ability to spell approaches zero. Although she designated such cases as having a special disability, she said that it is not due to a congenital localized neural lesion or to childhood injuries. Instead, the disability itself is "the very fag end of the normal distribution of spelling ability," which is determined by "unknown laws of variation and heredity." Consequently, Hollingworth concluded that such cases differ in degree but not in kind from normal spellers:

> By far the greater proportion of the sum total of bad spelling is, however, due to causes other than special disability in forming the bonds involved in learning to spell words. Over eighty per cent of the poor spellers in our Experimental Class spelled poorly from some cause other than special disability. General intellectual weakness, lack of interest, distaste for mental drudgery, intellectual inertia, previous learning in a foreign language, sensory defects, and bad hand writing are doubtless the most frequent causes of poor spelling.

Here we see a valuable point of view in Hollingworth's conclusion that disability is the fag end of normal distribution of spelling facility.

At the same time, she seems to reject innate endowment as a causative factor and seems to prefer environmental and emotional bases.

In 1923, Hollingworth published a book entitled *Special Talents and Defects*. She called attention to many people who possess a remarkable gift for reading. She maintained that usually—but not always—extreme precocity in reading is associated with a high general level of intelligence. She illustrated her position by citing a case report by Terman of a girl who, at the age of two, could read fluently from an ordinary primer, thereby equaling the reading ability of a typical six-year-old. When Terman later tested the general intelligence of this child, he obtained an I. Q. rating of 150. In other words, her reading ability outmatched her general level of intelligence. In contrast, Hollingworth added: "A few cases of superior ability to read occurring in combination with low I. Q. have also been reported by Bronner."

Hollingworth reported in considerable detail her own four-year study of a nonreader, giving an account of personality factors in this child as well as various remedial reading procedures used in treating him. Her contribution to remedial reading is found in part in the following:

> We see, therefore, that non-readers, of general intelligence much above the minimum level required for reading, do learn to read when special training is given. This training may stress phonics (Schmitt), it may stress the motor and kinaesthetic avenues of approach (Fernald and Keller), or it may stress visual perception (Gates). It may or may not proceed by use of the old "alphabet" method (Hinshelwood). . . . In fact, no investigator has established his or her method as the only successful approach to particular cases, by excluding other methods through experimental teaching. . . . For non-readers such as have been described under the criteria laid down by the investigators quoted, it seems highly probable that the best method would be that wherein all avenues of approach are fully utilized.

As to the cause of reading disability, Hollingworth said that the claim of Hinshelwood and many others that it was due to some congenital lesion or agenesis was "irreconcilable with facts known to psychology." Elaborating on this point she said:

Cases where a generally stupid child is innately gifted with special ability to master the mechanics of reading, for example, are no doubt as frequent as cases where a generally capable child learns them with difficulty. The theory of specialized lesions or other faults of structure might cover disabilities, but would it cover special talents as well?[5]

This question raised by Hollingworth is as pertinent today as it was in 1923. When a person is unusually gifted in mathematics, music, art, motor coordination, etc., it is not expected that hyperplasia in a certain part of the brain is to be found as the basis of the superior talent. More specifically, for the gifted few with eidetic imagery who can repeat the names, numbers and addresses on the page of a telephone directory after one perusal, no anomaly of the brain has been demonstrated. Also, no propitious confluence of emotional experiences in early life has been found as the cause of such talent.

---

[5]Hollingworth also speculated that there might be an inheritance of function as well as of structure.

Chapter III

THE ORTON STORY

*Within the heterogeneous community of poor readers
(slow readers, retarded readers) there exists a specific
syndrome wherein particular difficulty exists in learning
the conventional meaning of verbal symbols, and of asso-
ciating the sound with symbol in appropriate fashion.*
MACDONALD CRITCHLEY (1964)

THE MANY INVESTIGATORS mentioned in the foregoing chapters laid
the groundwork for more comprehensive contributions in the field
of language disabilities. A propitious combination of circumstances
placed the right man in the right place at the right time to make these
contributions possible. The man was Dr. Samuel T. Orton, a psychiatrist, a neurologist, as well as a neuropathologist; the place was the
Iowa State Psychopathic Hospital; the time was the mid-1920's.

Before going to Iowa, Orton had been the scientific director of the
Pennsylvania Hospital for Mental Diseases. He was recognized as an
authority in neuropathology, having worked with Dr. Elmer Southard
of Harvard University and having studied as many human brains
post mortem as anyone at that time.

In 1922, Orton was chosen to be the organizer and chairman of a
new department of psychiatry at the University of Iowa and the
director of the Iowa State Psychopathic Hospital. As his chief of staff,
Orton appointed Dr. Lawson G. Lowrey, who later became an outstanding leader in the child guidance clinic movement. He also chose
as the director of psychiatric social work Miss June Lyday, who later
became Mrs. Samuel T. Orton. She was a graduate of the Smith
College School of Psychiatric Social work, and she did her field training at the Boston Psychopathic Hospital.

The early 1920's witnessed great changes in both education and
psychiatry. In education, as part of the upheaval caused by the
advent of progressive education, the teaching of reading was emphasized. New techniques and new methods were constantly being tried.

[26]

In psychiatry, the exigencies of World War I had made demands on psychiatrists that changed the face of the profession. Psychiatry stepped outside the walls of the mental hospital and into the community through the establishment of outpatient clinics and, more specifically, of child guidance clinics.

As a pioneering step in this new trend, Orton established mobile or traveling clinic teams, each composed of a psychiatrist, a psychologist, and a social worker. These teams were based in the Iowa State Psychopathic Hospital, but they made scheduled trips to many communities in the state. They set up one-day clinics in various localities and gave special attention to problem children referred to them by the public schools. Concerning the work of these clinics, Orton said: "Among these children who were reported to the clinic as 'dull, subnormal, or failing or retarded in school work' was a fairly high proportion whose chief difficulty was in learning to read."

In the Greene County Clinic, fifteen children were found who fell within this description. Two of them fitted precisely Hinshelwood's description of congenital word-blindness. It was possible to bring one of the two—a boy named "M. P."—into the Iowa State Psychopathic Hospital for detailed study.

"M. P." was a sixteen-year-old boy in junior high school, but he had never been able to learn to read. On the Stanford-Binet test he came out with a mental age of 11 years-4 months, and an I. Q. of 71. On the Pintner-Patterson performance tests his results equalled those of an adult. By the Healy test his score was 90 out of a possible 100, which was a superior performance for adults.[1] At school, his spelling showed marked disparities from the normal. For example, he wrote:

"supr" for supper
"weit" for white
"blou" for blue
"gen" for green
"gary" for gray

Orton was immediately aware of the similarity of the symptoms found in brain-injured people to those found in "M. P." and some

---

[1]Orton called attention to the probability that the majority of "strephosymbolic" children would make a low score on the Stanford-Binet test because of their special disability which was not taken into account in the testing.

of the other children; but these latter children show no *other* evidence
of brain damage defects in their history, neurological examination and
other tests. They seemed particularly confused in attempting to remember whole-word patterns and the orientation of letters. To describe their difficulty, Orton coined the term "strephosymbolia"
(twisted symbols), which he looked upon as a developmental delay
which should yield in some measure to proper methods of treatment
and teaching. He did not consider the condition to be due to a "lesion"
in the brain or to an "agenesis" in a localized area.

Based on the study of "M. P." and other children in the clinic,
Orton presented a paper entitled "Word-Blindness in School Children"
before the American Neurological Association in May of 1925. This
was his first paper on "word-blindness," but he brought out many
points related to language in various cultures, to the role of dominance
or laterality, to handwriting (and mirror writing), to possible genetic
factors and to the frustrations produced in children who struggle with
language handicaps. He did not neglect the emotional elements involved in the causation of the condition and augmentation of the
symptoms. He disagreed specifically with Hinshelwood's ideas about
localized agenesis and about a division between mild (physiological)
and severe (pathological cases).[2]

In the decade following the publication of his first paper (November, 1925), Orton directed several neurologically-oriented research

---

[2]It is noteworthy that at the time this first paper was being published Orton was
preparing his lectures on neuropathology for publication in the *Archives of Neurology and Psychiatry*. In these lectures the phylogenetic development of the brain
was dealt with and the various cortices (cortical areas) such as the visual cortices,
the auditory cortices, the motor cortices, etc., received considerable attention. Of
particular significance was his hypothesis that there are three levels in the mantle
of man (the various cortices named above). He stated:

As a skeleton plan we may outline three levels as:
(1) The arrival platform, which is that area of the cortex in which a sensory
    path first debouches and which is devoted selectively to sensation of one
    particular type. Apparently, however, this cortex subserves sensations only
    and is not associated with recognition of the meaning of sensory impres-
    sions.
(2) The elaborative, or as I prefer to call it the recognitive, which extends as
    a zone around each arrival platform, and which apparently serves in con-
    junction with the arrival platform for the recognition of concrete objects.
(3) The associative areas, in which sensory material of various types is brought
    together to form the concept. It is probably here that the abstract mem-

programs with doctors, psychologists, social workers and teachers who were on his staff. These studies, which further elaborated on his original concepts, were presented in several medical and educational journals. (See bibliography.) His description of "strephosymbolia" in the *Journal of the American Medical Association* (1928) should be read by all who are interested in language disturbances. This article has been reprinted in the 1963 issue of the *Bulletin of The Orton Society*.

From the start of his interest in language handicaps, Orton was not unmindful of speech disorders, especially stuttering, and the speech disturbances resulting from "word-deafness." In these speech disorders he recognized the same constellation of associated findings that he had already noted in reading disabilities—namely, the lack of well-established cortical dominance, the family histories which revealed mixtures of speech, reading, spelling and motor coordination handicaps, along with the presence of both speech and reading disabilities in certain individuals. In cooperation with his colleague, Lee Edward Travis, investigative studies in speech pathology were started at the Iowa State Psychopathic Hospital in conjunction with the studies of reading disability. From this beginning, the University of Iowa became one of the leading speech centers in the country. Orton continued to be interested in speech disorders, but he became better known for his contributions in the field of reading.

Orton continued the study of the familial occurrence of these related disorders and elaborated on the role that confused dominance plays in their causation. Further details about dominance are found in an article which appeared in *School and Society* in 1928:

---

ories are stored which serve as the building material for ideation, imagination and, when operating in harmony with the two lower centers, for the recognition of the graphic, verbal and other symbols.

Also, in reference to the visual cortices, Orton said:

The angular gyrus, because of its strategic position at the junction of the occipital, parietal and temporal fields, has been considered as ideally located for associative processes but it also overlies a great mass of associative pathways linking these three zones, and the influence of deep lesions on these fiber tracts does not seem to have received sufficient attention. Without allowance for the influence of section of these pathways it seems incredible that this small zone could accommodate all the special functional elaborations which have been accredited to it.

The four activities which constitute the language faculty—
understanding the spoken word, understanding the printed word
(reading), speech and writing—seem to be controlled exclusively
from one hemisphere since destruction of certain areas of one
hemisphere causes loss of one or more of these functions while
destruction of exactly similar degree and in exactly the same part
of the other hemisphere gives no demonstrable result. This striking difference in functional importance of the two hemispheres
in the more complex functions underlying language constitutes
the problem of cerebral dominance and while much of the older
view of the exact pigeonholing of these functions into restricted
areas, predestined for that particular purpose, is under challenge
today, yet the general view of control of these functions from one
hemisphere is practically universally accepted.

As we have seen above, however, there is no such striking structural difference between the two hemispheres as we see between
their functional duties. The two halves are about equal in size and
in complexity and since the studies of Dr. Kappers of Amsterdam
and his followers have demonstrated that completed growth of
nerve-cells is largely influenced by the stimuli which they receive,
we must assume that the inactive (or non-dominant) hemisphere
has been stimulated as freely as the active (dominant) side and
we may further assume that such stimulation has left a record
behind it in the nerve-cells of both hemispheres. In other words,
we feel that both halves have been equally irradiated by nerve-
currents and that both bear impress thereof, but since the destruction of one side brings no aftermath we believe that one of these
sets of records is elided or inactive in the language-faculty and that
normally a physiological habit is established of using only one set
in reading, writing and speech. The two halves of the brain, however, while alike in size and design, are reversed in pattern, that
is, the left hemisphere bears the same relation to the right hemisphere that the left hand does to the right hand. It seems logical,
therefore, to conclude that the records (or engrams, as they are
called) of one hemisphere would be mirrored copies or antitropes
of those in its mate. If then there should be failure in establishment of the normal physiological habit of using exclusively those
of one hemisphere there might easily result a confusion in orientation which would exhibit itself as a tendency toward an alternate
sinistrad and dextrad direction in reading and in lack of prompt
recognition of the differences between pairs of words which can

be spelled backwards or forwards, such as was and saw, not and ton, on and no etc.

These alterations and confusions are exactly what characterize the efforts of retarded readers and moreover the frequency of their occurrence bears a very clear relation to the severity of the condition. Extended studies have shown that while many other types of errors occur, such as faulty vowel-sounds, faulty consonant-sounds, etc., confusion in direction bears a most significant relationship not only to reading-retardation in children of normal intelligence (specific reading-disability) but also to the amount of their handicap. In their earlier years these children have greater trouble than the average in telling b from d and p from q. Later they learn to tell these letters apart quite readily when seen alone, but they are apt to get them mixed when encountered as parts of words, or this may evince itself in written spelling as when a boy writes bady for baby and septemder for september and cannot see the error on rereading it. Still later these simpler confusions between letter-forms are entirely corrected, but errors due to wrong sequence or direction of reading are common. Here the most frequent are confusions of palindromic words like was and saw, as mentioned above, but we also very often find a few letters turned around in the middle of a word. Of this type my recent case-records show pardon read as pradon, maple as malpe, story as sorty and target as targret. Obviously such failure of the printed word to call up its sounds in proper sequence forms an obstacle to arousing that auditory memory of the word to which its meaning is attached, and reading is sadly blocked.

Orton said more than once that reading and other language problems are to be found in all degrees of severity as a continuous series. He said that they may exist in children of all levels of intelligence— they may even exist in a genius—as well as in those with complicating physical disabilities or with contributing environmental hardships or personality deviation.

He went on to explain the neurophysiological functions on which he based his concepts in an article published in 1934:

An interest of many years standing in the problem of aphasia and the other syndromes that I have been accustomed to call the alpha-privative group (aphasia, agraphia, alexia, apraxia et al.) has led during the recent past to an intensive study and, I believe, to a somewhat better understanding of the disorders and delays in the acquisition by children of the various fractions of the language faculty and to methods of treatment which are, in many instances at least, proving their efficacy.

In these disorders of acquisition we meet syndromes which very closely approximate the losses of a previously acquired language facility which follows lesions of the brain in the adult.

It was this close similarity that led Hinshelwood to use the term congenital word blindness and to assume that a failure of development of the cortex destined to serve as the visual word center was the cause. There is no precise evidence to support such a focal agenesis and much to suggest that, did it occur, adjacent brain areas would be competent to assume the function. Moreover, there seems to be reasonable ground to assume a physiological disorder rather than an obligate structural defect in explanation of these cases. There remains, however, so instructive a similarity of symptoms between failures of acquisition and loss of language that I believe that no study of either can be considered complete without a comparable investigation of the other.

The one outstanding peculiarity of the cerebral patterns underlying language in the adult is that of the much greater physiological importance of one hemisphere than the other in this faculty. This is the phenomenon of unilateral cerebral dominance. Stated briefly, in the adult losses in the capacity to understand the spoken word, to reproduce it, to interpret the graphic word, or to reproduce it, may or may not occur following destructive lesions of certain brain areas, dependent on whether or not the master hemisphere is involved. The master hemisphere is usually indicated by the master hand but here many uncertainties appear because of the existence of many mixed patterns and because of the influence on handedness imposed by early training. Mostly notably does this last factor affect the hand used for writing; which is the commonly accepted criterion of the handedness pattern of individuals in hospital records.

In addition to the group of functions above outlined as constituting the language faculty, viz., understanding and reproducing both spoken and graphic words, certain other functions are apparently controlled from the master hemisphere. Here we may mention the conscious representation of the body image, of which Schilder has told us, and many of the more complex postural and motor patterns whose disturbance is seen in the apraxias.

The principle of unilateral physiological superiority in the adult brain can be held to be established, however, only in these more intricate patterns of integration and obviously does not obtain at the projection level.

Between the projection levels, however, and those in which the physiological superiority of one hemisphere is generally accepted lies a sort of "No Man's Land" which receives relatively little attention in the literature of the aphasias although its disorders are frequently recognized when they exist as an isolated clinical picture. I refer here to the agnosias or disturbances of function of what may be called the second level of cerebral elaboration. The segregation of three distinct stages of elaboration of sensory material in the visual sphere is clearly indicated in our terminology by the three clinical concepts described as cortical blindness, mind blindness, and word blindness.

The Salmon Lectures

In 1936, Orton was chosen to give the Salmon Lectures at the New York Academy of Medicine. These annual lectures are in memory of Thomas W. Salmon, an illustrious American psychiatrist. Each year the lectureship is awarded to a person who has made a significant contribution in the field of psychiatry.

Orton's three Salmon Lectures were published in 1938 under the title *Reading, Writing and Speech Problems in Children*. This book, which has recently been republished, remains a classic text for those who are interested in language disorders.

In the foreword to these lectures, Orton said:

> In the present volume the writer offers a necessarily condensed summary of the findings of a ten-year period of intensive study of some disorders in the acquisition of the language faculty encountered by certain children, as interpreted from a much longer period of interest and study from the literature, in the clinic, at the autopsy table and in the laboratory, of cerebral localization and of aphasias.

Although a "condensed summary," the first lecture covered topics such as alexia (word-blindness), auditory aphasia (word-deafness), motor agraphia, motor aphasia, and apraxia. In the second lecture, he described all these syndromes as evidences of developmental lag, not as neuropathological or acquired disorders. He qualified the terminology to include the idea of lag, using the terms "developmental alexia" (reading disability), "developmental agraphia" (special writing disability), etc. He also included speech disorders, as well as combined or mixed syndromes, under the concept of developmental lag.

In this volume nine family trees were diagrammed, showing a mixture of left-handedness, ambidexterity, stuttering, defective speech, reading disability and writing disability. Also diagrammed were the educational profiles of several children with some language handicap. These profiles in which mental age and achievement in arithmetic, reading, spelling and writing are plotted against an axis of grade placement and chronological age are most revealing of a child's accomplishment and handicaps. They can be helpful to teachers and psychologists, but they are rarely found in psychological reports, in school records, or in case histories in child guidance clinics.

Orton devoted several pages to a section entitled "Emotional Reactions and Behavior Patterns." In each case he studied he made a special effort to ascertain whether any deviations in emotional development were manifest before the onset of the language difficulty. He found "a very considerable variability in the individual reaction to a given handicap dependent not only upon diverse factors in the child's own make-up but also upon the social, economic and educational status and ambitions of the family." However, "the reading disability cases as a group form a clear cut example of the appearance of emotional disturbances which are purely secondary to the academic obstacle. The great majority of these children have exhibited no deviation in either their emotional or intellectual development up to the time they have encountered reading in their first or second year of school." In his cases of developmental word-deafness, on the other hand, this did not hold true, probably because such a handicap reaches far back into infancy. Many other interesting nuances of differing emotional reactions in children with speech delays and apraxia were recorded. With reference to all kinds of language disturbances, Orton Said:

> As a child who carries any form of unrelieved language handicap grows older, there naturally ensues an accumulated emotional overlay which in many instances makes any effort to assign etiologi-

cal significance to either the organic or the emotional factors that
are present in the situation as purposeless as attempting to allot pre-
eminence to either the warp or the woof of a piece of cloth.

In later publications Orton extended and clarified his original concepts in certain respects. With particular regard to cerebral dominance
or laterality, we find the following in Orton's discussion of a paper
by John G. Lynn in 1942:

> One probably makes a mistake in attempting to associate too
> closely conditions like reading disability with handedness pattern.
> The great majority of my patients with specific reading disability
> are right handed. Many of them are also right eyed and right
> footed; in other words many of them have distinctly unilateral
> motor patterns, but this does not preclude the possibility of a con-
> fusion of dominance in the parts of the cortex which have to do
> with the reading process, and one sees the same symptoms as in
> those who do have confusion in the motor patterns.

At the end of his book *Reading, Writing and Speech Problems in
Children,* Orton made a succinct statement which has been referred
to as "The Orton Credo":

> The view presented here that many of the delays and defects
> in development of the language function may arise from a devia-
> tion in the process of establishing unilateral brain superiority in
> individual areas, while taking account of the hereditary facts, brings
> with it the conviction that such disorders should respond to spe-
> cific training if we become sufficiently keen in our diagnosis and
> if we prove ourselves clever enough to devise the proper training
> methods to meet the needs of each particular case.

From 1925 until his death in 1948, Orton devoted most of his time
and energy to research, teaching and clinical services in the field of
language handicaps in children. After leaving the University of
Iowa, he continued his broad research in language disturbances at
the New York Neurological Institute under grants from the Rockefeller
Foundation. In his research clinics, his teacher training programs and
his private practice, Orton and his associates demonstrated that children with specific language disabilities could be taught and showed
how they could be taught so that academic failures and the emotional
reactions accompanying them could be largely eliminated. In all of

his work he was ably assisted by Mrs. Orton, who continues to do remedial reading teaching with children and to train teachers for this special field.

The Orton Society

After Dr. Orton's death, The Orton Society was founded in 1949 by a group of doctors, reading and speech specialists, parents, and others who had been closely associated with his work and dedicated to this field of service. Mrs. Orton served as president of the Society from the time of its founding in 1949 until 1960. The *Bulletin of The Orton Society,* which is published annually, contains articles by prominent specialists from many parts of the world.

Volume VII (May, 1957) of the *Bulletin of The Orton Society* carried an article by Mrs. Orton called "The Orton Story." She mentioned that she was often asked the question: "What does strephosymbolia mean?" In answer to this question, she pointed out the following characteristics, several or all of which can be observed in children who have a reading disability of the strephosymbolic type:

1. Their attainment in reading is considerably below that expected for their mental age and their years of schooling and is often below their achievements in arithmetic.

2. They show no evidence of any significant impairment of vision or hearing, or brain damage, or primary personality deviation, or any history thereof.

3. They show great difficulty in remembering whole-word patterns and do not learn easily by the "sight method" of reading. They tend to confuse small words which are similar in general configuration.

4. They are poor oral readers and fundamentally poor spellers although they can sometimes retain memorized lists of spelling words for varying lengths of time.

5. In their early attempts at reading and writing, they show marked confusions in remembering the orientation of letters (b, d, p, q) and the order of letters in words or numbers in sequences (saw-was, on-no, felt-left, 12-21). They are sometimes called "mirror-minded" or "mirror-readers."

6. They usually show some evidence of delayed or incomplete establishment of one-sided motor preference (unilateral cerebral

dominance). They tend to be left-handed or ambidextrous or mixed in their motor choices, e.g., right-handed and left-eyed, or they may have been slow in the establishment of their handedness.

7. They often show delays or defects in more than one language area. In addition to poor reading, they may have delayed or imperfect speech, a poor ear for words, a poor oral vocabulary, or clumsiness in hand-writing or in other motor acts.

8. They usually come from families in which there is left-handedness or language disorders, or both.

9. They are three or four times as apt to be boys as girls.

Chapter IV

CONTINUATION OF THE ORTON STORY

*That both cerebral ambilaterality and dyslexia are to be
equated with immaturity of cerebral development, is the
view most widely held today among neurologists.*

MACDONALD CRITCHLEY (1964)

THE ORTON STORY would not be complete without a detailed account
of the contributions made by some of the persons who had worked
directly with Orton.[1] Neither would it be complete without reference
to the work of several others, some of whom became interested in
Orton's concepts and carried forward his work through their own
individual research, and some of whom worked independently.

Orton's Direct Followers

Lauretta Bender, who started her psychiatric career with Orton
at the University of Iowa in 1926, is known as the originator of the
Visual-Motor Gestalt Test (1937)[2] This test commonly known as
the Bender-Gestalt Test, measures the degree of maturation of the
visual-motor Gestalt function. It calls for the reproduction of a series
of varying configurations and is a valuable guide in revealing maturation of perceptual motor Gestalten, especially in young children.

---

[1]Psychiatrists who worked directly under Orton were: Paul Dozier, Edwin Cole,
Earl Chesher and David Wright. Several speech specialists—Edward Lee Travis,
Bryng Bryngelson, Katrina de Hirsch, and Ellen Donohue—also worked with him.
Orton trained several educators in remedial reading: Anna Gillingham, Page
Sharp, Warren Koehler, Charlotte Pardee, Elizabeth Peabody, Peter Gow, Helene
Durbrow, Harlin Sexton and Sally Childs. (Sally Childs was president of The
Orton Society.) One pediatrician, William Langford, worked with Orton at the
New York Neurological Institute.

[2]The German word *Gestalt* means form or pattern—the shape things have. Stated
quite simply, Gestalt psychology is based on the theory that physical, psychological
and biological events do not occur through the summation of separate elements,
such as sensations experienced or reflexes, but through formed patterns of these
integrated units which function singly or in interrelation—configurationism. Each
of these patterns is called a Gestalt (plural, Gestalten).

Wertheimer, in 1912, formulated the ideas that developed into Gestalt psy-

According to Bender, children with reading disabilities show many of the following disorders on this test:

1. Figures tend to be more primitive, more fluid, and full of movement of the primitive vortical whirling type.

2. Squared figures become rounded, dots are replaced by loops, diamonds are squared, oblique lines become vertical and sometimes even horizontal.

3. There is disorientation on the background, usually by rotation of mobile figures, or verticalization tendencies.

4. There is a tendency to close open figures.

5. There is a tendency to convert figures, especially those that are verticalized and closed, into a "man" (body image projection) by drawing a face in the closed figure.[3]

Bender has followed, in the main, Orton's concept of "developmental lag," but she has elaborated on this and other aspects of language problems. In an article published in 1958, she summarized the results of her studies. Her explanation of "maturational lag," as she preferred to call it, was as follows:

It is based on a concept of functional areas of the brain and of personality which mature according to a recognized pattern longitudinal-wise. A maturational lag signifies a slow differentiation in this pattern. It does not indicate a structural defect, deficiency or loss. There is not necessarily a limitation in the poten-

---

chology. He defined a Gestalt as "a whole the behavior of which is not determined by that of its individual elements but where the part-processes are themselves determined by the intrinsic nature of the whole." His colleagues, Kohler and Koffka, then elaborated the Gestalt theory. The studies of Bender and others go far beyond the "whole-word" concept in the application of Gestalt psychology, as is evidenced by the Bender-Gestalt Test.

Some psychologists and educators had pointed out long before the advent of Gestalt psychology that many young children are able to recognize short but whole words before they know the individual letters. They devised the "whole-word" or "look-say" method of teaching reading, which became labeled as an application of Gestalt psychology. However, in Gestalt psychology emphasis is on structure, the way things are put together, the way parts make up the whole. Actually, the "whole-word" method is more an application of Pavlov's conditioned response-psychology.

[3]See reference to Tolor and Schulberg (1963) for an evaluation of the Bender-Gestalt Test.

tialities and at variable levels maturation may tend to accelerate, but often unevenly. Again one has to use the concept of plasticity in the way the embryologists use the term, being as yet unformed, but capable of being formed, being impressionable and responsive to patterning, and carrying within itself the potentialities of patterns which have not become fixed. This is also characteristic of a primitive state. It is this particular characteristic of developmental lags that effect such a variety of symptoms that defy classification and make it possible for each investigator to emphasize those factors that best fit his experience and theories. However, most significantly it is these qualities in developmental lags in children that offer us the greatest opportunities for understanding of hitherto little-understood conditions and also afford methods of training and therapy and opportunities for adaptive development.

* * *

The basic postulates for the understanding of language lags are that those parts of the neopallium which serve the specifically human functions of unilateral dominance, unilateral handedness for tool or pen and pencil usage, unilateral eyedness for close focus, auditory and visual recognition of signs and symbols, and the learning process for the spoken and written language, show a wider range of maturation age than do parts associated with other maturation or habit patterns.

In this same article Bender made a much broader statement which encompasses related fields:

Our insights in child psychiatry have been influenced by (1) studies in gestalt psychology and the knowledge that perceptual motor experiences have a known genesis from motility, action and movement and a maturational pattern determined, for example, by the visual motor gestalt test (Bender); (2) Paul Schilder's teaching concerning the body image, the most specific and complete perceptual motor gestalt, the maturation of which can also be followed by the Goodenough draw-a-man test among other ways; (3) psychoanalytic material and egopsychology, which also give us an understanding of the genesis and maturational patterning through childhood; and finally (4) Paul Schilder's emphasis on the patterned postural reflexes of childhood, which also pass through maturational patterns.

Lags or disturbances in maturation of any of these areas can be readily recognized by the standards indicated. Arnold Gesell, in his *Embryology of Behavior,* has shown the relationship between the tonic neck reflex attitudes of the foetal infant and all subsequent action patterns and suggests the beginning of cortical dominance. Today, the postural reflex position which will reveal increased tone and therefore a higher position of the dominant hand is the best but still least-known test for dominant handedness.

Paul Schilder,[4] mentioned above, was a neurologist, psychiatrist, and psychoanalyst who contributed a great deal to the thesis that delays in maturation are the essential problem in language disorders in children. He concluded that there was insufficient development of the cerebral centers upon which the development of the faculty of reading depends:

> These variations are probably due to a different development of those parts of the brain which are indispensable for the process of reading—a dysfunction of a cortical apparatus—which expresses itself in the differentiating and integrating difficulty, in optic mistakes concerning letters, and increased mirror tendencies, all of which increase the primary trouble in agnostic intellectual function.

After extensive study, Schilder (1944) wrote an article entitled "Congenital Alexia and Its Relation to Optic Perception." In addition to right-left disorientation (reversals), he found other kinds of perceptual difficulties, such as difficulty in recognizing single letters, in coordinating the sound of letters into whole words, and in breaking down the word into its component sounds.

The relationship of the hearing element to the reading process had been noted before by Bronner and others. This point is an important one, but it is frequently overlooked. We hear and speak words long before we read and write them. Reading is then the translation of symbols of sound (letters and words) into blocks of sound that make sense. If the correct hearing of words is lacking, reading will be impaired at least to some extent. Also, the majority of children with reading disability tend to spell "by ear," because they lack a clear-cut visual memory pattern of words. If, in addition, they have no clear-cut hearing of words, their handicap is augmented.

---

[4]For several years, Bender and Schilder worked together at Bellevue Hospital. Lauretta Bender is Mrs. Paul Schilder.

Studies by Bender, Schilder, Gesell and others of the maturation of motility patterns in children have shown that there are marked changes between the ages of five and seven—just when they start reading. Normally, at this time the tonic-neck-reflex becomes submerged; dominance with right-left orientation is established, and there comes the ability to handle oblique lines and diamond Gestalt structures in drawing. A retardation in any one of these developments is often associated with some lag in the other developments and may predict retardation in language skills. Also, since space and time are interlocked and time itself has many different Gestalten, it is not surprising that maturational lag may manifest itself in the concept or perception of time.

Bender called attention to a number of similarities between childhood schizophrenia and the developmental lags in language, such as dyslexia. She interpreted childhood schizophrenia on the basis of maturational lag and pointed out that schizophrenic children, as well as dyslexic children, retain primitive and plastic responses and show instability of perceptual behavior. She said:

> There are a number of similarities between childhood schizophrenia and developmental lags in language like dyslexia, which at times make even the differential diagnosis difficult. Children with severe reading disabilities show lags in neurological patterning or "soft neurological signs" also; they are awkward in their motor control or motility, and retain the immature tonic-neck reflex attitude for a longer time than other children do. Their motor tone is more variable; electroencephalographic patterns are of the dysrhythmic, immature type, as attested to by Kennard, Klingman, Taterka and Hill; general behavior is disorganized and impulsive; motor-perceptual patterns or capacity to develop gestalten remain primitive and full of motion and fluidity; and personalities are immature, impulse-ridden, and dependent, so that they are often taken for post-encephalitic, retarded, or schizophrenic children. They also suffer from anxiety and feelings of inadequacy which lead to various symptom formations.

However, she pointed out certain differentiations between childhood schizophrenia and dyslexia: "The language lags are more strongly localized in the area of language, dominant cerebral control, and mentation, and are therefore not as all-embracing or as severe as in childhood schizophrenia."

Bender also called attention to the difference between dyslexic children and mentally retarded children or those with organic defects:

> Children with language lags are quite different from children with a general mental retardation or with organic defects to the extent that they have capacities for accelerated development or learning, sometimes not until a delayed stage in maturation has been reached, but always while the principal features of the disability are retained. They also have capacities for vivid compensations in related areas of cerebral function.

Bender was among the first to point out that children with organic brain damage may be afflicted with various language disability syndromes, although they had shown no language handicaps before encephalitis, head trauma, or other agents had produced the brain damage.[5] She was also among the first to claim that reading disability could be predicted in the preschool child.

It is obvious that Bender took into account the whole child in his milieu and included in her studies the personality problems of children with maturational lags:

> Their personality is immature, impulse-ridden, dependent, so that they are often taken for post-encephalitic, retarded or schizophrenic children. They suffer from anxiety and feelings of inadequacy which lead to various symptom formations. Other life problems may increase their learning difficulties or be increased by them, leading many workers to consider these problems primary to the retardation in learning.
>
> Everyone working with these children knows how rewarding they can be and how rapidly they can overcome their disabilities if the relationship to the tutor, the motivation, and the remedial techniques at all coincide with the children's needs. On the other hand anxiety, feelings of inadequacy, inability to identify with age-

---

[5] The writer did some pioneering work in this field. Between 1930 and 1935 he became sensitive to the possibility that several children who were referred to a clinic as behavior problems had brain damage. Between 1935 and 1940, a follow-up study of these children revealed that almost all of them had some language learning impairment. In some, there was definite evidence that the handicap had not existed before the organic damage. The report of this study was not published until 1946 because war service intervened.

level children or with authoritative teaching adults, withdrawal even with regression, antagonism, paranoid attitudes, antisocial behavior, all may be the result of failure to over-come the handicap or find compensatory activities. Defenses against these attitudes may fall into any category of neurotic symptom formation or personality deformations.

After working several years with hundreds of children at Bellevue Hospital, Bender concluded that over 50 per cent of the boys who came to her psychiatric service with behavior disorders were nonreaders or severely retarded in reading, "It is also recognized," she said, "that this [reading disability] is one of the most common causes, and a correctible one within limits, of social or emotional maladjustment, behavior disorders, delinquencies, etc., in our young people."

Basically, the studies carried out by Bender and her associates confirmed the Orton concepts, although she added new dimensions to his work, especially in the field of Gestalt psychology. The characteristics she found in children with language lags paralleled almost identically those found by Orton:

1. Poor establishment of cortical unilateral dominance.

2. Right-left confusion—involving the child's own body and others.

3. Slower development of motor skills, awkwardness in motor control and mobility, longer retention of tonic-neck-reflex-attitude responses, more variable motor tone, etc.

4. The number of boys affected was several times that of girls.

5. Family histories that included other individuals with the same or related problems.

6. The possibility of predicting reading disability before the child enters school.[6]

As an extension of Bender's work, attention is called to a follow-up study made in 1961-62 by A. A. Silver and Rosa A. Hagin of twenty-

[6]Attention is called to the first Percival Bailey Lecture delivered by Lauretta Bender in October, 1960, entitled "The Brain and Child Behavior." While the lecture focused on childhood schizophrenia, Bender gave an inclusive review of the contributions of "the giants" who had studied child behavior from many interrelated aspects. Her lecture started with a quotation from Percival Bailey: "I seached in vain—for any awareness of the other variable which seems to me so obvious, namely, that we might be dealing with an organism defective by constitution or development."

four children with specific reading disability who were among the forty-one originally studied by Bender at Bellevue Hospital between 1949 and 1951. These adults were given the same battery of tests that they had taken ten to twelve years earlier. The general conclusion was that "their specific perceptual problems and lack of clear-cut cerebral dominance persist, although in less severe form."

Some details from the study of Silver and Hagin are of significance because they also reviewed the records of the forty-one children in Bender's original study. Concerning these children, Silver and Hagin said:

> In the perceptual area, immaturity was found, particularly in the visuo-motor field, where nine out of ten children had specific difficulty in spatial orientation and in visual figure-background perception. Five out of ten had problems in auditory perception with inability to grasp the temporal relationships of sound. In the neurological area there was outstanding defect in right-left discrimination and evidence from the "extension test" that cerebral dominance was not clearly established.

Concerning the "extension test" as described by Schilder, these writers stated that it may "point to a basic biological defect in the reading disability, namely, the lack of clear-cut cerebral dominance."

Other psychiatrists, neurologists, and pediatricians who were associated directly with Orton have produced many valuable studies and clinical reports that were confirmatory of Orton's findings and of Bender's Gestalt interpretations. Among the psychiatrists, R. S. Eustis and E. M. Cole published several papers in a variety of journals— bringing the topic of reading disability to the attention of pediatricians, ophthalmologists, and general practitioners of medicine. A recent article by Cole (1964) entitled "Reading and Speech Problems as Expressions of a Specific Language Disability" demonstrated the intimate relationship of reading disability to various speech disturbances, including stuttering. He reviewed the writings of several well-known speech specialists, all of whom tended to divorce stuttering from the general group of language disabilities, especially developmental dyslexia. However, he expressed his own opinion by saying: "We do not agree that stuttering is an isolated problem. We consider stuttering, or stammering (we use the terms interchangeably) as being one aspect of an over-all language handicap, part of the specific language disability that we are attempting to describe." Also, Paul Dozier wrote an important paper on word-deafness in which he stressed an aspect of language disability which had been pointed out by Orton.[7] (See p. 55.)

J. Roswell Gallagher—whose fundamental training was in pediatrics and who was associated with Mrs. Orton in clinical work—has written informative articles on language disabilities based on his experiences as a physician in a preparatory school for boys and in the adolescent unit of Children's Hospital in Boston. In 1958 Gallagher visited several centers in Europe where special attention was given to reading disability, and the report that resulted from his observations showed that the problem is equally prevalent in other languages. As a result of his visit and largely through his interest and effort, Knud Hermann's book on reading disability was translated from Danish into English.

In his book, *Medical Care of the Adolescent,* Gallagher (1966) summarized many aspects of the topic. Concerning causation, he said:

> Many educational psychologists reject the belief that there are hereditary and cerebral causes of dyslexia and object to the use of the words "congenital" or "hereditary." Perhaps they consider them to imply that the condition is unlikely to improve. . . . Finally, though many seem to emphasize one or another special factor, they believe dyslexia the result of such causes as inadequate readiness for initial reading, intellectual backwardness, social and cultural poverty, personality, emotional and adjustment difficulties, irregular school attendance, and defective teaching.
>
> There are few, if any, who would question the importance of any of those matters and would not wish to give them consideration, but at the present time it is difficult to believe that any one of these or any combination of them can constitute the *basic* cause of the difficulty in a high percentage of those young people

---

[7]The numerous and excellent contributions of the educators and psychologists who were directly associated with Orton are recognized. The writer considers it to be beyond the range of neuropsychiatric experience to deal with all the intricate details of psychological studies and remedial reading techniques. However, consideration of these fields must be taken into account in the understanding of the total problem, and a few references to such studies will be found elsewhere in the text and in the bibliography.

who exhibit the characteristics of a specific language disability. The frequency with which any of these factors seems to be the primary cause of trouble and the frequency with which no difficulty in learning to read or spell occurs in their presence need further to be investigated.

Other Contributions Related to Orton Concepts

Many psychiatrists, neurologists, psychologists, and educators who were not associated with Orton have written articles and books on developmental dyslexia that deal with the main concepts of the "Orton School." In these publications will be found agreement with and elaboration of several of his concepts, disagreement with some, and rejection of a few. As will be seen later in Chapter V, some of the literature—especially from psychoanalytic and psychological sources—gives no consideration to Orton-like concepts.

In European countries several fundamental studies of "congenital word-blindness" (the term still used by some writers) were published after Orton's original article in 1925. Many of these studies corroborated Orton's theories and findings, although a few differed in certain aspects. Some of the European investigators came to the same conclusions that Orton did, but it seems that they were not directly influenced by him.

In Germany, Bachmann (1927) and Solms (1948) gave lengthy bibliographic reviews as well as their own points of view *ueber kongenitale wortblindheit* (concerning congenital word-blindness). In France, Ajuriaguerra (1951), Launay (1952), Chassagny (1954), and others wrote about reading "inaptitudes." In all of these reports, the clinical descriptions followed very closely those of Morgan, Hinshelwood, and Orton and observed the errors in spelling including reversals, confused dominance, familial tendencies, etc., that characterize developmental dyslexia.

From Sweden and Denmark came some classic studies, only a few of which can be mentioned here. The treatise by H. Skydsgaard (1942) of Denmark entitled *Den Konstitutionelle Dyslexi, "Ordblindhed"* has been referred to by many writers. In addition to a clear description of word-blindness as found in Danish people, Skydsgaard produced geneological tables which indicate that heredity is a conspicuous feature in dyslexia.

However, it remained for Bertil Hallgren (1950) to carry out more detailed and controlled genetic studies in Sweden. In a study of the families of 112 cases of reading disability, Hallgren found reading and speech problems in other family members in 99 of the families (88 per cent). He came to the conclusion that "specific dyslexia with a high degree of probability follows a monohybrid autosomal dominant mode of inheritance." In other words, a single gene is involved in a dominant non-sex-linked form of inheritance. From his study of twins, Hallgren reported that in three pairs of uniovular (identical) twins there was concordance for word-blindness in all three pairs, but in three pairs of binovular twins there was concordance in only one pair. Later, Knud Hermann and Edith Norrie (1959) reported concordance for reading disability in all nine pairs of uniovular twins studied by them, but in thirty pairs of binovular twins there was concordance in only ten pairs. Although the number studied was statistically small, these findings in twins indicate that heredity is a definite factor in dyslexia.

Early interest in word-blindness had prompted the Danes to form a national association for word-blindness in 1943 and in the same year to establish the Word-blind Institute in Copenhagen. Knud Hermann, Edith Norrie,[8] and others who have worked at the Institute since its origin have carried out several studies. One important book, *On Medfordt Ordblindhed,* by Hermann (1955) resulted from these studies. It was revised and translated into English in 1959 under the title of *Reading Disability.* This book presents a clear and detailed description of Hermann's clinical findings. His observations followed in general and corroborated the findings of Orton and others, especially with regard to the clinical syndrome, the evidence of confused dominance, and the hereditary aspects. He postulated his initial statement as follows:

> Congenital word-blindness presents an impaired development of certain symbol functions, involving principally reading and writing, but also other symbols such as numbers and musical symbols.

---

[8]Edith Norrie, a word-blind case herself, was the founder of the Word-blind Institute.

The symptoms occur as primitive characteristics which are to be found also in the incompletely developed person as a manifestation of normal variation.

Of the various contributory causes of congenital word-blindness, only one factor is found to be invariable, *viz.* heredity, which must be regarded as the specific pathogenic factor.

From this premise, Hermann went on to develop the similarity of the reading disability syndrome to Gerstmann's syndrome.[9] Although Hermann was not the first to call attention to the similarity between dyslexia and Gerstmann's syndrome, his detailed studies reported in 1955 were impressive if not completely convincing.

After discussion of Gerstmann's syndrome and case illustrations of dyslexia, Hermann summarized his views:

> Comparative analysis shows the symptoms of Gerstmann's syndrome and constitutional dyslexia to have so many features in common, that it is very likely that the fundamental disturbance in these two conditions is identical, viz. a defect involving the categorical sphere of function which may be termed directional function.
>
> The directional disturbance is related to a failure of lateral orientation with reference to the body-scheme, such that concepts of direction are either uncertain or abolished; the individual consequently has difficulty in orienting himself in extra-personal space. This difficulty in orientation has particular consequences for the ability to operate with symbols such as letters, numbers, and notes. Such difficulty with symbols can be described in terms of a failure of Gestalt function: the latter cannot operate in a

---

[9]In 1924, Josef Gerstmann, an Austrian neurologist, described a group of symptoms occurring consistently after brain damage in a circumscribed area of the parietal lobe of the dominant hemisphere, which involved sequential ordering and a Gestalt disturbance related to "body image." The four main symptoms were:
1. Disorientation or confusion about the right and left sides of the body.
2. Finger agnosia (inability to identify individual fingers touched or moved).
3. Dyscalculia (impaired calculating ability).
4. Agraphia (disturbed handwriting).
From the literature, including further contributions of Gerstmann, and from the writer's clinical experience, it appears that the four symptoms are not an all or none proposition. Finger agnosia does not mean complete obliteration of finger recognition, agraphia does not mean complete inability to write, and dyscalculia does not mean inability to add two and two. In fact, at least one function in the quartet of symptoms may show little if any impairment.

sufficiently differentiated way when concepts of direction and sequence are impaired or poorly developed.

The directional uncertainty in congenital word-blindness is shown directly by confusion between right and left, and also by certain types of error—especially reversals, rotations, and disfigurements (whereby parts of letters are drawn in wrong directions).

The agraphia of Gerstmann's syndrome is identical with the disordered writing of word-blindness, and it must also be noted that the errors presented by normal and word-blind subjects (in both reading and writing) also show no essential difference. This similarity is particularly marked in relation to the errors of normal subjects in their first years at school. This feature does not justify rejection of the theory that congenital word-blindness is a specific abnormality, which can be traced to one causal factor. When children in their first years of schooling commit certain elementary errors (reversals, rotations, etc.), this is an indication that their directional function is not yet fully developed. Directional concepts probably become established at about 9-10 years of age. If these special types of error persist beyond this age, they are most probably due to congenital word-blindness.

The defect of directional function can explain the dyscalculia in congenital word-blindness, and also the slight speech difficulties which may occur in word-blindness and whose most characteristic feature is a transposition of syllables. These cases of dyslexia with speech disturbances may possibly represent a transition between word-blindness on the one hand and audimutitas on the other. The experience at the Word-blind Institute has been that persons suffering from audimutitas always show difficulties with reading and writing, similar to those found in word-blindness.[10]

---

[10]Concerning Hermann's consideration of Gerstmann's syndrome, attention is called to a more recent study by M. Kinsbourne and E. K. Warrington (1963) entitled "The Developmental Gerstmann Syndrome." These writers started their paper with the suggestion that this syndrome may appear in children on a developmental basis and, if so, what effect it has on their acquisition of educational skills. They reported on seven children who had this syndrome, but it appeared that all of them showed some evidence of acquired brain damage. They said: "Reading retardation of varying degree was present in all but one of the cases, though it was characteristically somewhat less severe than the retardation in spelling." In their explanation of reading retardation, they brought in Gestalt principles and went on to say:

The developmental Gerstmann syndrome reveals its fullest expression in a child who, backward in reading, and still more in spelling, fails tests

Hermann recognized that there are other causes of reading difficulties, such as intellectual retardation, brain damage, and environmental factors. He said, "It has never been denied from medical quarters that a series of exogenous factors may interfere when children are learning to read and write."

However, Hermann and others have contended that dyslexia is a definite constitutional disorder and not just the "fag end" of a continuum that extends upward to eidetic imagery. Citing Jaederholm's data as shown on a curve of general intelligence and mental defect, Hermann pointed out that the skewness of the curve consisting of a small hump in the region of I. Q. < 45 "can be taken to indicate that dyslectics are not simple variants of the normal, but represent one or more morbid conditions of a special nature." Hermann continued, "The supposed gradual transition from the group of normal readers to the dyslectics is often used as an argument against the medical conception of dyslexia as a specific abnormality."

Hermann's point is well taken, but the skewness of the curve may be due in part to an accumulation of dyslexic cases (unrecognized) at this particular level on the curve. On the other hand, if we accept developmental dyslexia as a maturational lag, there must be a continuum in gradation of facility from the nonreader to the average reader and above. All gradations of reading facility are passed through by the average or normal child as he develops from age five to ten. Also, there is a similar continuum of development or maturation in color vision, motor coordination, tone acuity, etc., without a definite line being drawn to distinguish those persons who lag behind in any of these respects while progressing in others.

In the United States, Ralph D. Rabinovitch and his associates have

---

of finger differentiation and order, confuses right and left, makes errors of letter sequence in spelling, and of rank of digits in calculation, and, poor in "spatial" and constructive tasks, performs significantly less well on the performance than on the verbal scale of the W.I.C.S. . . . One might expect sometimes to encounter the syndrome in a less complete form, particularly if the child is examined during a transitional period in which a delay in cerebral cortical development is finally overcome.

In final summary they stated: "The developmental Gerstmann syndrome may arise on a constitutional or traumatic basis, and may exist in isolation or in a setting of other neurological disorder. It may cause reading and writing retardation of characteristic type."

carried out studies of "reading retardation," as he prefers to call the
condition. In 1959 Rabinovitch was quite clear in describing reading
retardation cases and placing them in one of three major groups:

1. Capacity to learn to read is intact but is utilized insufficiently
for the child to achieve a reading level appropriate to his intelligence. The causative factor is exogenous, the child having a normal
reading potential that has been impaired by negativism, anxiety,
depression, emotional blocking, psychosis, limited schooling opportunity, or other external influences. . . . They are diagnosed as
secondary reading retardation.

2. Capacity to learn to read is impaired by frank brain damage
manifested by clear-cut neurologic deficits. The picture is similar
to the early-described adult dyslexic syndromes. Other definite
aphasic difficulties are generally present. History usually reveals
the cause of the brain injury, common agents being prenatal
toxicity, birth trauma or anoxia, encephalitis, and head injury.
These cases are diagnosed as brain injury with reading retardation.

3. Capacity to learn to read is impaired without definite brain
damage suggested in history or on neurological examination. The
defect is in the ability to deal with letters and words as symbols,
with resultant diminished ability to integrate the meaningfulness
of written material. The problem appears to reflect a disturbed
pattern of neurologic organization. Because the cause is biologic
or endogenous, these cases are diagnosed as primary retardation.

Concerning primary reading retardation, Rabinovitch was quite
explicit:

Although definite statistics are not available, it is likely that the
large majority of children presenting total or severe reading retardation have a primary problem, with secondary or exogenous
causation higher in the less severe cases. There is a strong predominance of boys in the incidence of primary retardation. The
proportion of boys to girls is probably greater than 10 to 1. Many
workers have suggested a hereditary factor with which this sex incidence is related, and there is much evidence in support of such a
view, although further research in this area is indicated.

Andrew L. Drew (1956), who was associated with Rabinovitch,
published an article entitled "A Neurological Appraisal of Familial
Word-blindness." Admitting that there was variability in symptoma-

tology from patient to patient, Drew's general findings were as follows: "Right-left confusion, various extinction or inattention phenomena, cortical sensory disturbances, mixed hand-eye preference, non-specific motor awkwardness, dissociated dysgraphia, and speech and spelling abnormalities are all variously combined with reading disturbance." He called attention to the fact that many characteristics of dyslexia are similar to those found in Gerstmann's syndrome and that the symptoms are consistent with the auditory-visual-phonetic disintegration described by Schilder. He also claimed that in dyslexia there is a basic disturbance of Gestalt function:

> No constant neurological sign is present but if these various findings are interpreted as Gestalten disturbances, then the entire symptom complex becomes a coherent entity. It is believed that the inconsistencies, confusion and apparently diametrically opposed findings reported in the literature and observed clinically can best be resolved by interpreting the findings in a configurational setting. . . . There is some reason to believe that delayed development of the parietal lobe is the anatomical substrate of this disturbance in Gestalt recognition.

In this article, Drew gave his findings in three cases of familial word-blindness which occurred, in varying degrees, in a father and his two sons by different marriages. He expressed the idea that a comprehensive theory of word-blindness should include heredity, since present-day neurological opinion does not accept a discrete "reading center" in the brain that could be selectively controlled by a dominant gene.

In connection with configuration distortion and reading disability, A. A. Fabian (1945), working at Bellevue Hospital with children who were severe nonreaders, was one of the first to point to the significance of verticalization as a sign of immaturity in the Gestalt figure. When presented with horizontal figures, 76 per cent of these children rotated them to the vertical position. Fabian then tested 586 other children in a public school and found that 51 per cent of the six-year-olds rotated figures from the horizontal to the vertical, while only 22 per cent of the six-and-one-half-year-olds made the same rotation. The percentage dropped sharply at age seven and was practically absent at seven and one-half years. He pointed to this finding as one of the prevailing signs of reading disability but interpreted it as one of the infantile ego responses to personality problems.

Arnold Gesell (1949) described the preschool child as struggling against the tendency to verticalize all constructions, especially the oblique ones. He said that when this difficulty persists, together with reading disability beyond the sixth year, it was of diagnostic significance and indicated the seriousness of the reading retardation and evident immaturity of the growing action system.

A more recent study by the Bellevue Hospital group should also be mentioned. Silver and Hagin (1960) reported on neurological and perceptual disturbances in nonreaders: "Our neurological evaluation indicates that 92% of children with specific reading disability have defects in right-left orientation; immaturity in postural reflexes and a discrepancy between the hand used for writing and the dominant hand as determined by extension tests."

Many other contributions to the topic of dyslexia that are in keeping with Orton concepts will be reviewed in Chapter VII, which deals more specifically with neurological and neurophysiological studies.

Contributions on Topics Related to Reading Disability

As previously pointed out, reading disability does not stand alone as a distinct entity. Almost invariably it is part of a general disturbance in language function. Many writers have focused attention on the allied disabilities, such as spelling, writing, word-deafness, dyspraxia (abnormal clumsiness), etc. Speech disorders are "allied," to be sure, but it is beyond the scope of this book to include a field of such magnitude.[11]

---

[11]From speech therapists we find confirmation of the close relationship between speech disorders and other language disturbances. Jon Eisenson (1958), a specialist in speech (and hearing) disorders at Queens College was convinced that Bender in her discussions of reading disabilities "was talking about the same kind of children whom I have seen throughout the country with the diagnosis of aphasia, aphasoid delayed speech, or language retardation." He said, "In our files at Queens College, we have repeated instances of children who began their experience with us with a diagnosis of delayed speech and who continued or returned to us two or three years later with a designation of reading disability."

Falck and Falck (1962) stated, "Many children referred to a clinic because of obvious speech problems have somewhat less obvious (but equally real and handicapping) language disabilities in the area of reading, writing and spelling. . . . To ignore these non-oral language problems when training students is to limit their potential effectiveness and worth."

For many years educators have been concerned wi
all too often they have considered spelling to be di:
from reading and other language functions. Morgan, ᴗ.
many others have pointed out the specific characteristics that occur
in both the oral and written spelling of dyslexic children. The "spelling
by ear" or "just as it sounds" is one of the characteristics, as is the tendency to reverse the sequence of letters. Also, in these children there
is a frustrated gazing into space, as if searching for a visual image
of the word they are trying to spell.

Although there have been many studies concerning poor spelling
ability, very little has been written about the champion spellers who
win national contests. It is the writer's surmise that these champions
have some prodigious visual memory and an unusual facility in
auditory-visual associations of language symbols along with a thorough
knowledge of spelling rules. Surely, great facility in spelling is not the
result of brain damage or of hypertrophy of an area in the brain, nor
can emotional motivation be the primary explanation.[12]

Although illegible handwriting is common among adults (doctors
included) as well as among children, there are some persons who do
not seem able to learn to write. Orton described such a condition as
"developmental agraphia (special writing disability)." Helen C. Durbrow (1960) gave a comprehensive summary of this condition in an
article "Children Who Cannot Write" (*Bulletin of The Orton Society,*
May, 1960).

Word-deafness, a term brought forward from the early pathological
studies, has been included with developmental reading and speech
disabilities. Orton gave an excellent account of this aspect of developmental lag and showed its relation to other language handicaps.
Word-deafness was definitely a part of the larger complex considered
by Bender and Schilder. The role that word-deafness plays in speech
disorders is very definite but often overlooked.

Paul Dozier (1953), who was associated with Orton, wrote a paper
on "The Neurological Background of Word Deafness." Concerning
"developmental word-deafness," he said:

---

[12]In the psychoanalytic literature, E. Sterba (1943) wrote an article entitled
"On Spelling," bringing in many of the emotional or experiential factors men-
tioned by Strachey, Blanchard, and others in their studies of reading disability.
(See Chapter V.)

I remember that Dr. Orton mentioned casually to me one time that there was one more characteristic of these children, and I have seen it borne out almost without exception, and that is that they have a certain ruthlessness. I know why it is, I think. The children are frustrated. Since they can so obviously hear ordinary sounds in the environment—the closing door, the dinner bell, someone calling their name—no one understands why they do not seem to react to the spoken word as do normal children, and so they feel frustrated, starting as they do with normal intelligence. The common reaction in a very small child, as well as in some older children, is ruthlessness.

* * *

When we are speaking of word deafness, we are not speaking of something that is the same in every child who is afflicted with it. I can only compare it with reading disability—and say that we can have about every degree of it, from just a dash of it to a totally disabling difficulty, and when we have a severe degree of this peculiar inability to remember, to understand the spoken word of others, then we get an intellectual deprivation, and most of these children are, for educational purposes, probably most practically grouped in most things as feeble-minded.

Although Dozier compared developmental word-deafness with word-deafness resulting from brain damage, he recognized that the origin of developmental word-deafness is constitutional. He also recognized the accompanying behavioral disturbances, and he found evidence of mixed dominance in the large majority of his cases, as well as mixed laterality in the families.

In conclusion, Dozier said:

We have a similar condition here to strephosymbolia or specific reading disability, but it is a more severe one because all four divisions or departments of language function, as I have before mentioned, are found to be affected in the course of it. There are all degrees of it. Severe degrees allow the child to be confused with the retarded, with the deaf. The mild degrees are probably only recognized or usually recognized after school starts and the inevitable reading disability appears, although some of them are recognized at the nursery school period when they come with the presenting complaint of persistent infantile speech or have delayed speech.

Some of the early writers on word-blindness observed extreme clumsiness or poor motor coordination in the children they described. Orton called attention more than once to what he termed "developmental apraxia" (abnormal clumsiness) as part of the syndrome of strephosymbolia. Later, William S. Langford (1955) gave an excellent description of developmental dyspraxia based on clinical and personal experience. He related this disability to the other handicaps found in language dysfunctions. He called attention to the varying degrees of clumsiness:

> In some children the dyspraxia seems to run the whole gamut. At six or seven or eight, they are still so clumsy in walking that they fall upstairs or fall downstairs or over door jambs, they are always knocking things over and in many of them, when they sit down to write or do something that calls for a lot of concentration, we see a sort of motor overflow into their feet similar to what we see in the cerebral palsy child.

*   *   *

> They seem to have trouble in taking their old, more simple patterns and developing new sequences out of them. We see this in the larger and in the small motor muscle activities. Some of these children with severe dyspraxia do not have any associated reading disability or any academic handicap and in a sense they are fortunate because they can compensate with academic success and intellectual achievement. However, many of these children do have concomitant reading difficulties which prevent this compensational achievement in academic lines and theirs is a difficult lot.

*   *   *

> There seems to be a difficulty not only in getting the concept of the movements as a whole but also in maintaining the kinaesthetic memory of the pictured movement once they have been through it. This does not seem to be ameliorated as the child grows older and one could think of it as being of the same order as the difficulty of the child who has trouble in getting sequential patterns and letters and words in reading. It is the difficulty in getting a Gestalt impression of things. . . .

Recognizing the accompanying emotional problems, Langford said:

> Personalitywise, these children seem to develop many inferiority feelings because of their motor disability. Boys are expected to compete with their peers in sport activities. Girls are expected

to be graceful and when we see a girl who is clumsy, this is quite hard on her family as well as herself.

In the last sentence of his article Langford stated that he was the "doubly left-handed" child in his family, "always knocking things over and always falling over things, and in my own family, where I know parts of three generations, there is a large mixture of these things."

Another study entitled "Clumsy Children: Developmental Apraxia and Agnosia" was published by J. N. Walton, E. Ellis, and S. D. M. Court (1962). In the five children they studied, there were no positive neurological findings, but four of the children showed some evidence of ambilaterality or ambidexterity. Two had been diagnosed as mentally backward, but on the Wechsler Scale for Children the verbal score of all five showed them to be of normal intelligence. However, there was a marked discrepancy between their verbal and performance scores.

Failure in arithmetic is in many respects allied to language disability. A child who reverses figures and their sequence as he does letters will be handicapped in ordinary addition, multiplication and subtraction. In fractions and decimals, in algebra, geometry and calculus the handicap will be more than doubly compounded. Moreover, if he is unable to read an arithmetic problem correctly, he is destined for complete failure.

On the other hand, there are children and adults who read well but still cannot "figure" accurately. Many writers have dealt with this subject, but particular attention is called to an article "Congenital Arithmetic Disability and Acalculia" by Erich Guttmann (1936). He found that some "cases may be regarded as specific arithmetic disabilities, arising from structural or functional anomalies of the brain." He claimed that in some cases there was no difficulty in reading numerical figures and that in some children with reading disability there was no "figure-blindness." It is difficult to accept Guttmann's hypothesis that one specific area of the brain is the center for calculation and other arithmetical functions. Gerstmann's syndrome and the Gestalt interpretations, which include acalculia, appear to be a much more acceptable explanation.

The above remarks do not deny that there are persons with arithmetical ineptitude in contrast with those who are "mathematical geniuses;" but the latter may not have special aptitudes in other fields.

Music is still another "communication" function that is related to language abilities. In many ways reading a music score, sense of rhythm, tone sensitivity (perfect pitch *versus* tone-deafness), motor ability, etc., cannot be divorced from language abilities and disabilities. Quite early in the discussion of word-blindness Peters (1908) mentioned this relationship in his paper, "Ueber Kongenitale Wortblindheit." He called attention to the difficulties encountered by the word-blind when they attempt to read music. Claiborne (1906), in an article entitled "Types of Congenital Amblyopia," went on to say and illustrate that many persons have imperfect appreciation of or memory for musical sounds. He used the term "amblymusia" in this connection.

To conclude the discussion of "allied" disabilities, the following paragraph is quoted from Hermann's book *Reading Disability*:

> It should be mentioned that note-blindness is inherited in the same way as word-blindness, and two colleagues have given me interesting information on this point. One of them is himself note-blind, but is a competent cellist and has had to devise his own "system" in order to read music. He is not word-blind, but his son is markedly so. The other colleague is himself word-blind but not note-blind. He now reads without difficulty, but still has trouble in writing, and needless to say this handicap is a considerable embarrassment when he has to write prescriptions. In the course of time he has worked out a system of checking to guard against mistakes of this kind. Both of his sons are note-blind but not word-blind. They have found an outlet for their musical interests through playing by ear, but they have been unable to learn to read music. In these cases it is remarkable how word-blindness and note-blindness have alternated in the two generations. This indicates that in all probability these two disorders have a common basis, which applies to number-blindness as well, since this also occurs in word-blind families.

Chapter V

EMOTIONAL AND ENVIRONMENTAL FACTORS IN READING DISABILITY (REVIEW OF PSYCHOANALYTIC LITERATURE)

> *But a thing once said sinks in the mind. That which has struck the brain often from time to time comes back again, and in the breast of simple infancy lives unexplained full many a mystery.*
>
> VICTOR HUGO

M ANY OF THE WRITERS mentioned in the previous chapters referred to the existence of emotional and environmental factors in various types of language disturbances. However, in most instances these writers considered emotional factors to be secondary to the language disability, sometimes being the direct result of the difficulty, sometimes coexisting with it, and sometimes even augmenting it. They did not consider emotional disturbances to be the direct or primary cause of language dysfunctions.

In cases where brain pathology has produced aphasia, Hughlings Jackson recorded that during emotional episodes aphasic patients were able to say things and otherwise overcome aphasic handicaps, which they could not do in a more quiescent state. In contrast to the aphasics who are aided by their emotions, many stutterers may be able to talk with ease in a tranquil atmosphere, only to become completely blocked when asked to speak before an audience. This observation does not necessarily prove that all stuttering is caused by emotional inhibitions. Also, there are children with "birth palsy," who have overcome athetoid movements and speech defects, only to have a return of such symptoms in the presence of strangers or when they are embarrassed.

Even persons without any special disability may at times have difficulty listening to a lecture or reading a book. Much of a person's receptivity, inner elaboration and retention depend on interest, motivation and concentration which, in turn, may be emotionally and environmentally conditioned. For example, a boy in a reading class at school may be "looking out the window," daydreaming of football or fishing. On the other hand, he may be preoccupied with and anxious about strife in the home that unsettles his fundamental security. He may feel hostile toward the teacher who is a parent substitute. His emotional distractions—whatever they are—will reduce his efficiency in reading, arithmetic, or spelling. The reduction in efficiency may vary in keeping with his interest and facility in the subject matter.

A child may have such unusual facility in some field other than language—in sports, music, mathematics, or dramatics perhaps—that motivation and interest in reading and spelling may be submerged. Also, a child may not have much ability in any direction; consequently, the resultant ego frustration leads to inertia and resistance in all educational pursuits. No child likes to be a "dub" in the eyes of his peers or his parents in any field of action. Certainly, this applies as much to reading, spelling and writing as it does to ball games, dancing or social activities. It is taken for granted that emotional reactions will accompany and have a bearing on these activities.

However, the assumption that emotional blocks or inhibitions within the individual may continuously be the fundamental and only factor in the causation of language disabilities (particularly reading) is a different tenet. Some writers are of the opinion that emotional inhibitions are the fundamental cause of language disability, while others find the cause outside the individual—in teaching methods, in the home atmosphere, in the socioeconomic status of the family. In either approach, the innate facility of the individual child often receives little consideration. In other words, "somatic compliance," to use Freud's expression, is overlooked.

Freud's Concepts

When Sigmund Freud published his monograph on aphasia in 1891, he was primarily interested in neurology. In this monograph he was the first to put his finger on an important point in language disabilities when he said:

There were cases of aphasia in which no localized lesion needed to be assumed and the symptoms could be attributed to an alteration of a physiological constant in the speech apparatus. Aphasia simply reproduces a state which existed in the course of the normal process of learning to speak and read.

When Freud wrote this monograph, he was a neurologist, but his interest was already shifting toward psychoanalysis.

In Freud's voluminous writings in the field of psychoanalysis, there are no articles that specifically concern reading, spelling, or writing, but his observations about "slips of the tongue" are well-known. In his *Psychopathology of Everyday Life* (1901) there is a chapter on mistakes in reading and writing, but this chapter does not concern itself with reading disability *per se*.

In Freud's early psychoanalytic contributions will be found statements that have a bearing on language disturbances. In his first lecture in the United States at Clark University during September, 1909, Freud referred to Breuer's first case in which psychoanalytic principles were used (1889-1892). Among the great variety of hysterical symptoms presented by the patient, "her eye movements were disturbed and her power of vision was subject to numerous restrictions." Hysterical disturbances of vision, which naturally might include inability to read, had been described long before 1889. Such hysterical disturbances, however, are different from reading disability.

Some important concepts that have to do with disturbed vision and indirectly with impaired reading ability are found in Freud's *Three Essays on Sexuality* (1905). He dealt with the various sensations and the manner in which they participate in sexual functions:

> Visual impressions remain the most frequent pathway along which libidinal excitation is aroused; indeed, natural selection counts upon the accessibility of this pathway when it encourages the development of beauty in the sexual object. On the other hand, this pleasure in looking (scoptophilia) becomes a perversion (a) if it is restricted exclusively to the genitals, or (b) if it is connected with the overriding disgust (as in the case of voyeurs or people who look on at excretory functions), or (c) if, instead of being preparatory to normal sexual aim, it supplants it. The force which opposes scoptophilia, but may be overridden by it (in a manner

parallel to what we have previously seen in the case of disgust), is shame.

Freud (1910) wrote a contribution to a *Festschrift* in honor of a Viennese ophthalmologist. The title of the paper translates as "The Psycho-analytic View of Psychogenic Disturbances of Vision." In this article Freud focused on hysterical blindness and made no specific reference to reading, but he again described the connection between the repression of scoptophilic impulses and the outbreak of psychogenic visual disturbances. He said:

> Let us suppose that the sexual component instinct which makes use of looking—sexual pleasure in looking (scoptophilia)—had drawn upon itself defensive action by the ego-instincts in consequence of excessive demands, so that the ideas in which its desires are expressed succumb to repression and are prevented from becoming conscious; in that case there will be a general disturbance of the relation of the eye and of the act of seeing to the ego and consciousness. The ego will have lost its dominance over the organ, which will now be wholly at the disposal of the repressed sexual instinct. It looks as though the repression has been carried too far by the ego, as though it had emptied the baby out with the bathwater: the ego refuses to see anything at all anymore, now that the sexual interest in seeing has made itself so prominent. But the alternative picture seems more to the point. This attributes the active role instead to the repressed pleasure in looking. The repressed instinct takes its revenge for being held back from further physical expansion, by becoming able to extend its dominance over the organ that is in its service. The loss of conscious dominance over the organ is the detrimental substitute for the repression which had miscarried and was only made possible at that price.

Freud stated this point of view in other words and pointed out the role that scoptophilia plays in inhibiting the taking in of knowledge through the eyes, which would naturally implicate the process of reading:

> As regards the eye, we are in the habit of translating the obscure psychical processes concerned in the repression of sexual scoptophilia and in the development of disturbances of vision as though a punishing voice was speaking from within the subject, and saying: "Because you sought to misuse your organ of sight

for evil sensual pleasures, it is fitting that you should not see anything at all anymore," as though it was in this way approving the
outcome of the process. The idea of talion punishment is involved
in this, and in fact our explanation of psychogenic visual disturbance coincides with what is suggested by myths and legends.
The beautiful legend of Lady Godiva tells how all the town's in-
habitants hid behind their shuttered windows, so as to make easier
the lady's task of riding naked through the streets in broad day-
light, and how the only man who peeped through the shutters at
her revealed loveliness was punished by going blind.

It is of considerable interest to note that, in conclusion, Freud expressed his definite belief that mental phenomena are ultimately based
on physical ones. He stated:

> We may ask ourselves whether the suppression of sexual com-
> ponent instincts which is brought about by environmental influence
> is sufficient in itself to call up functional disturbances in organs, or
> whether special constitutional conditions must be present in order
> that the organs may be led to an exaggeration of their erotogenic
> role and consequently provoke repression of the instincts. We
> should have to see in those conditions the constitutional part of the
> disposition to fall ill to psychogenic and neurotic disorders. This
> is the factor to which, as applied to hysteria, I gave the provisional
> name of "somatic compliance."

Freud continued to express from time to time his stand about the
physical or constitutional basis of behavior. His viewpoint about
somatic compliance has considerable importance in language disabilities and will be referred to later.

Elsewhere in Freud's writings and in those of other psychoanalysts
will be found specific details as to what may happen as a result of the
looking and seeing experiences in early life. Two experiences in this
realm seem to stand out as sources of inhibition or distortion in later
life. They are: (1) the witnessing of the sexual activities of the
parents (the so-called primal scene), and (2) the observation of the
differences in the sexual organs. Children experience both of these
activities much more frequently than parents and others seem to realize.

To a small child, the sexual activities of his parents—whether he
witnesses them by eye or by ear—usually mean an attack or an aggres-

sion in which the mother is being overcome or hurt in some mysterious way. This seems wrong and frightening to the child, and at the same time he may feel guilty because he is peeping or eavesdropping. From these emotional experiences, the child concludes that looking and listening in order to find out new things should be avoided.

Concerning the seeing of the genitals of the opposite sex, peeping is a common and natural expression of sexual curiosity. The exhibitionistic experiences that practically all children share in some form or other may be associated with shame and guilt. The children themselves do such acts in a very secretive way, knowing they will be shamed and punished if they are caught. Even more fundamental in the personality structure may lie "castration anxiety," the boy wondering if he will be punished by removal of the penis and the girl thinking that she has already been punished by its removal. Because reassurance on this point cannot be obtained, the looking and showing tendencies may become insatiable, sadistic, and displaced to areas other than the genitals. Since the eye starts the chain reaction, then the eye may stop it or choose not to take in knowledge about such startling and anxiety-provoking matters. Since knowledge of new things may come through the reading of books, the eye may choose not to absorb knowledge from this source.

Because looking to satisfy curiosity may be traumatic in more ways than one, the child tries to refrain from looking. Many psychoanalytic writers follow this explanation and frequently refer to "taking in knowledge through the eyes." If this psychoanalytic interpretation is valid for the eyes, the same paradigm should apply to the ears. However, word-deafness is much less common than word-blindness.

The majority of the subsequent writers in psychoanalytic literature who deal with reading disability—frequently referred to as learning inhibition by analysts—start with the above concepts and go on with their own elaborations.

Contributions of Other Psychoanalysts

A few references to reading by other analysts appeared in the early psychoanalytic literature, but reading was not the main topic under consideration. For example, Ernest Jones, the well-known translator and biographer of Freud, referred to school subjects in his article

"The Child's Unconscious" published in 1923. He said that "disabilities for a particular school subject were often due to an inhibition of interest because the subject was unconsciously associated with some disagreeable idea or topic and that after the unconscious associations were brought into consciousness through psychoanalysis the individual was able to master the subject which had been failed previously."

The first article in the *International Journal of Psychoanalysis* in which reading was the main topic appeared in 1930 under the title "Some Unconscious Factors in Reading." James Strachey, the author, pointed out in detail the oral and anal factors that might be related to reading, and he mentioned expressions such as "devouring a book," "chewing-up words," which would have an oral connotation. He said that reading represents a sublimation of certain primitive biological tendencies which are seen at the beginning of life and that "mental energy employed in reading is to some degree derived from certain unconscious trends." He identified these trends with scoptophilia, anal eroticism, and oral impulses, but he dealt mainly with oral impulses. He said that smooth, passive and easy reading represented oral-receptive (drinking, sucking) impulses to the reader; but, on the other hand, difficult reading represented oral-sadistic (biting, chewing) impulses.

Strachey said that in children who have reading disability, these impulses are unstable or incompletely repressed and sublimated, so that the act of reading threatens to bring about release of these urges to their original primitive form. The possibility that these urges might be released in primitive form is so frightening that the child refuses to read at all. He also postulated that, in a child's unconscious, reading may have the significance of taking knowledge out of the mother's body and that fear of robbing her is an important factor for inhibition in reading.

Concerning the general process of reading, Strachey claimed that the average reader reads word by word, often pronouncing the words to himself and even moving his lips as he does so (an oral manifestation of some libidinal significance). Reading aloud might have some element of a kinesthetic significance, but Strachey did not mention this point.

In contrast to reading disability, Strachey cited the prowess of "Lord

Bowen, the famous Victorian judge, of whom the story was told that he could simultaneously read down the seven columns of a page of 'The Times' by merely moving his eyes slowly from the top of the page to the bottom." Strachey surmised that Lord Bowen must have started reading word by word, but through some special facility he went on to his prodigious accomplishment. However, Strachey did not attempt to explain this special facility on the basis of extremely fortunate emotional conditioning in the early life of the good judge.

There is nothing in Strachey's article about any language disability that might be innate or acquired through organic damage. He leaves the impression that all reading disabilities must be attributed to emotional or personality developmental factors that occur in the process of the child's passing through the oral and anal stages and in his relationship to his mother. In a more general way, he implied that there is a sadistic element in the inhibition of reading. It must be recognized that, according to the subject of his paper, he was not called upon to mention factors other than unconscious ones.

Almost coincident with Strachey's article, Melanie Klein (1931) published an article entitled "A Contribution to the Theory of Intellectual Inhibition." She said that in the unconscious the mother's body (so far as the child is concerned) is equated with everything desirable. It is the only source of desirable things, but they can be obtained only if the taking of them is not damaging. Fears about the results of his curiosity, which the child looks upon as an aggressive act that may be damaging (probing or penetrating curiosity, so to speak), lead to inhibitions of curiosity about pregnancy, birth, death, the difference between the sexes, and the specific relationships between mothers and fathers.

Inhibitions in these areas may become so marked that not only would curiosity about pregnancy be interferred with, but even thoughts about the geography of the mother's body might be suppressed; indeed, even facts about the geography of "mother earth," or the subject of geography at school might be avoided as dangerous. If, in a child's conceptualization, looking into things is forbidden or dangerous or damaging, then he may not learn, or learn to read, or learn from reading.

Klein's summary of her analysis of a seven-year-old boy illustrated some of her theories concerning intellectual inhibition: "I should like to add that it is essential for a favorable development of the desire for knowledge that the mother's body should be felt to be well and unharmed. It represents in the unconscious the treasure house of everything desirable, which can only be got from there; therefore, if it is not destroyed, not so much in danger and therefore not so dangerous itself, the wish to take food for the mind from it can more easily be carried out." As a final statement, she said: "The presence of excessively strong early anxiety-situations and the predominance of a threatening super-ego derived from the first stages of its formation are fundamental factors, not only in the genesis of the psychoses, but in the production of disturbances of ego-development and intellectual inhibition."[1] From this, it would appear that disturbances of ego-development and intellectual inhibition should be found together.

Phyllis Blanchard started writing about reading disabilities in 1928, but her psychoanalytic interpretations came later (1935 and 1947). Her first approach was that of a clinical psychologist. In her original study of a small number of clinical cases, she found a relation between reading disabilities and maladjustment or behavior problems: "Some of the common causes of reading disability seem to be undiscovered vision defects; emotional conditionings in the early years of school life; inadequate teaching in the early grades or changes from one pedagogical method to another during the acquisition of the fundamental skills which are necessary for reading proficiency."

In her later publications, after she became a psychoanalytically trained therapist, Blanchard suggested that a common etiological factor found in children with reading disability is the difficulty in handling aggression that is involved in learning or looking into things "with a piercing eye." This aggression has excessive guilt and anxiety connected with it, particularly over hostile and destructive impulses and fantasies that are, in a manner of speaking, oral in form. Blanchard also pointed out that reading disability often disguises hidden motives and satisfies the guilt need for punishment by exposing a child to

[1]Much background material had already been expressed by Klein (1924) in a paper entitled "The Role of the School in the Libidinal Development of the Child." Running through most of her articles is a theme that castration fear is a basis for many inhibitions and that repression of the active masculine component in both boys and girls may be the chief cause of inhibitions in learning.

failure at school and criticism both at school and at home. This, of course, was in line with Strachey's idea about the sadistic element in reading disability.

It must be recognized that Blanchard brought to her writing on reading disability a broad point of view and extensive clinical experience. Her reviews of the literature were comprehensive and included studies by neurologists, psychologists, and educators. She compared reading disability with neurotic symptomatology, but she estimated that only 20 per cent of reading disabilities were of neurotic origin. She considered that the other 80 per cent were nonneurotic in origin, but that this group had emotional and personality problems which preceded the reading problem. She noted that 80 per cent of the cases were boys, but instead of considering heredity as a factor contributing to this predominance among males, she accepted an explanation offered by Nunberg in 1932. This explanation was based on the psychosexual development of girls, claiming that their active, aggressive strivings tend to be held in check by passive, feminine tendencies, seldom reaching the same strength as in boys; therefore, girls do not have as much need as boys to sublimate aggressive drives.

Another contributor who wrote about the experiential factors in the causation of reading retardation was Gerald Pearson. He had a medical background with clinical experience in child psychiatry. In his book, *Common Neuroses of Children and Adults* (1937) which he co-authored with Spurgeon English, he recognized that in some children language disturbances are due to brain damage. Under discussion of speech disorders, there was reference to Orton's "strephosymbolia" and to the role of cortical dominance. In this connection Pearson stated that cases of aphasia indicate:

1. That the function of speech comprehends more than spoken speech, including also the ability to understand heard words, seen words (reading) and the use of written words (writing).

2. That the total function of speech is based on unimpaired associations between the auditory receptive centers, visual receptive centers, the motor center for the use of the hand and of the motor speech organs.

3. That in right-handed people this complex association of centers which results in the function of speech takes place in the

left cerebral cortex, in left-handed people in the right cerebral cortex.

Pearson and English added that reading difficulties as an attempt to solve a conflict have various sources:

1. Some unpleasant and painful experience may have occurred during the early efforts of the child to learn to read and, as in cases of arithmetical disability cited above, the child becomes conditioned against reading.

2. Reading may be the one subject stressed by a hated and severe parent. The child, unable to express his antagonism to the parent openly, does so indirectly through refusal to learn to read.

3. Reading is the acquiring of knowledge through looking. If a child has been severely inhibited in his peeping activities, all acquisition of knowledge through looking may come under the ban of the child's superego. The problem then is not the inability of the child to learn to read, but his fear to use his vision to acquire knowledge. The best treatment for these cases is that which will reduce the severity of the child's superego, i.e., analytic treatment for his neurosis, of which the reading disability is only a symptom.

4. As in the cases of stammering, the words and letters themselves may come to represent curious anal-sadistic phantasies. In a case reported by Blanchard the child's distortion of words and reversals of words and letters represented a magical spell by which he poured forth his hate and his fear of various people. He was so consumed by these emotions that he had the compulsion to distort everything he read or wrote, and consequently could not learn to read properly. Such cases in which the reading difficulty is symptomatic of a definite neurosis require analytic treatment.[2]

In 1954, Pearson published a book entitled *Psychoanalysis and the Education of the Child.* In this book, he enumerated many factors

---

[2]As an interesting sidelight, Pearson and English stated:
The child who has a reading difficulty is totally or partially unable to read. If the school he attends uses the older methods of teaching reading, i.e., the use of a uniform text for the whole class, he may appear to have no difficulty at all and so be advanced year after year. In one case a boy had reached the eighth grade before it was noticed that he could not read. He had an excellent memory, and through listening to the other children memorized the entire book. He would then be guided as to what was being read by pictures or marks on the page and, with a few errors as to the right place to start, would recite a page or two almost perfectly.

outside neurotic conflict that may be involved in disturbances of the learning process, but the emphasis was on psychoanalytic interpretations. He listed fear of sibling rivalry, dread of castration, disturbances in relation to reality, and the other possibilities mentioned in the psychoanalytic literature. He said that "some reading disabilities may be due to strephosymbolia or to other causes I have already mentioned, but certainly these causes do not explain the severe cases. Blanchard's studies seem to indicate that they are cases of difficulties in digesting and assimilating learning material. In my cases this inability to digest was always associated with a disturbance of the ability to take in and to give out, because of severe intrapsychic conflicts. . . ."

Pearson went on to say: "I am still not certain whether or not such phenomena as reading readiness really are the result of maturation, or myelinization of the cortical association tracts. More careful investigation may show that they result from the lessening of the child's intrapsychic conflict after the solution of the edipus conflict and the consequent beginning of the latency period."

Pearson's book contains provocative discussions concerning the psychoanalytic principles that are related to education, but it fails to take into account innate or organic factors that bear upon the learning process. Again, one is left with the impression that in the psychoanalytic concepts presented are to be found the fundamental causes of reading disability and all inhibition of the learning process.[3]

Margaret Mahler (1942) wrote an intriguing article captioned "Pseudoimbecility: A Magic Cap of Invisibility." Starting with the myth about the cap that made a person invisible in the presence of others, she applied it to clinical cases, showing that "pseudo-stupidity enables children as well as infantile adults to participate to an amazingly unlimited extent in the sexual life of parents and other adults." Elaborating on this mechanism, she said:

Erotization of the intellectual function of the ego has been

---

[3]However, with an "about face" in the same book, Pearson became concerned about the trend in psychiatric reporting and cautioned: "It is necessary to re-emphasize it (the organic) because at the present time when there is so much emphasis on the importance of intrapsychic processes in all phases of medicine and education, psychiatrists tend to become over-enthusiastic about dynamic intrapsychic processes to the complete neglect of physiological and organic processes, for which they seem to have a psychic blind-spot."

shown to cause the ego to give up this function in order to escape conflict. It is known also that intellectual restriction is often used to disguise aggression in order to escape retaliation. Pseudo-stupidity, in addition, has been described as a display of castration to escape fear of literal castration and the loss of a loved object.

* * *

In my cases the manoevre of the children was emotionally fully reciprocated by a parent or sibling because it met the adult's own unconscious desire, isolated from his feelings of guilt. The utilization of stupidity is widespread because mutual sexual desires are gratified on a preverbal affective level, without becoming conscious through word pictures, which renders repression or other defense measures unnecessary.

It is evident, then, that Mahler would consider the failure to acquire language functions to be the hallmark of stupidity, thereby permitting the child and the adult concerned to go on in this infantile manner.[4]

Emmy Sylvester and Mary Kunst (1943) in their article "Psychodynamic Aspects of the Reading Problem" stated:

In short, the learning process may become conditioned by anxiety which is generated by: 1. inadequate capacity for mastery; 2. fear of loss of love; 3. patient's own destructive threat towards the persons on whom he depends. The reading disability thus becomes a defense against anxiety which may be stimulated by curiosity. . . . It is our conclusion that the disturbances in reading are disturbances of the exploratory function and that symptomatic treatment by pedagogical methods is not enough.

Concerning this "exploratory function," Sylvester and Kunst said that when the child's zeal to explore is blocked by emotional problems he often interprets exploration as dangerous and unacceptable. On the other hand, exploration already indulged in could be threatening because he had seen more than he could experience without anxiety. Reading, as an exploration, would then become a danger to be avoided.

As a specialist in pediatrics, Edward Liss turned to psychoanalysis

---

[4]It should be noted that Freud (1908) discussed a connection between suppression of sexual curiosity and intellectual inhibition. Also, Ernest Jones (1913) wrote on "Simulated Foolishness in Hysteria," and C. P. Oberndorf (1939) wrote about "The Feeling of Stupidity."

and child psychiatry. Between 1935 and 1955 he published at least six papers pertaining to learning difficulties in children with normal intelligence. Most of his material can be applied to reading disability and related language disorders. In 1941, as an aspect of his approach to learning difficulties, he wrote:

> In a previous publication we called attention to the phenomenon of learning as an erotic, sensuous experience. Because of this libidinalization the intellectual activity was equated with masculine or feminine practices. This constellation conditioned the acquisition of knowledge in proportion to the individual's own attitudes toward himself or herself as a specific biological entity with certain preponderant cultural practices which are pertinent to that particular sex. In other words, where the acceptance of one's biological destiny is within the norm, and the learning process has been eroticized as a practice pertinent to that sex, the learning process functions with a minimum of conflict.

In 1955, Liss summarized several of his ideas in a paper entitled "Motivations in Learning." The word "motivations" draws attention to the fact that many of the psychoanalytic writers were concerned mainly with motivation rather than with the inner elaborative processes that go on after words are seen or heard. However, Liss did consider how these complex functions that are related to understanding what is seen or heard might be blocked or inhibited by experiences in earlier life.

Emanuel Klein (1949), in discussing "Psychoanalytic Aspects of School Problems," gave considerable attention to reading. He started with the child's experience of separation from home when he enters school:

> The attitudes to the teacher, the classmates and to the schoolwork are an important bridge between early attitudes to the parents, the siblings, and the self, and their later expression in adult life. The component instinctual drives, sado-masochistic trends, scoptophilic and exhibitionistic impulses, oral and anal strivings, and narcissistic attitudes play basic roles in the learning process and its impairment. . . . Difficulty in learning to read is often a rebellion against this shift from being read to and corresponds to difficulties in being weaned. A child with strong passive oral wishes will shrink from this change. In boys this goes with a strong oral

attachment to the mother, or with the development of passive homosexual feelings to the father. Being read to then represents being at mother's breast, or at a different phase the fulfillment of fellatio wishes toward father.

Klein found reading difficulties much more prevalent in the male sex. He accounted for this prevalence through the following explanation:

One large group of boys with reading difficulties especially in the first few years of reading are passive boys, with strong oral dependent traits, closely attached to the mother, with fear of a stern father. As they approach the genital stage, the castration anxiety is too great, there is regression and reinforcement of oral traits, renunciation of masculinity, development of passive homosexual wishes on an oral basis. These boys tend to withdraw from boys' athletic games and street fights, they insist on being dressed to a late age, are clumsy in tying their shoelaces. They clung strongly to breast or bottle, resisted the first weaning and all subsequent weaning processes, like the shift from being dressed to dressing, from being washed to washing themselves, and combing their hair. They are fearful of the first school experience and resist leaving the mother. If the first teacher is very gentle, they may adjust to school after a little while but on encountering the first stern teacher they develop a great fear of the teacher, the school and the school work. If matters are less extreme they may gradually accept the school activity, learn some of the school arithmetic but develop the difficulty in reading, especially if the mother's reading to them has represented an important substitute for giving up the breast. In these patients the female genital is reacted to, as though it were a breast, with a hidden penis from which nourishment can be gotten, with a consequent predeliction for cunnilingus. In the case of the girl where passivity normally plays so large a role in personality development, retention of passive attitudes is much less likely to be a disruptive influence. In this connection it is interesting to note that reading difficulties are four times as common in boys as in girls.

Klein also observed that "the shape, appearance and sound of letters often play a role in reading, writing and spelling difficulties, in that they may stimulate oral, anal, urinary or genital fantasies."

In Volume X (1955) of *The Psychoanalytic Study of the Child,* a paper by Victor Rosen appeared under the title of "Strephosymbolia: An Intrasystemic Disturbance of the Synthetic Function of the Ego." From Rosen's review of the pertinent literature, it is evident that he was well-acquainted with the writings of Hinshelwood, Orton, Bender, and many others. At the outset, Rosen stated that "the present paper will attempt to demonstrate that the so-called strephosymbolic disturbance consists of a failure to synthesize the ordinal aspects of the word, which is a function of its phonetic qualities, with the visual elements of the word. An attempt will also be made to demonstrate that this disturbance resembles a phylogenetic phase in orthographic evolution, namely, the transitional stage between idiographic scripts and the syllabary alphabet."

Rosen then presented an abstract of his analysis of a young man. The patient manifested a gift in mathematics, but he had a disability in reading and spelling "of the so-called strephosymbolic type." In summarizing his analysis, Rosen stated:

> Evidence is presented to indicate that his writing errors arise from oscillations between attempts to reproduce words in phonetic fashion without regard to their visual appearance or alternatively in idiographic fashion without regard to the ordering of phonemes necessitated by the sound of the word. It is suggested that phylogenetically his disturbance is similar to a transitional stage in the development of writing between idiographic forms and a syllabary alphabet with incomplete development of the concept of phonetic writing. It is suggested that the basic conflict in this case arises from the primal scene fantasy which associates father with visual activities, mother with auditory functions and which conceives of them as two separate unloving human beings who are incapable of producing a child except by artificial insemination. It is further suggested that secondary autonomy has been achieved in the visual and auditory perceptual functions of the ego when utilized separately, and that conflict invades these areas only in their synthetic function related to recognizing and evoking phonetic words and images. At this point their synthetic product becomes invested with primal scene significance. The genetic origin of the disability may be due to precocious maturation of certain ego sectors in visual and auditory perceptual processes so that they become involved in the oedipal conflict at a crucial stage of their development. Thus they are prevented in their synthetic relationship from

forming a new, completely autonomous structure as they might have, had their maturation been somewhat delayed. An attempt is made to indicate the relationship between this disturbance of interperceptual synthesis and the enhancement of preconscious problem-solving operations in mathematics which utilize "unsolidified" images.[5]

In an article that was far-ranging in scope, Vivian Jarvis (1958) discussed "The Visual Problem in Reading Disability." Starting with home conditions and visual defects as the two most frequent causal factors in reading disability, Jarvis stated that the two are "inextricably bound up with each other." Concerning the problem of vision, Jarvis said:

Only it may not primarily be a problem of fusion, aniseikonia, astigmatism, or, in other words, a physical or physiological problem, but rather one that has unconscious meaning bound up with it. It is this visual problem in the retarded reader of average or better-than-average intelligence and its ramifications as we pursue its relation to the oedipal conflict, the problems of aggression and identification, to the fantasy of the preoedipal mother, to scoptophilia and exhibitionism, and to the defense mechanisms it provokes that will be the subject of this paper. . . . We may presume that if a situation or symptom "plays out" the oedipal conflict, we shall see compounded therein oral and anal derivatives as well.

With several references to psychoanalytic literature and with considerable case material for illustration, Jarvis concluded:

There is a need to deepen our understanding of the underlying causes of reading disability by focusing attention on the visual problem as a looking (scoptophilic) rather than a vision problem. Further, the looking has been regarded as an activity with active and passive aspects. It is the active part of looking necessary to establish the automatic skill of reading which is felt to create a major difficulty for the retarded reader rather than the reading content. Its counterpart outside of school is an inability to identify predominantly with one's own sex. It is highly probable that

---

[5]Reference has been made elsewhere to Bender's note (1958) about Rosen's case report. She said that Rosen pointed out the same mechanisms described by Schilder in 1935. Schilder gave a neurophysiological explanation for the very same mechanisms. Rosen, though quoting Schilder, gave a psychoanalytic interpretation.

so-called nonreaders have a greater reading vocabulary than is suspected, but that alphabetical letters and words lend themselves to a quick association with the underlying fantasies relating to reading and make it necessary for the retarded reader to resort to the mechanism of denial to keep these fantasies repressed.

A central notion in the fantasies is that of the phallic or castrating mother. Another notion is that stupidity (equated with craziness, badness, inability to read) may result from masturbatory activity with injury displaced to the head but on a deeper level it is regarded as a symbolic castration and thus both ideas serve as the denial of real castration in either sex. An understanding of the denial of voyeurism and compensatory exhibitionistic activities or fantasies should have important implications for reading therapy and for the teaching of reading in normal situations.

With regard to the fact that boys far outnumber girls with reading disabilities, Jarvis offered two possible explanations:

1. Bearing in mind that poor readers are usually boys, we are reminded of Oedipus who blinded himself. It may be that "reading cases" are boys who have blinded themselves symbolically and thus create the problem of vision.

2. Another result of the inability to read is stupidity. Stupidity represents, among other things, a symbolic castration and thus real castration is avoided. Perhaps this is the reason why we see so many boys at a reading center: they are still under the sway of the castration complex, whereas most girls have already made peace in some way on this score (acceptance of castration) and can use their eyes with less anxiety. The girls who have reading and looking difficulties (in connection with feminine identification) may be clinging to an illusory penis.

During a symposium on learning problems at the 1958 annual meeting of the American Orthopsychiatric Association, Jerome Silverman, Margarette Fite and Margaret Mosher presented a paper entitled "Clinical Findings in Reading Disability Children—Special Cases of Intellectual Inhibition." Their case material came from the Special Reading Services which had been established by the New York City Board of Education in 1955. Silverman, Fite and Mosher, who represented a full clinical team, had studied thirty-five children (twenty-nine boys and six girls) who were selected "because of the severity of their learning problems." Their paper started as follows: "Reading disabilities occurring in children in the critical period from eight to ten years are so widespread and disabling that parents and school authorities are greatly concerned. Moreover, work with these children has shown repeatedly that the reading disability is only one aspect or symptom of a more basic disturbance in the child's emotional life."

Silverman, Fite and Mosher constructed a profile of a child with typical reading disability:

This child would be male, nine years old, and in the fourth grade. He would have at least average intelligence—usually above average intelligence—and probably would be doing nearly as poorly in arithmetic as in reading. In the classroom he would appear to suffer from severe anxiety, hyperactivity, depressive trends and fearfulness. He would usually have periods of excessive daydreaming and distractibility. These symptoms occurred in two-thirds of our children. In his early school history we would probably find an absence of kindergarten experience, a chronological age of below six years on entering the first grade, and various unfortunate early school experiences such as frequent changes of school or teacher, serious illnesses or accidents, excessive absences.

Frequently, there would be only one parent actively concerned or present in such a child's family. In addition, this child would manifest severe rivalry with siblings. In his early development there would be evidence of a disturbed and deprived relationship with his mother, especially around feeding and toilet training situations. Childhood curiosity about birth, differences between the sexes and relationships between parents would be found to be very poorly handled. The parents themselves, of such a child, would often be found to have suffered from a disturbed traumatic childhood, and frequently have histories of mental illness or breakdown. They would probably be involved in serious marital discord. One or both parents, moreover, would have undesirable attitudes regarding academic achievement and apply undue pressure on the child, perhaps because they themselves had had learning difficulties. The data showed that there was a surprisingly high incidence of school failure and learning disability on the part of parents and siblings of the typical child.

In this typical child, occasionally other problems such as prematurity, speech defects, variation of visual acuity, and handedness problems may be further handicapping factors—other sources of frustration. These physical and developmental factors, then, while they do not appear crucial in the origin of the reading problem, may be contributory. There may be some possibility that the reading disability child may more frequently have an irregular constitutional and physical background which might influence his subsequent psychic maturation and structure.

These authors, while recognizing the Orton concepts, the possibility of confused dominance, and hereditary factors, summarized their point of view as follows:

> Disabilities then may occur 1) because of the child's conflict in acquiring knowledge—he suffers a general inhibition in learning and does not allow himself to learn generally or to learn by learning reading or by reading; and 2) through conflicts displaced to use of vision for learning arising during the important phases of his psychosexual development. There must be freedom for the active and aggressive purpose of seeing and knowing, and utilizing "giving out" what is seen and known; freedom passively to take in and without conflict, and with gratification to chew or digest the food of knowledge. Indeed, since seeking knowledge can represent aggressive activity, if the child has learned this is dangerous or prohibited for him, he cannot permit himself the aggression or curiosity necessary to search or look actively for knowledge, or even the aggression necessary to enable him actively to master a skill—reading. Moreover, one may learn to read but not be able to derive pleasure of any sort from the reading skill. The ability to learn to read does not necessarily imply the ability to experience pleasure in reading itself, or the ability through reading to accumulate or use knowledge.

At the same symposium Ben O. Rubenstein and his associates presented a paper entitled "Learning Impotence: A Suggested Diagnostic Category." Regarding the terminology of their paper, they said, "We prefer the term 'learning impotence' to learning impairment for we wish to emphasize the picture of almost complete powerlessness these children present in their attempt to overcome their difficulties. In addition, the interference with psychosexual development which is evident in these cases makes the term appropriate." They also constructed a profile of a reading disability child, although they did not call it that:

> This paper emphasizes the need for intensified study of children whose primary symptom is learning impotence. We have used this label to denote a symptom complex involving children with adequate intelligence whose major characteristic is the permanent, diffuse, and self-defeating nature of their learning disability. Allied symptoms include moderate obesity; poor physical coordination; unusually poor object relationships with their peers and adults expressed in both passive and aggressive ways; resultant unpredictable behavior bordering on the bizarre or pseudodelinquent, or both; a very low frustration tolerance; marked orality; and a negatively charged pathological attachment to mother leading to difficulty in achieving a separate identity. . . . These children see "nonlearning" as a successful form of separation from mother, for which they are isolated and punished. The child experiences the learning task as surrender, as the giving up of precarious individuality. As a result of this conflict, energies which normally should be available for the more advanced ego functions remain restricted and fixed at pregenital levels. The skills required for the learning process thereby suffer in development.

Bessie Sperry, Nancy Staver, Beatrice Reiner and David Ulrich (1958) of the Judge Baker Guidance Center in Boston studied seven boys of normal physical and intellectual endowment whose school achievement was below normal in reading and to some extent in spelling and arithmetic. They emphasized the aspects of renunciation and denial in learning difficulties and said, "Our focus was on the problem these boys had with the taking in of knowledge in school rather than on how much they were able to produce in the school situation."

Concerning the boys' motivation, they stated:

> At this point in our study of these boys two factors appear most prominent in their own motivation to fail—fears and guilt about some external event which no one could actually control, and guilt about a complicated unresolved oedipal problem. . . . In summary, these boys have responded, for various reasons, to a family pattern in which they were most eligible for the role of the unsuccessful one. In this situation they have presented them-

selves as unaggressive, compliant, and in need of help. The symptom of school failure reflects this adjustment on the child's part, serving very well to secure some dependent satisfactions from the parents.

Sperry and her co-workers reported at other times (1952 and 1959) on studies of other aspects of learning problems that have to do with destructive fantasies and motility. It has been noted frequently that many of the children with learning problems are hyperactive and distractable. With regard to motility, Sperry observed, "Essentially it seems to us that successful motor activity to these boys represents the assertion of their autonomy and masculinity. With the conflict involved, it is not surprising that there is a marked vacillation in the amount of activity and fears about it in all of them. The most active are never sure, and have to demonstrate again and again that they are able to master their conflicts by activity, while the most inactive engage briefly in counterphobic behavior or repetitive legitimate activity in an effort to assert some sense of mastery. Such defenses, however, are not appropriate for the successful mastery of school learning."

Prentice and Sperry (1956) wrote an interesting article concerning their experience in combining remedial reading techniques with analytically oriented psychotherapy. They used this method with children who had what they called "primary neurotic learning inhibitions." They said that their group of children (all boys) "specifically excludes learning problems in the context of organicity, delinquency, or major psychopathologies." No mention was made of developmental dyslexia, but they observed that their pupils showed accident-proneness, clumsiness and hyperactivity which are characteristics frequently found in dyslexia. In their brief presentation of two cases, the first boy was left-handed, suggesting the possibility of confused dominance, which is often a part of dyslexia. The second boy, when asked to write "medical hospital" wrote "medikill hopstable." In spite of the fact that such spelling errors are found in dyslexic children, a purely psychoanalytic interpretation was given:

> During the rest of the hour he was hyperactive as he associated to his own hospitalization and surgery. He recalled wanting to run away. Charlie's spelling errors appeared to condense his wish

to retaliate for what he perceived as a sadistic attack upon him ("I-kill"), together with his attempted denial through hyperactivity of the passive vulnerable position ("hops-table"). In other spelling errors as well, Charlie's activity-passivity conflict was dominant.

Ego Development and Reading Disability

Discussion of the psychoanalytic approach would not be complete without calling attention to the growing emphasis that psychoanalysts now place on the importance of ego development in personality structure. Ego development concerns the child's gradual recognition of himself as an entity or individual different from others and from the world about him. His recognition of himself gives him an orientation about his own functioning in relation to his milieu.

Ego development is influenced by a multitude of factors—parental attitudes, the family constellation, sibling rivalry, and many other environmental influences. On the other hand, constitutional endowment may help shape the ego identification and either strengthen or weaken it.

As we have seen, Schilder and others stressed the importance of the body image in ego development. More specifically, Rosen's concept of ego development in relation to reading disability was revealed in his paper "Strephosymbolia: An Intrasystemic Disturbance of the Synthetic Function of the Ego." Melanie Klein called attention to the role of early anxiety situations and a threatening superego in the production of disturbances of ego development and intellectual inhibition. Fabian, after having demonstrated some definite Gestalt disturbances, said: "Reading disability, which is much more common in boys, is a symptom of an ego disability."

Kephart (1960) suggested that the differentiation and utilization of the self (ego) are necessary for an individual's orientation in external space. He said that a child who has not differentiated one side of the body from the other has difficulty in achieving directionality in space and, therefore, cannot appreciate directionality in letters and words. This may seem to be an extreme application of ego psychology and may not be applicable to the child with confused dominance. Is the directionality difficulty the result of ego dysfunction, or did it— as a constitutional factor—influence ego development?

Perhaps a clearer and somewhat different approach is to be found in a report by John Doris and Albert J. Solnit (1963). Although they were writing about "brain damage and associated school problems," their observations are applicable to dyslexia in general. They said:

> The assessment of the handicapped child's ego strengths and deficits through psychotherapy and the assessment of his environment are crucial for enabling the child and his environment to achieve an optimal mutual adaptation. This formulation indicates that continuing contacts with the family (especially the parents), educators, and others who observe and interact with the child are essential for the diagnostic, therapeutic, and counseling processes involved in this clinical research and its application.

> * * *

> In children with central neurological difficulties the handicap can be described in terms of ego deficits and these deficits can be approached in terms of treatment, education, and corrective experiences. It is important to state again that work with the skills and adaptations representing the ego deficits is not sufficient. These children also need to be helped to develop simultaneously the intact sectors of their ego in order to maintain a balance of development that protects self-esteem and the motivation to work at overcoming the handicap. This balanced help establishes the basis for an integration of sectors of handicap and normal functioning so necessary for mastering the tasks of development and forming a healthy character structure. Hartmann (1956) has stated: ". . . the child is born with a certain degree of preadaptiveness; that is to say, the apparatus of perception, memory, mobility, etc., which help us to deal with reality are, in a primitive form, already present at birth; later they will mature and develop in constant interaction, of course, with experience; you know that the very system to which we attribute these functions, the ego, is also our organ of learning." In the brain-damaged child the degree of preadaptiveness is curtailed, and sufficient accommodation by the environment for this limitation is usually necessary to promote the child's optimal development.

> The ego handicaps of the brain-damaged child can be described in terms of: perceptual impairment; relative inability to postpone discharge or accept substitute gratifications; poor motility control; disturbed body image; defective speech development and control;

differentiated or diffuse difficulty in the use of the symbolic process (e.g., a visual-motor handicap or speech deviation); relative inability to transform impulses, i.e., to sublimate and to have available the psychic energies necessary for the trial-action functions of speech, thought or memory; and inability to cope simultaneously with outer stimulation and inner needs.

Parents of Dyslexic Children

Several studies of the parents of children with "learning inhibitions" have been carried out. Most of these parents had children with a reading disability which was consistent with the description of developmental dyslexia.

Rubenstein, in his article that dealt specifically with learning impotence, referred to one of his earlier articles (1957): "It may appear that we have largely ignored the oedipal conflict in these children and the role the fathers played in their illness. This phase of their difficulty was discussed in another paper. In brief, these fathers were likened to the early roving American frontiersmen who rode the 'business range' and left the home and children in the mother's hands."

Ilse Hellman (1954) recorded "Some Observations on Mothers of Children with Intellectual Inhibitions." Summarizing her findings, she said:

> The mother's part in the establishment of oral fixations, their influence on the fate of the component instincts of curiosity and looking were discussed and it was shown which circumstances had made it possible for the children to enter latency and develop sublimations successfully. . . . The cases show close similarity to the well-known structure of pseudo-imbecility and learning inhibitions. An additional factor in establishing the symptom was found in the mother's symptom of lying and secretiveness, which reinforced the impairment of the children's ego functions of memory, reality testing and synthesizing.

Margaret Grunebaum (1962) and her associates focused attention on the fathers of children with learning inhibitions, but they also included considerable information on mothers. The summary of this paper was as follows:

> In this paper we have presented our observations on the way in

which the fathers' attitudes influence the development and mainte-
nance of inhibitions about achievement and mastery of elementary school children referred for longstanding primary neurotic
learning inhibitions. We have seen how these fathers persisted
in their self image of inadequacy and resignation despite objective indications of educational and occupational adequacy. We
have observed how their deep sense of deprivation led them to
adopt a passive or explosively demanding orientation to their wives
and to view their sons as competitors for mother's support and
admiration. Our clinical material indicated the ways in which the
fathers unconsciously subverted the child's achievement strivings
in the face of their conscious wish that the child succeed. We
have described how the mothers, through their own need to maintain an image of masculinity that was dangerous or devalued, also
unconsciously limited the son's attempts to form an achieving
masculine identification. Finally, we attempted to summarize the
ways in which the neurotic attitudes of the parents are internalized
by the child and the factors which promote his displacement of
the conflict to the school situation.

Validity Study of Psychoanalytic Concepts

Walters, Van Loan and Crofts (1961) said that psychoanalysts have
attributed reading disability to three supposedly related factors: fear
and avoidance of looking; hostility, primarily toward the same-sex
parent; and failure to identify with the same-sex parent. In an attempt to test the validity of these assumptions, they devised certain
ingenious psychological tests for this specific purpose. They gave the
tests to a group of school children with low reading ability and also
to a control group of good readers. The differences found between
the two groups were not conclusive and certainly not supporting of
the assumptions. The investigators concluded that the differences
found could be accounted for by other than psychoanalytic hypotheses.

Chapter VI

OTHER ENVIRONMENTAL FACTORS

And if you can't read
Pray endeavor to spell,
For by frequently spelling
You'll learn to read well.

The Franklin Primer (1831)

IT IS RECOGNIZED that the several factors mentioned in the psycho-analytic literature as causes of reading disability or learning inhibition stem from the child's milieu. In other words, these factors are neither innate nor the result of brain damage, but are absorbed from the environment and become internalized as a part of the child's personality very early in life. However, many writers outside the psycho-analytic field take the view that other conditions in the environment external to the child's personality are the causes of reading disability.

For example, William S. Gray (1921) listed the following causes of "poor reading": irregular school attendance, poor health, malnutrition, nervous disorders, nationality, inappropriate methods of instruction, inadequate reading, visual defects, vocal defects, breathing irregularities, auditory defects and defects in brain tissue. A little later, Blanchard (1928) stated: "Some of the causes of reading disability seem to be undiscovered vision defects; emotional conditioning in the early years of school life; inadequate teaching in the early grades or changes from one pedagogical method to another during the acquisition of the fundamental skills which are necessary for reading proficiency."

To be sure, any of the factors mentioned above can cause poor reading in any child, but many authorities contend that they are not the *fundamental* causes of reading disability of the dyslexic type. That these external factors contribute to and often aggravate an already existing dysfunction is readily admitted.

Some people have claimed that the cause of reading disability lies in the structure of the English language, saying that it is too unphonic

[86]

and has too many irregularities. As an alphabetic language, English—along with French and German—is imperfect because of the many sounds and combinations of letters. In comparison, Spanish is nearly perfect. Even in this so-called perfect language, reading disability does occur. In fact, Claiborne referred to a paper on this topic published in Buenos Aires as early as 1903. And more recently—in 1961—Antonio Subirana of Barcelona, Spain, wrote about language dysfunctions among Hispanic peoples.

John Money (1962) stated: "One has heard claims that developmental dyslexia does not exist in Spanish-speaking schools because the language is so perfectly phonetic. I have no documentary evidence one way or the other, but would presume that developmental dyslexia does exist. Phonetic regularity is of no help to the child who cannot remember the name and sound of each letter, and it does not totally abolish the problems of mirror writing and reading." Also, Money referred to a report about a twelve-year-old Japanese boy who had great difficulty with the more recent syllabary, phonetic system (Kana script), but learned with greater facility the Kanji script based on the ancient Chinese ideographic method.

Many well-known and well-documented studies have been made in Germany, France, Sweden, Denmark and other countries, indicating that specific reading disabilities are just as prevalent in other languages as they are in English. It appears, then, that the cause of reading disability is not to be found in the characteristics of language structure.

Teaching Methods and Reading Disability

Rudolph Flesch (1955) in his popular book *Why Johnny Can't Read* made several startling statements by asking these rhetorical questions: "Do you know that there are no remedial reading cases in Germany, in France, in Italy, in Norway, in Spain—practically anywhere in the world except in the United States?" "Do you know that there was no such thing as remedial reading in this country either until about thirty years ago?" "Do you know that the teaching of reading was never a problem anywhere in the world until the United States switched to the present method around about 1925?"

Most people tend to accept Flesch's statements as valid and place the blame for reading retardation on teaching methods. It is understandable that Flesch's view has a direct appeal to parents with children who have difficulty in reading; it is easy to make the teachers the culprits. It is easier to project the fault onto someone or something outside the family than to look for the causes in the home or in the child.

However, if the child's innate endowment, emotional factors in the family, and the possibility of brain damage are fully considered, then it appears that teaching techniques are of secondary importance and could not be the fundamental cause. Unquestionably, a teaching method may make the existing disability more or less evident and secondarily increase or decrease it, depending on the method used.

Among the many proponents who champion teaching methods as the cause of reading disability, there is considerable disagreement. The debate usually centers around the phonic *versus* the look-say approach in the teaching of reading. The history of the shift from the "old-fashioned" alphabet, phonic, word-make-up method to the whole-word or look-say method and, now, to a middle-ground attitude has been well-documented elsewhere.

According to some historians, Horace Mann started the shift away from the phonic approach over a century ago. In his report to the Board of Education in Massachusetts in 1838 he said that "presenting the child with the alphabet is giving them what they never saw, heard, or thought before. . . . But the printed names of known things are the signs of sounds which their ears have been accustomed to hear, and their organs of speech utter. It can hardly be doubted therefore that a child would learn to name 26 familiar words sooner than the unknown, unheard of and unthought of *letters* of the alphabet." Flesch attributes the shift to a teacher named John R. Webb, who suddenly changed over to the whole-word method in 1846. Others have claimed that the change came after the introduction of Gestalt psychology about 1912. Around the turn of the century some psychologists—Huey, Dodge and others—were advocating the whole-word or look-say system of teaching reading. In fact, Huey suggested that phonics should be discarded entirely.[1]

---

[1]It appears that these psychologists based their advice on studies of eye movements which showed only two or three fixations per line of reading. However, the experiments were made with adults who had had a few years of experience with reading and not with beginners.

W. S. Gray (1957), an outstanding pioneer in the study of reading, summarized his conclusions in his Burton Lecture, "The Teaching of Reading: an International View." He gave particular attention to the conflict between the two approaches—the mastery of word elements (phonics) and the use of sight vocabulary (look-say). He took a middle-of-the-road stand, and he mentioned "the eclectic trend which emphasizes from the beginning both meaning and the skills of word recognition." He stated that "all children and adults do not learn to read equally well by a given method. This implies that there are factors other than the method that influence progress in learning to read, such as the teacher, the home and school environment, and varying abilities and other characteristics of the learners." He did not elaborate on the "varying abilities," nor did he place any emphasis on specific reading disability.

Nonetheless, Gray's leaning toward the whole-word approach was revealed in his following statements:

> It has been found that most children usually perceive things (including words) as whole, often inaccurately at first, but gradually in greater detail. Furthermore, both children and adults learn words more effectively when the reading activities are purposeful and meaningful to them. . . . Such findings tend to limit the scope of the remaining controversial issues with respect to initial methods of teaching reading. With but very few exceptions, even the ardent advocates of the use of phonics are now basing the initial identification of letters and sounds on the study of word wholes.

A different point of view was expressed by Charles C. Walcutt (1961). He wrote a chapter entitled "The Reading Problem in America" in the volume *Tomorrow's Illiterates,* which he edited. Here there was a strong indictment of the neglect of phonics and other basic principles in the teaching of reading. Walcutt said that "at first ailments like 'mixed hand-eye dominance' and 'specific reading disability' were defined by such theorists as Dr. Samuel Orton and Dr. Russell Gallagher[2] in such a way as to account for students of average or superior intelligence who failed to read successfully." Then, after describing a school in which no reading problems occurred, a school

---

[2]The reference is to Dr. J. Roswell Gallagher.

which used his phonic system, Walcutt went on to say that reading disability "is entirely due to the methods of reading instruction generally followed in our public schools."

Attention is called to a research group in Nottingham, England. This group stresses the greater use of phonics and all that term implies in the teaching of reading. One of the more articulate members of this group, Hunter Diack, wrote many articles on reading problems. In joint authorship with J. C. Daniels (1954) it was stated:

> . . . that an alphabet is a way of writing down the sounds of speech, that the order of letters in a word signifies an order of time, that the idea that children see words as immediate wholes is based on careless observation of children who can be observed in the process of analysing the words, that the "general shape" of a word is purely adventitious, that the only logical visual analysis of printed words is into letters, that in learning to read children are in fact learning to translate symbols of sounds (letters) into blocks of sound that make sense.

In a later monograph (1960) Diack devoted one chapter to "The Rise and Fall of Gestalt Theory." He stated: "For upwards of thirty years writers on the teaching of reading have leaned upon Gestalt theory. They have continued to do so even after the Gestalt system of thought has crumbled under logical analysis supported by more precise experimental work than any carried out by the founders of Gestalt theory." Diack's point about Gestalt theory is important, but the claim that children see "words as wholes" is only a small part of Gestalt psychology. As previously mentioned, Gestalt psychology is concerned with structure, the way the parts make up the whole. The whole-word method of teaching is more an application of Pavlov's conditioned response psychology than of Gestalt psychology.

Mary C. Austin and her associates (1961) wrote *The Torch Lighters: Tomorrow's Teachers of Reading*, which was published by the Harvard University Press. This study was concerned with the training of teachers of reading. It was based on questionnaires answered by faculty members in 371 institutions of higher learning and on personal interviews with some of them. Concerning word recognition skills, the study revealed:

> Each instructor interviewed expressed a firm commitment to a

"balanced" or "eclectic" approach to the teaching of word analysis skills. Invariably, students were introduced to systematic procedures, usually those outlined by the author of the class text, for giving children skill in using context clues, word-form clues, phonetic analysis, structural analysis, and the dictionary as the best way to figure out unknown words independently. All instructors were unalterably opposed to excessive emphasis on the teaching of phonics; and the inroads that a number of phonic-oriented reading systems are making in various school systems throughout the country are causing great concern. The general impression gained from the responses to this question of the word attack problem is that instructors were fairly well convinced that the present method advocated by authorities in the field of reading (who themselves hold to a balanced system of word analysis techniques) will produce the desired pupil learning outcomes.

On the basis of personal interviews, Austin found that in regard to causes of reading disability the blame was "scattered as though it came from a shotgun." She concluded: "Their replies indicated four causal factors: poor classroom teaching; lack of leadership at the administrative and supervisory levels; poor organization and use of materials within the schools; and difficulties particular to the children themselves. The people who received the most censure were the classroom teachers."

Concerning the fourth cause, difficulties particular to the children themselves, it was stated: "Lack of readiness was the most frequently cited, caused either by an ineffective readiness program in the school or by poor preparation at school and/or poor home environment. Furthermore, children were evidently handicapped by false ideas about their own abilities, ideas which were sometimes reinforced by pressure from well-meaning but uninformed parents."

The above findings shed light on the attitudes of teachers and "teachers of teachers of reading." However, in the twenty-two recommendations for improving the teaching of reading for tomorrow's teachers, the child with dyslexia remained in the shadows of the torchlight.

The San Francisco Curriculum Survey Committee prepared a report for the Board of Education, which was submitted April 1, 1960. The committee was composed of faculty members of the University

of California and Stanford University, who represented various disci-
plines. The first caption of the committee's report was "Reading:
The Basic Importance of Phonics." The first sentence of this section
was explicit: "We recommend a systematically phonetic approach
to reading."

This committee did not mention innate capacity as an explanation
of reading retardation, but the arguments in favor of the phonic approach in the general teaching of reading were clearly stated. The
following quotation is an example of the stand taken:

> The exponents of look-say have built elaborately on one very
> minor recent discovery, but they have largely ignored a vastly more
> important discovery made at least three thousand years ago by the
> Phoenicians. We refer, of course, to the alphabet. The whole
> purpose of the alphabet is to break up all the sounds of human
> speech analytically into a small number of fundamental com-
> ponents, which are then represented by an equally small number
> of symbols. Knowing these symbols and their sounds, the six-year-
> old can with little drill sound out and recognize from a printed
> text a large proportion of the 10,000 words he has already learned
> by listening and talking. Quite apart from the practical advantage
> of being infinitely more effective, phonics has an immense peda-
> gogical advantage over look-say: it encourages the child to think
> rather than to guess.

The committee's final paragraph on reading was forthright and
optimistic:

> If the phonic method does for San Francisco children what it
> has done for children of other communities, it should soon bring
> about a marked improvement in reading and thus make possible
> a more solid and more rapidly progressing curriculum. Moreover,
> spelling should cease to be the nightmare it has been in recent
> years. English spelling is far from being completely rational, but
> it is rational enough to open itself very considerably to the phonic
> key.

James B. Conant made a valiant effort to set the record straight
for the public on the issue of phonics *versus* look-say. He arranged a
conference of reading experts, which was held in New York City
in September, 1961. It was attended by twenty-eight experts who

were known to have divergent views on the use of phonics in reading instruction. With only one dissenting voice, the conference participants agreed on the following statement:

> It is not true that our schools, in general, use primarily a "sight-word method." It is not true that our schools, in general, do not teach phonics.
>
> We hold that reading cannot be taught through "sight-words" (look-say) alone. Such teaching would require our children to memorize, word by word, the mass of printed words. No reading authority advocates so impossible a procedure.
>
> We consider phonics one of the essential skills that help children identify printed words that they have not seen before and then understand the meaning that those words represent. Without phonics most children cannot become self-reliant, discriminating, efficient readers.

The report of the proceedings of this conference on "Learning to Read" was a valuable one, but there was only fleeting reference to variation in individual capacity to learn to read. More attention was given to external influences and motivation. Mention was made of lack of teacher training and "large classes, meager libraries, inadequate equipment, insufficient books and supplies, poor public support—both moral and financial."

A more recent item on phonics appeared in the *New York Times* January 5, 1964. Since it showed clearly the continuing debate and the trend toward phonics, one statement warrants repetition here:

> The Reading Reform Foundation, an admittedly partisan organization dedicated to the return of phonics—teaching of letters of the alphabet rather than whole-word recognition—to reading instruction, last week claimed substantial victories. In a year-end survey, the foundation said phonic systems of teaching are now in use in more than one-fourth of the nation's schools.

Albert J. Harris (1963), in a pamphlet on reading compiled by the National Education Association, stated that "every reading expert believes in the importance of teaching phonics, but opinions vary on when and how to teach phonics and on how much it should be stressed."

The specialized teachers of reading who were trained by Orton and other teachers experienced in remedial reading have advocated a return to the use of phonics in the teaching of reading for all children. Although they do not claim that any method of teaching is the basic cause of reading disability, they have found through experience that about 25 per cent of all children do not learn to read with facility through the look-say method, that children with reading disability progress when phonics are combined with other sensory modalities, and that practically all children profit by and enjoy the knowledge of word make-up and the origin of sound in language.

The proponents of the look-say or whole-word system of teaching reading are not so articulate in championing their approach as they were some time ago, but they continue to advocate the look-say method. For example, Flesch quoted from an article by E. A. Betts, a recognized authority on reading, which appeared in the January 1954 issue of *Education*: "For the past 150 years, the phonics fad has come and gone. Right now the fad has again taken over reading. While there is need for improving the phonics program through the teachers, it should be obvious that this one gimmick will not make much of a dent in the reading problem."

Flesch also referred to a statement made in 1928 by Arthur I. Gates: "That it will be the part of wisdom to curtail the phonetic instruction in the first grade very greatly is strongly implied; indeed it is not improbable that it should be eliminated entirely." As late as 1963 Gates had not changed his view. In a pamphlet published by the National Education Association he said that "some of the recent popular books on reading assume that all the problems can be solved by the exclusive use of extreme, time-consuming, formal phonic systems as those in use more than a half century ago."

Turning to another aspect of teaching not directly related to phonics *versus* look-say but still concerned with inappropriate teaching, some arresting statements were made in the *Encyclopedia of Mental Health* published in 1963: "The main reason why Johnny (children in the public schools of the United States) is having difficulty with reading is probably because of the overcrowded condition in the classroom. . . . No studies have been done so far which show that one method of teaching reading is superior to another." No one would deny that overcrowding in classrooms adversely affects both pupils and teachers.

However, overcrowding cannot be held responsible for producing the clinical picture of dyslexia with all of its characteristics.

Socioeconomic Factors

Concerning the more intimate social aspects of the family situation as related to learning inhibition and reading retardation, Chapter V covered the roles of the mother and father. Here, we go beyond the family and embrace the socioeconomic factors found in the immediate neighborhood and the community.

First of all, many psychiatrists, psychologists and other professional workers in the field of mental health have come to believe that mental retardation may be due to socioeconomic causes. The "Manual on Terminology and Classification in Mental Retardation," a monograph supplement to the *American Journal of Mental Deficiency* (1961), included the following types of mental retardation: "(1) psychogenic mental retardation associated with environmental deprivation, and (2) psychogenic mental retardation associated with emotional disturbance."

Elaborating on these types of mental retardation, a report from the Group for the Advancement of Psychiatry (1963) stated:

> Social factors, such as physical and psychological deprivations, are also important in the etiology of mild mental retardation. Current studies on deprivation indicate that it is impossible to develop normally if there is inadequate emotional and intellectual stimulation. . . . Psychological factors that can cause a child to function on a mentally retarded level range from severe anxiety to early infantile autism. The developmental history of such children gives evidence of original intellectual potential, but the longer the psychological stress continues, the more the child may become indistinguishable from those with biological mental retardation.[3]

If, then, it is accepted that a general retardation of mental or intellectual functions may be due to socioeconomic situations, it appears logical that reading, spelling and writing might be retarded by the

---

[3]It is interesting to note that McCready (1926), writing about word-blindness and word-deafness, pointed out that children with such handicaps are likely to be considered feebleminded. He went on to add that "these children may eventually become feebleminded by deprivation unless their condition is exactly recognized and proper treatment instituted."

same factors. A child who has missed a year or two of schooling because of illness, family disruption or frequent moves will be retarded in reading, spelling and writing along with all other school subjects. A child who comes from a home in which there are no books or in which the parents do not even read a newspaper will be handicapped in reading, but not in reading alone.

The contention that socioeconomic stress impairs only reading, spelling, and writing (or speech) and leaves other school subjects and other intellectual functions unimpaired is open to question. The contention is all the more to be doubted when the clinical picture of dyslexia with the accompanying reversals of letters, confused dominance and other characteristics is considered. It is probably true that reading and its related language functions are more vulnerable to the influence of early deprivation than other educational attainments. However, more important than deprivation so far as reading is concerned may be the role of "somatic compliance" (Freud's term) in determining an individual's vulnerability to social, economic and emotional stress.

Regardless of the above contentions, several studies have been made of the role of socioeconomic factors in reading retardation. For example, Irving D. Harris (1961), in his book *Emotional Blocks to Learning*, reported on his studies of the influences of the environment on learning and more definitely on learning to read. Harris, as a psychoanalyst on the staff of the Illinois Institute for Juvenile Research, was concerned with the milieu and the mores surrounding the language-blocked child of average intellectual endowment. He gave attention to emotional blocks arising from conditions such as social class, family disorganization, parental ambition and birth order. Concerning socioeconomic status, Harris found a significantly greater proportion of boys from lower middle-class or lower-class families in the nonlearner group than in the learner group. Granting a lower level of intelligence in the children of lower-class families, there were also the factors of lack of motivation, lack of stimulation and lack of parental anxiety about the boys' accomplishments.

In family disorganization, the crucial situation was found to be a combination of parental incompatibility and a mother who worked outside the home. This particular combination seemed to produce

(1) difficulties in concentration, (2) reading problems, and (3) repetition of grades. "These manifestations were attributed to a chronic feeling of anxious insecurity in the boy as to whether his home would stay intact or come apart. This feeling, in turn, was traced to the personality of the mother who was unable to function as a homemaker or rejected that role."

Parental ambitiousness was a more complicated factor in the learning process than was economic status or an absentee mother. Parental ambitiousness was closely related to birth order. Harris stated that "youngest or last-born boys were found almost twice as frequently in the group with learning problems." Many other interesting observations on first- and last-born children were recorded by Harris, and in the appendix of his book he added a chapter on birth order.

Many statements that involve socioeconomic problems have been made by persons in position of authority. For example, the superintendent of a city school system was quoted in a newspaper article as saying that the inability to learn at a satisfactory rate usually stems from three causes: poverty, poor home conditions or a physical impairment. He was quoted as saying: "Why can't the student read? Is it because he comes from a poverty stricken home or lives in an adverse family atmosphere and, as a result, is emotionally upset or disturbed? Is it because he has a physical handicap, maybe an eyesight problem?" He made no mention of individual endowment or even of teaching methods. The public was left with the impression that reading disability is due to poverty, emotional turmoil in the home or poor eyesight.

There is a growing trend in some quarters to turn the equation around and claim that reading disability is a common cause of poverty. In fact, the *Reader's Digest* (November, 1962) published an article by Lester Velie which related illiteracy to poverty. The article carried the provocative title of "Who Will Weep with Willie McGee?" Velie, one of the magazine's roving editors, explained the title by saying: "Though countless jobs go begging, Willie and his children are on relief. Why? Because Willie—like one out of every ten American adults—is functionally illiterate and can't be retrained for a place in our industrial society. His problem is one which every community must come to grips with."

In confirmation of his claim, Velie said: "When Chicago relief administrators tested relief recipients in one neighborhood recently 50.7 per cent were found to be 'functional illiterates.' They had less reading and writing ability than an average fifth-grade child." He turned up similar facts in Philadelphia, Detroit, and other cities. Velie noted that programs to combat illiteracy have been instituted in some cities and that those on relief are required to study reading.

Not all illiterates have a specific reading disability, to be sure, but the chances are good that a large percentage of them do have some degree of dyslexia. The writer has been unable to find a study that defines the proportion of dyslexics among illiterates.

Related to illiteracy is the problem of school dropouts and their subsequent unemployment. President Kennedy recognized the seriousness of the dropout problem when he said in his State of the Union Message, "Today an estimated 4 out of every 10 students in the fifth grade will not even finish high school."

Daniel Schreiber (1962), director of the National Education Association Project on School Dropouts, said: "Studies from every section of the country testify that the average dropout is at least two years retarded in reading ability by the time he quits school. . . . A nationwide study conducted by the U. S. Department of Labor showed that 70% of the dropouts had registered I.Q. scores about 90. . . . The majority of dropouts come from families of the lower socioeconomic categories. . . ."

In listing nine causes for school dropouts, Schreiber started off with "reading retardation" and said: "To my mind, the greatest factor in school dropouts is reading retardation." He referred to a study by Ruth C. Penty of Teachers College which found that three times as many poor readers as good readers drop out of school.

The National Education Association devoted one issue of its *Newsletter* to "Project—School Dropouts" (April, 1963). In this *Newsletter* there was a reference to a study which showed "a close correlation between the ability to read well and various home influences such as the size of the family, the level of parental aspiration for the child, the educational level of the parents, and the occupational status of the father."

Dyslexia is a prominent factor in illiteracy and school dropouts, both of which play an important part in unemployment. Unemployment, in turn, is a basic cause of poverty. From the above, a step-by-step progression can be diagrammed with almost tragic precision:

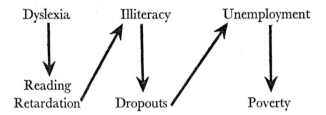

Chapter VII

FURTHER NEUROLOGICAL STUDIES

Despite a century of study, the mechanisms of speech and aphasia remain as challenging problems.

LAMAR ROBERTS (1959)

A DISCUSSION OF FREUD's classic monograph *On Aphasia* (1891) terminated the review of the early neurological contributions to the understanding of language disturbances. The discussion of further neurological contributions was interrupted because our attention was shifted to Morgan (1896) who "discovered" congenital word-blindness.

From 1896 until 1925, when Orton published his first article on word-blindness, it was mainly the ophthalmologists who called attention to congenital or innate reading disabilities; almost all of them tried to attribute this handicap to an agenesis or a lesion in a particular part of the brain. During this thirty-year period, the neurologists and neuropathologists continued to focus their attention on speech disorder as the term aphasia implied. During this time psychiatrists and professional workers in child guidance clinics paid little or no attention to reading disability.

Contributions of English Neurologists

With particular attention to motor aphasia and speech disturbances, some outstanding neurologists in England provided leadership in the study of organic aphasia. The work of Hughlings Jackson has already been discussed.

Sir Henry Head published detailed studies of aphasic cases; he reviewed the history and formulated a new classification and terminology (1920). He agreed with Hughlings Jackson in his opposition to the concept that there are specific centers in the brain, such as a word-memory center. Although he made definite reference to organically produced reading and writing disturbances as well as word-hearing disabilities, he did not describe clearly innate dyslexia.

With his attention on speech, Head recorded some pertinent observations about organic language disorders:

> To the group of functions which suffer in these high-grade disorders of speech, I have applied the term "symbolic formulation and expression. . . ." Acts of symbolic formulation and expression are integrated on a level superior to that of motion, and are of higher order than sight or hearing. Consequently, the clinical manifestations cannot be classified as "motor," "visual," or auditory defects of speech. Moreover, the clinical facts fail to bear out the contention that the various forms assumed by these disorders in the use of language can be classified in distinct categories as faults of speaking, reading, or writing. These are purely linguistic terms for diverse human actions, and do not correspond even to groups of physical functions. . . . Disorders of this kind cannot be classified as isolated affections of speaking, reading and writing, for these acts are more or less disturbed whatever the primary nature of the defects. Nor can they be attributed directly to the destruction of auditory or visual images or to any other analogous processes, which belong to a relatively low order in the psychical hierarchy. Each clinical variety represents some partial affection of symbolic formulation and expression; the form it assumes depends upon the particular modes of behavior which are disturbed or remain intact.

Lord Brain (W. R.) wrote extensively on aphasia. His recent book *Speech Disorders* (2nd Ed., 1965) showed that he, too, was more interested in or cognizant of speech disorders than of reading and writing disorders. He gave an excellent review of the history of medical opinion about aphasia with details about exact brain localization as claimed by Broca and Wernicke, but denied by Freud and Jackson.

Most of the chapters in Lord Brain's book dealt with organic disorders of speech, but he did have a section on developmental disorders of speech in which he described developmental dyslexia. He said that "developmental dyslexia is much commoner than congenital auditory imperception. . . ."

Elsewhere in the book he discussed the pathology of agnosic alexia: "In agnosic alexia the patient suffers from an inability to read, because he fails to recognize the visual symbols of speech, that is, written and printed words, but he can still write both spontaneously and from dictation, and other speech functions are normal. . . . In agnosic alexia, on the physiological hypothesis adopted in this book, the essence of the disorder lies in a failure of the visual presentation of letters and words to arouse the visual word-schemas which play an essential part in the recognition of written and printed words and the evocation of their meanings."

Concerning the anatomy of word-blindness, Lord Brain stated:

> In order that the physiological process just described may occur, it is necessary that nervous impulses derived from the visual cortex of both occipital lobes should reach in right-handed persons the left angular gyrus and its neighbourhood. There is general agreement that the lesion responsible for pure word-blindness is so placed as to interrupt this pathway. . . . Impulses from the right visual cortex may be interrupted in the splenium of the corpus callosum or in the subcortical white matter between the splenium and the angular gyrus. . . . It will be noted that all the areas named fall within the territory of supply of the posterior cerebral artery, and in most cases pure word-blindness is caused by a vascular lesion resulting from arteriosclerosis of this vessel or its branches.

Macdonald Critchley published important studies of aphasia, but perhaps more important was his book *The Parietal Lobes* (1953). The chapter titles indicate the varied disturbances of function which may result from lesions in the parietal lobes: disorders of tactile function and of motility; apraxia; Gerstmann's syndrome; disorders of the body image; visual defects; disorders of spatial thought, of language, and of symbolic thought. These are the same disorders of function that come up for discussion again and again in consideration of developmental dyslexia.

It is impossible to do justice to the implications in Critchley's disquisition that relate to the subject at hand—developmental dyslexia. Briefly, however, Critchley said, "Lesions of the parietal lobe of the dominant hemisphere are at times followed by impairment in symbolic thought. The principal evidence of such disorder consists in disturbances in reading and calculation."

The writer knows that Critchley recognized that language, motility and tactile dysfunctions can be caused by developmental lag as well as by a lesion in the brain. With regard to the aphasias in general, Critchley followed the concepts of Hughlings Jackson, Freud, and others in maintaining that there is no specific word-memory center in the brain or other exact localization for the specific parts of language functions.[1]

Contributions of American Neurologists

During the first half of the twentieth century many neurologists and neurosurgeons in the United States and Canada were interested in aphasia. Except for Orton and his associates, little attention was given by neurologists to the reading and writing aspects of aphasia, although these aspects were noted as part of the over-all picture.

J. M. Nielsen (1937) wrote an article "Unilateral Cerebral Dominance as Related to Mind Blindness." Later (1941) in his *Text Book of Clinical Neurology,* he discussed the aphasas at considerable length. This was followed by his very detailed studies of case material as published under the title of *Agnosia, Apraxia, Aphasia. Their Value in Cerebral Localization.* In this study he regrouped and renamed the various language disturbances resulting from brain damage.

In the latter book Nielsen stated that alexia may result from pathological changes on three different physiological levels as follows:

1. Agnostic alexia is the failure of recognition of letters, figures, syllables, and words. The lesion which can cause this type of alexia may involve only the white matter of the left occipital lobe or this plus involvement of the splenium of the corpus callosum.

2. Aphasic alexia is the loss of ability to comprehend statements of a simple character, the words being properly recognized. Henschen believed, and subsequent investigation has proved him correct, that the angular gyrus cannot, as a rule, serve for interpretation of written or printed matter if anatomically dissociated from the area of Wernicke. For this reason acoustic verbal agnosia

---

[1]The above paragraphs were written before it was discovered that Critchley published a monograph on *Developmental Dyslexia* in 1964. This monograph is an expansion of his Doyne Memorial Lecture for 1961 on the subject of "Inborn Reading Disorders of Central Origin." Critchley agreed with Orton and others that no cerebral pathology had been found to account for developmental dyslexia.

is usually accompanied with alexia. A lesion between the angular
gyrus and Wernicke's area has the same effect.

3. Semantic alexia is the loss of the ability to comprehend complicated statements, although the patient is still able to grasp
simple ones involving a few words. This type, like semantic aphasia
itself, results from a lesion of the temporal lobe involving Wernicke's area and the language formulation area.

Elsewhere, with regard to certain language centers of the brain,
such as the angular gyrus which functions for recognition and re-
visualization of the written word, Nielsen said: "The patterns are
spread diffusely over the cortex and the superiority of the major (side)
is great. . . . The minor angular gyrus in most instances has its
engrams so crudely made that, after destruction of the major side in
adulthood, many years are required for it to perform at all well.
Unless the major is destroyed early in life, the minor rarely attains
a degree of perfection comparable to that of the major."

Nielsen made the interesting statement that "there is hardly an
element of agnosia, apraxia, or aphasia established as resulting from
organic lesions that has not also been noted in purely functional
states." It is not entirely clear as to what Nielsen meant when he
used the word "functional," but he had been discussing the psychological approach of Hughlings Jackson, Head, and others as
viewed from the standpoint of physiological development.

Outstanding among Canadian contributions by neurologists and
neurosurgeons is the work by Penfield and Roberts described in their
book *Speech and Brain-Mechanisms*. No one has carried out more
meticulous and extensive studies of brain localization than Wilder
Penfield. As a neurosurgeon, it was possible for many of his observations to be based on the results of removal of brain tissue or on the
effects of electrical stimulation applied to selected areas of the brain.
As the name of the above-mentioned book indicates, the fundamental
interest was in speech mechanisms, but references to reading and
writing appear in the text. The following quotation concerning localization of functions in the brain represents the authors' viewpoint:

In summary, much has been learned about aphasia since Broca's
time. It would seem that most authors agree that lesions in specific
localities produce definite clinical types of aphasia. The closer the

lesion is to Broca's area (the posterior part of the third frontal convolution) and the adjacent precentral face area, the more the motor components of speech are involved. The nearer the lesion is to the vicinity of the junction of the parietal, temporal and occipital lobes, the more reading and writing are affected; and the more the posterior superior temporal region is involved, the greater the difficulty in the comprehension of spoken words.

Neurologists of today do not believe that there is a word-memory center in the brain, a "pure" alexia or a "pure" aphasia. Speech is not an independent function; all aphasias comprise not only a disorder of speech but a disorder of language. Since the use of language is a highly individual mode of behavior, an aphasia will constitute an aberration of the pattern of total behavior. According to Critchley, an aphasic is a brain-injured person who is struggling to cope with an artificial situation by means of the reduced mechanisms available to him at the particular moment. The same concept applies to the person with developmental dyslexia, although he is not brain-injured. Moreover, with reference to developmental dyslexia, Critchley said: "It is not wise to seek too close an analogy between the non-appearance of a function, and the loss of a function through disease. In any case, the term 'aphasia' should not be applied to a failure in the development of a language-modality, but should be reserved for loss or impairment of a mature linguistic endowment."

Cerebral Dominance

The expression "cerebral dominance" means that the cortex in one side or hemisphere of the brain is dominant over the other side in the choice of functions that can be carried out by one side of the body. From the time of Hippocrates it has been accepted that the two sides of the brain, although appearing alike, do not function alike. For people who are definitely right-sided, the centers that control language functions are almost invariably located in the left side of the brain. However, for left-sided people, the opposite is not always the case. Moreover, the anatomical arrangement is such that one side of the brain is a mirror image of the other side, just as one hand is a mirror image or the opposite of the other hand.

In the early descriptions of congenital word-blindness by Morgan,

Hinshelwood, and others, no emphasis was given to the role of mixed or confused dominance in spite of the fact that in the illustrations used there were numerous examples of reversals and confusion in the spelling of words. It remained for Orton (1925) to call attention to this evidence of confused dominance and to express the idea in his term "strephosymbolia," which means distorted or twisted symbols.

Orton expressed the view that many of the delays and defects in the development of language functions may arise from a deviation in the process of establishing unilateral brain superiority. He made it clear that this is a very complicated problem which involves far more than handedness or ambidexterity, and that brainedness does not always match handedness. He said that "if there should be failure in establishment of the normal physiological habit of using exclusively those (engrams) of one hemisphere there might easily result a confusion in orientation which would exhibit itself as a tendency toward an alternate sinistrad and dextrad direction in reading and in lack of prompt recognition of the differences between pairs of words which can be spelled backwards or forwards, such as was and saw, not and ton, on and no, etc."

Handedness is only one of several functions related to laterality, and it may be a very misleading one. If a person states that he is right-handed and demonstrates right-handed writing, it is not conclusive proof that he is a dextral (right-sided). Early in life he may have been trained to use his right hand when he showed evidence of being a sinistral (left-sided). There is little necessity for a dextral to train his left hand; but for the sinistral, the parents, the teachers, the individual himself and the exigencies of life combine to force or coerce training of the right hand.[2]

Regardless of the combination of laterality functions, the problem may not be an all or none proposition—either right-sided or left-sided —but rather one of ambilaterality. Critchley (1964) said, "That cerebral ambilaterality and dyslexia are to be equated with immaturity of cerebral development, is the view most widely held today among

_____

[2]In addition to handedness, eyedness and footedness are often recognized; but not earedness. Articles have been published on tonguedness and smiledness. Besides, some people raise one eyebrow in preference to the other and some can wink only one eye.

neurologists." This statement is confirmatory of opinions expressed earlier by Orton, Gesell, Bender, Schilder, Hermann and many other writers. Critchley expressed the opinion that true ambidexterity is a rare condition but that acquired ambidexterity is found in left-handers who have trained their right hand. Also, there is good evidence from detailed studies that left-handers are not as left-handed as right-handers are right-handed.

In his work on aphasia,* Brain gave considerable attention to handedness and cerebral dominance. He estimated that 5 to 10 per cent of people in Great Britain and the United States are left-handed and that left-handedness is about twice as common in males as in females. He said:

> The preference for the right hand is usually the result of heredi-
> tary predisposition, and there is evidence that right-handedness
> is inherited as a Mendelian dominant and left-handedness as a
> recessive. . . . Either hemisphere can function alone for language
> if the other is severely damaged early in life; in children, aphasia
> occurs more frequently as the result of right-sided lesions than in
> adults, and moreover is more transitory. Hence, at birth, it would
> seem that the two cerebral hemispheres possess an equal poten-
> tiality for the localization of the speech functions, but there is a
> natural tendency, presumably inherited, for the large majority of
> individuals in the course of learning to speak to establish their
> speech centres in the left cerebral hemisphere, to some extent inde-
> pendently of whether they are right-handed or left-handed.

While doing his outstanding work in the field of cortical dominance, Oliver L. Zangwill (1962) was fully aware of the problems of dyslexia. He recognized that reading difficulty and cerebral ambivalence could be taken as evidence of a constitutional maturational lag. He cautiously suggested the possibility that children without firm lateral preference may be vulnerable to stress. He did not delineate how this vulnerability would lead to the picking out of reading, spelling and writing as an evidence of stress except on the basis of confused dominance.

Vernon B. Mountcastle (1962) edited the report of an international symposium on "Interhemispheric Relations and Cerebral Dom-

---

*Speech Disorders, 2nd Ed., 1965.

inance." Richard Jung, who summarized the Mountcastle report, brought out a factor that is not usually considered: "We know very little about inhibitory mechanisms that may be at play between the right and left brain. . . . If inhibition did not occur in the cortex, we would all be epileptics, and if it did not occur between the two hemispheres, we would not develop skilled voluntary movements. For a neurophysiologist, it seems evident that interhemispheric coordination and all of the functions which have been discussed, including transfer of training, can only occur with a considerable amount of inhibition." Hughlings Jackson spoke about inhibition in this context many years before, and Orton pointed to the factor of inhibition or lack of it in strephosymbolia.

At the same symposium Arthur L. Benton summarized certain points as follows: "There can be no question that the relationship between handedness and cerebral dominance for language deserves continued scrutiny. . . . The least controversial fact in this area is that the left hemisphere is dominant for language in the very great majority of right-handed persons. On the other hand, we now know that the second part of the classic formula (i.e., that the right hemisphere is dominant in sinistrals) does not hold. . . . In short, in contrast to the situation obtaining with dextrals, the dominant hemisphere for language in sinistrals is essentially unpredictable."

Discussion of cerebral dominance would not be complete without consideration of the functions of the corpus callosum, which is made up of the large band of nerve fibers which connect the two sides of the brain. This body (corpus) was formerly considered to be nothing more than a telephone pole that supported wires from one side of the brain to the other side, but in the last decade studies have shown that this cross communication structure has some very complicated functions. A few of these functions appear to be relevant to perception in general and to reading in particular.

R. W. Sperry and his colleagues have made important contributions in this field by animal experimentation and through observation of patients with epilepsy in whom the corpus callosum was divided to provide relief from convulsions. Sperry's article entitled "The Great Cerebral Commissure," which appeared in *Scientific American* (1964), summarized most of the research studies related to this area of the brain. In this article he referred to the observations of Norman Geschwind who "noted that a patient with a damaged corpus callosum, and similar individuals in the medical literature have shown effects such as word-blindness, word-deafness, and faulty communication between the right and left hands."

Geschwind wrote a chapter on "The Anatomy of Acquired Disorders of Reading" for the book *Reading Disability: Progress and Research Needs in Dyslexia* (edited by John Money). Geschwind reviewed the studies of pure word-blindness and discussed the role of the corpus callosum in word-blindness. Other investigators, many of them stimulated directly by Sperry, have recognized that there may be a difference between reading disability resulting from organic lesions and reading disability of the innate or developmental type.

Biochemical Considerations

Attention is called to recent discoveries in the biochemical field that are related to learning, perception, and memory. Out of studies focused on genetics came the discovery that DNA (deoxyribonucleic acid), an offspring of RNA (ribonucleic acid), may be the molecule in the cell which determines heredity. Many experiments tend to confirm the theory that RNA is somehow involved in the learning-memory process, at least in flat worms and rats. Moreover, senile humans with gross memory disturbances have shown remarkable improvement in memory after injections of RNA.

That a metabolic disorder in the enzymatic reactions of RNA and DNA would disturb only the perception and memory functions related to reading, spelling and writing appears most improbable. Equally improbable is the conjecture that the nerve cells which perform in language functions may have some specific metabolic disorder, either in lack of certain chemicals or in overaction and inhibitory effects of chemical processes. However, no one has injected RNA into a human being to determine its effects on reading disability.

Brain-damaged Children and Dyslexia

Practically all the earlier writers on congenital word-blindness (mostly ophthalmologists) postulated that the cause of the disability was some kind of brain pathology. For them it had to be some anomaly

—an agenesis or lesion in a certain region of the brain. Orton was the first to deny explicitly that agenesis or a lesion was necessarily the fundamental cause. As a neuropathologist he was fully aware that brain pathology could produce reading disability even in children, but he thought that the major cause of word-blindness was a developmental lag and not a pathological condition in the brain.

Approaching the problem from a different direction, Bender, Schilder, and others—including the writer—became aware of the fact that brain-damaged children frequently showed evidence of dyslexia along with their neurological and behavioral abnormalities. These children often had a suggestive or definite history of some type of central nervous system disorder.

Usually, if evidence of brain damage is found in a child's medical history, in the electroencephalogram (EEG),[3] in minor neurological signs, and/or in any of the psychological tests, there is a strong tendency to decide "this is it" in regard to dyslexia and all of the child's other problems. Consideration of the possibility that language disability may have been present as an innate factor deserves attention. In other words, since about one child in ten has some degree of language disability, it is possible that the dyslexia may have stemmed from causes outside the organic damage, at least in some instances.

The above observation is not intended to deny that dyslexia may be the direct result of brain damage, especially in early life, even *in utero*. Passamanick and his colleagues have given strong evidence that such damage may occur. Kawi and Passamanick (1958) found that in 16.6 per cent of 205 children with reading disability there were pregnancy complications such as preeclampsia symptoms, bleeding, hypertension, etc., while in a control group of normal readers, the pregnancy complications occurred in only 1.5 per cent.[4]

Arnold Gesell (1947) said, "The surprising prevalence of reading

---

[3]A few writers have claimed that abnormal EEG tracings have been found in a high percentage of children with reading disabilities. Reference is made to the reports of Hughes *et al.* (1949), Kennard *et al.* (1952), and Cohn (1961). Concerning these reports and other studies, there remain questions about the interpretation of EEG abnormalities (especially in children), the selection of cases for study, and the lack of control groups. As Benton (1963) said: "Actually, a specific association between EEG and reading disability has not been unequivocally demonstrated."

[4]Early in the literature about congenital word-blindness, Fisher (1910) and McCready (1910) focused attention on birth injury and prenatal factors. In

disabilities, so-called, and their frequent association with minimal birth injuries tend to support our thesis that these injuries are more common than is ordinarily supposed."

Lillian Wagenheim (1959) in a study of 674 elementary school children found a significant relationship between the occurrence of measles in the first three years and later reading achievement. This was true for boys, but not for girls. In the same study, no significant relationship was found between early measles and level of intelligence. Wagenheim, however, was reluctant to accept completely her findings as final proof that virus diseases acquired in the first three years could produce a specific crippling effect upon the learning process.

Critchley (1964) in his chapter dealing with maternal and natal factors in the etiology of developmental dyslexia was doubtful of perinatal causes. He stated: "Most neurologists, however, would be reluctant to visualize in developmental dyslexia any focal brain lesion, dysplastic, traumatic or otherwise, despite the analogy of the acquired cases of alexia after brain damage. To do so would be to ignore the important factor of immaturity as applied to chronological age, cortical development, and processes of learning. In all probability the cases of reading retardation which have been observed after brain traumata at birth are of a nature different from the genuine instances of developmental, i.e. specific, dyslexia." In this statement he admits pathological causes of reading disorder, but he does not give points of differentiation between reading disability caused by brain damage and developmental dyslexia.

It appears, then, that there are many "shades of gray." The writer's opinion is that, in the majority of cases, reading disability is due to a physiological developmental or maturational lag which in itself may be accompanied by other signs of immaturity in "soft" neurological, dominance and psychological test findings. That the developmental lag has an hereditary anlaga, predisposition, or diathesis cannot be denied. That minimal or "soft" insults to the brain from various sources during the perinatal period and early infancy might enhance or even produce the developmental lag cannot be disproved. Hence, the "shades of gray."

---

reference to McCready, Bronner said, ". . . but he further adds as causes, defective intrauterine development, injuries at birth, acute infectious diseases in infancy, and defective post-natal development."

Chapter VIII

ILLUSTRATIONS OF DEVELOPMENTAL DYSLEXIA

*Some years ago, when I went to consult one of your
Editors, and having blurted out to him that I could not
read, he unfolded what was, to me, the new and wonderful story of word-blindness. I came away rejoicing.*

ANONYMOUS

WITHOUT A DESCRIPTIVE PICTURE of those persons who suffer from
language disability, the story remains lifeless. It is desirable to go
beyond objective description and attempt to portray the personal experiences—the embarrassment, frustrations, anxiety, and defeats—of
those who have to live with their word-blindness. Some of the best
descriptions come from men and women who have had the courage
to struggle with their handicap and the courage to tell about it openly.
They can speak for themselves more authentically than any clinician
can record his observations. After they have spoken, the clinician
will have his turn.

Autobiographies

An English woman wrote a vivid description of her life as a word-
blind sufferer. Her account was published anonymously in the *British
Journal of Ophthalmology* (1936):

> I have been asked to write my experiences of word-blindness.
> I am not sure that I shall be able to convey the daily difficulties
> which this condition causes, partly because one unconsciously ex-
> pects others to understand without explanation and also partly
> owing to the sufferer getting more or less used to the condition
> and consequently failing to analyse it.
> My father and his only brother were both stammerers, their
> sisters being normal. I had two brothers and a sister older than
> myself and a sister and brother younger than I. . . . The governess
> who started us "took no trouble over me," "was bored with me

because I was so slow," she told me this some forty-five years later when I happened to meet her after that interval. Meanwhile she had had a boys' school. She also volunteered that she knew now that she ought to have taken all the more trouble. "Reading with tears" was used for me, but without either of the desired results. My brothers and sister went ahead—while I never got properly started. A German governess took her place when I was seven years of age. She tried punishing me for being lazy and inattentive—which I am sure I was, for I found reading was so very difficult, almost impossible; the book was a blank and conveyed nothing to me and I was so weary with trying to learn to read. "Dunce," written in large black letters on a white cardboard hung on my back while I had to sit alone at the side table during luncheon with my back to the room—the butler and footman handling food looked on. I felt very foolish and self-conscious. I kept peeping around to see how they all took this exhibition. I was quite sure that I was an idiot or feeble-minded. And with those awful silent thoughts, I often cried in bed in the dark.

My mother offered to give me ten shillings if I would read a book. I tried to get through "Black Beauty." I was devoted to horses and this book about a pony attracted me. I worked away at it alone and with the governess month after month. I made a little "V" on the page to show how far I had got. I never finished the book or, of course received the ten shillings, and "Black Beauty" is a nightmare to me. Governesses came and went. A special one was employed for me alone in the hope that concentrated effort in a separate room might hasten my reading.

I was rather good at mental arithmetic and sums, and at these I beat my younger sister. Geography was a star turn for me, also handcraft, and I "sewed beautifully."

Perhaps I was about twelve years of age when I started going to Queen's College in Harley Street. In the reading class there, each girl had to read out loud a paragraph of about two inches of rather small print.

This lesson was simply agony to me, I dreaded it, my heart thumped from anxiety. I used to endeavor to sit in the back of the room and try to get the girl next to me to read my paragraph over to me in my ear, so that when my turn came I should know something about this wretched passage. Nevertheless, I made a lamentable exhibition of myself and I always failed to get the sense of the words I was trying to read. Neither did I know what the other girls had read, as I was worrying about my turn and paragraph. Sometimes this class was small in numbers and then I was forced to sit near the mistress—then the girl at my side could not help me as she would have been overheard. Just before my turn came I would scratch the inside of my nose and, having produced some blood, I was allowed to leave the room because "my nose was bleeding."

My mother has since told me that the Principal of Queen's College wrote to her to ask if my eyes were perhaps the cause of my difficulty in reading. I was duly seen by our family doctor who reported that there was nothing wrong. . . .

Not long after I married, in the course of conversation, my youngest brother said to my husband: "Oh, so you've discovered that she cannot read." I can read to myself very slowly, it is a physical effort. I tackle The Times daily. I think the shortness of the lines helps me, and I do not lose my place and my line quite so often as I do when reading a book. Constantly I have to read the lines several times to get the sense. I have to read each word by itself. I do not use my lips. Long words I have to spell out and I generally fail to appreciate the different syllables of which the word is composed.

I am still very ashamed of my inability to read. I carry this dreadful secret always. I live in fear of having to read out something. At all costs I must conceal my ignorance—a habit which dates from my childhood. . . .

I serve on several committees, both in London and in the country. Lately I was asked to be Chairman of one of the committees. I was very much pressed to take it. I should have liked to have been able to do so. Privately I thought the Chairman might have to read out loud—and I cannot. I had to refuse. It was a miserable and depressing business and I realize I am now labelled a sugarer, with no sense of duty, and selfish. . . .

I am very fond of music and I belong to a choral society. . . . I am an alto, and I find reading the words and the music almost impossible—for I have not time and cannot keep up with the rest. I have to let the words go and learn them by heart at home. . . .

Reading letters is a serious effort, as if reading was not bad enough without having to cope with what is always to me an undecipherable handwriting.

I write slowly and do not talk very much, and cannot speak in public—not even to open a bazaar. My husband says cheerfully of me: "She is a very intelligent woman and a very badly educated one." My eldest brother says: "Considering how slow she was in reading, and backward, it is wonderful how clever she is now; and she always has originality and efficiency and did her jobs especially well.

I have one child, born when I was 40 years of age. At her infant school she was considered clever, though slow in reading. She has forged ahead, she is now at a University. In the "vac." I know she reads about a novel a day. But she tells me that when it comes to reading history, she can only read slowly—much more so than the other students.

It has always been a grief to me not being able to read out loud to my girl, from her childhood upwards. I often tried. I am so morbid about her I see only lions in her path.

Some years ago when I went to consult one of your Editors and having blurted out to him that I could not read, he unfolded what was, to me, the new and wonderful story of word-blindness. I came away rejoicing.

"X"

Another anonymous account was dictated to the writer by a woman physician:

It has been suggested that I record briefly some of my difficulties in the field of language. Having more or less surmounted these disabilities, I believe that my experiences and observations may be helpful to others.

I did not talk until I was just over four years of age. I remember this very well and my mother recorded it in her diary about me. I confess that I had my own gibberish vocal productions long before the age of four and sometimes my mother and others seemed to recognize snatches of it. Undoubtedly my parents had some understanding of the problem and a teacher was engaged to teach me to speak "English." (Only English was spoken by the family.) This teacher was quite successful, because when I started school at six I was able to talk with others fairly well.

However, in school I was soon aware of difficulties in reading and writing. I was more naturally left-handed, but I was urged to use my right hand. I could do mirror writing better than I did regular writing. To start at the right side of the page and go to the left side was so natural, but reading and writing went the wrong way for me. I lagged behind the class in reading, spelling, and writing, but did well in arithmetic and later in geography. Again, my parents with considerable insight came to the rescue and employed a special "remedial" reading teacher. In some ways she was of great help, but I do not know just how, unless it was by constant repetition. She did not teach phonics and to this day I have little knowledge of such. Nor did she use any kinesthetic method. It was almost entirely a visual approach, showing one word after another until I memorized the exact sequence of letters in each word.

In college I did well in zoology because I could understand the illustrations. As to the long scientific terms, I simply memorized the exact sequence of the letters without any idea of the derivation or the look or sound of the term as a whole. I had trouble with foreign languages because I could not visualize the words or pronounce and write them as I seemed to hear them. The grammar and sentence construction in a foreign language was baffling.

I am sure that I do not depend on hearing lectures or conversation for my learning, although I understand all that I hear. I try to spell "by ear" any new words I hear but the result is often quite erroneous. There is some deafness in my family and when I "goof" on spelling or pronunciation I sometimes wonder if I hear well, but tests show no evidence of impairment. Also, visual tests show nothing that could be relevant to my difficulty.

I recognize now that I have had some kind of disability in language, especially in reading and spelling along with confused dominance and a speech problem in early life. If it had not been for the understanding help provided by my parents during my earlier years I probably would not have gone through college and medical school.

Very few anonymous reports on the experiencing of dyslexia could be found in the literature. Hermann (1959) included in his book an anonymous report of a dyslexic which had originally appeared in a newspaper. Skydsgaard (1942) included in his book a personal account written by an elderly lawyer.

The writer has attempted many times to persuade dyslexics to write their personal experiences, but without success. It is possible that these people are sensitive about their handicap; or that they have glossed over and forgotten or repressed the details of traumatic experiences; or that they may still have difficulty in putting their experiences into correctly spelled written words. For this reason, they may be reluctant to reveal any vulnerable spot to a secretary or someone available to do the writing for them.

Dyslexia in Adults

Critchley (1964) in his chapter entitled "The Dyslexic Child Grows Up" cited several instances where an individual had surmounted his language handicap and gone on to some creditable accomplishments. He cited the case of Karl XI (1655-97) who was judged to be "one of Sweden's wisest kings," whose "progress in reading was extraordinarily slow and in adult life he always relied upon personal interviews rather than on a study of reports. If handed a document he might be seen to hold the page upside-down and to pretend that he was reading the text. Throughout his life his spelling was highly unorthodox, the errors being quite unlike the usual mis-spellings of the uneducated. He would reverse words, omit letters, or start with letters belonging to the middle of a word. . . . Reversals and other such spelling mistakes were habitual with him up to the time of his death."

Many adults who have had a language handicap in childhood do overcome the disability to a considerable extent, but usually some remnants remain. The writer has observed several colleagues in medicine who had difficulty with spelling and, of course, with writing. Not all of these physicians had a specific disability, but certainly some of them did. One was given to mispronunciation, saying "stench" for stance and calling a refectory table a "refractory" table. Obviously, he could not visualize words and he spelled by ear.[1]

---

[1] The unintentional use of words or phrases when something else was intended, heterophasia, is not always a Freudian slip of the tongue. Frequently, dyslexics make errors of this type. In addition to their reversals of palindromic words such as was for saw and god for dog, space and time words may be confused: up for down, ceiling for floor, first for last, often for seldom. Saunders mentioned the boy who said, "The day after yesterday . . . I mean the day before tomorrow," when he really meant the day after tomorrow. Spoonerisms or malaproprisms as well as the scrambling of clichés occur quite frequently in the expressions of dyslexics. (It seems probable that the Rev. Spooner and Mrs. Malaprop were dyslexics.) As examples of this form of heterophasia, corkscrew was used for shoehorn in reference to getting into a tight girdle; in a dense fog it was remarked,

Two residents in psychiatry gave antithetical descriptions of their learning abilities. One said that he had depended very little on textbooks or reference reading because he was able to absorb most of his information from lectures, discussions and laboratory work. He admitted that he was a slow reader and obtained little enjoyment from reading. The second man was forthright in saying that he had trouble in taking in details heard in lectures and conversations, but depended on going to the books and other visual aids for his knowledge. In a group discussion of this topic at coffee-break time, he admitted that he missed two or three of the points in the conversation.

In a talk given before The Orton Society in 1956, the author told about two medical students who had definite reading disabilities. Regarding the first one, a professor of pediatrics came to the author with an examination paper of this student, who was starting his third year in medical school. The handwriting was quite juvenile; the many spelling errors showed reversals in letter sequence; and one answer was about a different although related topic. It was suggested that this student had a specific reading disability, that he be seen for further study, and that he be given an oral examination. The pediatrician said that he had heard about reading disability, and he agreed to give the student an oral examination. The following day an instructor in obstetrics came with an examination paper of the same student. The same observations and suggestions were made. Before the writer examined the student, both faculty members reported that on oral quizzing this young man appeared to know more about the subject than the majority of his classmates.

When the writer interviewed the student, he admitted that he "never could read much." Throughout his education his mother had read everything to him, and in medical school his wife was reading aloud all books and references. His father had had the same trouble, but he graduated from medical school with the aid of his wife's reading to him. However, the father could not pass state board examina-

---

"you can't see your face in front of you"; and an embarrassed girl said, "and was my nose red." Corey Ford, the humorist, wrote about what he called "double-take talk" or "skid-talk," giving as examples: "I was left holding the jackpot"; "he tells me something one morning and out the other"; "we miss you almost as much as if you were here"; and "I believe in being dumb to kind animals."

tions, because he could not read them. Later he became a professor in one of the preclinical sciences and wrote a textbook for his field.

Efforts to find the medical student's examination papers in the preclinical departments were unsuccessful. The faculty members there remembered him as a bright student who could not write or spell very well, but who managed to make passing grades. From personal interviews, it became obvious that the student had a specific reading disability. Arrangements were made for him to have expert and intensive remedial reading instruction during his vacation time, and psychiatric interviews were continued until he received his M.D. degree. There was some opposition to his continuance in medical school on the part of the dean and one other faculty member, but the opposition subsided as the student made rapid strides in overcoming his disability during the remainder of his medical schooling.

After his graduation a report came from a distant medical school hospital stating that this man was the best intern they had had for some time. He passed his American boards in internal medicine and became the head of a group practice clinic in a large city. More recently, by telephone (not by letter) he said that the explanation of the nature of his disability had been the turning point in his career and had helped as much as all the remedial reading tutoring. Before that time he had been "in the dark." He had felt frustrated and inferior, but when he came to understand his problem he could cope with it in the open.

The second medical student was referred for consultation while he was hospitalized with a gastrointestinal disturbance. He had become ill toward the end of his first year in medical school. After clinical and laboratory studies, the internist had made a diagnosis of anxiety reaction. Early in the psychiatric interviews with the student, he said that he was on the verge of failing the beginning course in physiology because he could not keep up with the assigned reading. This clue led to questioning about the student's other subjects. In anatomy he had been able to see and even feel what he was learning about. In physiology the subject matter was not so visible, there was more assigned reading, and the terminology was new to him. As in the case above, he admitted that reading was his weak point and that he had depended on being "read to" throughout his education. He had most of the characteristic signs of dyslexia, including confused dominance and reversals in spelling.

Before taking his final examination in physiology, he dropped out of school for one full year. During that time he received intensive tutelage in remedial reading. Faculty members were understanding and provided him with part-time work taking care of equipment in the physiological laboratory. Upon resumption of his studies the next year, he progressed without difficulty and continued work on his reading problem. In his senior year he was an honor student and became a member of Alpha Omega Alpha, the honorary medical school fraternity.

As an example of reading disability in an older person, a woman of about fifty years of age came to work as a ward maid in a hospital. She appeared to be younger than she was. She made an excellent impression on the staff, and she conversed with the doctors and nurses in an enlightened manner. She had finished the eighth grade and had married early, so her ambition to be a nurse was denied. She had been a widow for over ten years and had worked at a specialized manual job in order to help her four children get a college education.

Several months after starting her hospital work, she came to the writer with what she herself thought to be anxiety symptoms—a rapid heart rate, trembling hands, perspiration and fear of losing control of herself. At the end of the second interview, she suddenly said, "My trouble is that I can't read." She then revealed an almost complete illiteracy. She couldn't read the names on the food trays which she carried to patients, but she had found ingenious ways through adroit questions of getting the right food to the right patient without error or too much embarrassment. When a patient showed her a cartoon with a caption beneath, she laughed heartily without knowing what it was all about. She was unable to spell except by guessing and she rarely attempted to write a letter to her children.

She was greatly relieved by an explanation of her word-blindness— she had never heard of this condition. She recalled some of her earlier traits such as a tendency to be left-handed and a tendency to confuse letters and words that are reversible. With the realization that she was not "just dim" and with a frank facing of her handicap, her anxiety subsided. She carried on quite well until she fell in love with a bachelor doctor. Then her anxiety symptoms returned, partly because of the fear that he would become aware of her "secret failing."

Dyslexia in Children

Richard R., when he was almost ten years old and in the fourth grade, was referred to a school psychologist because of stealing, untruthfulness and inability to read listed in that order. Based on the Stanford-Binet Test, the psychologist said: "This lad demonstrated that he was functioning within the 'average' category with an obtained mental quotient of 102: mental age 9-8, chronological age 9-6. Following success through the VII year level, he achieved some success until total failure at the XII year level. This intratest variability reflected very poor memory functions both for meaningful and non-meaningful materials, but that visual memory (including visual-motor coordination) was better than auditory-recall memory. Vocabulary development was at about his mental age level, but abstract ability was quite good, as was practical reasoning ability."

On the reading evaluation (Gray's): "No reading score was obtained on the oral reading paragraphs. A consistent reversal tendency was noticed, b for d, p for g, etc. The same happened with numbers. . . . He wrote his name, 'Ricdnp'. It was the impression of the examiner that this boy has a definite language handicap and is badly in need of remedial therapy. His difficulty is typical of children who have 'strephosymbolia'."

On the personality evaluation (C.A.T.): "The stories elicited by the pictures reflected that this boy has a great deal of inner emotional conflicts which have further complicated his adjustment to his environment. Actually, he has anxieties which stem from rather deep-seated fears and feelings of basic insecurity. He may have a better relationship (unconscious) with women due to particular dependency needs, yet, he may also have some antagonistic feelings toward them due to earlier inconsistencies in their dealing with him; that is, his patterns of insecurity could stem from his feelings of an inadequate mother-person in early training periods. Relationship with men may also be conditioned by the fears which the mother may have had in this child's youth. At this point, the stories, produced from phantasy, bear out the history of this boy. He has reacted in a somewhat aggressive manner and it was felt that some of his aggression toward his peers has been related to his inability to gain educational status in competition with them."

In discussion, the psychologist went on to state: "Actually, it is possible that his lack of achievement in school could be a major factor in precipitating symptoms of his basic emotional problems. That is, had he been able to achieve success in school, then he may have been able to feel accepted and closer to his authoritative figures and peer group; however, finding school to be an unrewarding experience, regardless of effort, he has gradually been overwhelmed by his conflicts."

The boy's history was filled with some of the most unfavorable hereditary and experiential factors to be found in any case history. The maternal grandfather went through the fourth grade and later worked as a carpenter. He was a drifter, a poor provider for his seven children, frequently unemployed and often absent from home. Nothing specific was recorded about the maternal grandmother, except that she ran a boarding house to support the family. No information was available on the paternal grandparents.

Concerning the mother, it was recorded that she had difficulty in learning during the first few years in school but progressed up to high school level. At the age of fifteen she met her future husband and a year later started living with him. They lived together off and on for about fourteen years before they were officially married. In the years just prior to the marriage, two boys were born, the younger one being Richard. Both pregnancies were unwanted, and the boys were rejected from birth on.

The father completed the sixth grade and then worked as a butcher until he entered the army, so he must have been able to read enough to meet service qualifications. It was after his two years in the service that the boys were born and the marriage took place. The father died before Richard was two years old, and the boys lived with the mother and various relatives until she was sent to a state hospital when Richard was five years old. The boys were placed in a foster home on a small farm where the foster parents lived on a low margin of subsistence, depending largely on A.D.C. income. Richard and his brother remained in this home for about seven years. There were other foster children in this family, including a mentally retarded boy just younger than Richard.

Many other details about the emotional, economic and cultural deprivations that persisted could be added. Both boys maintained strong hope of a re-established home with mother, but she continued to deteriorate and the boys lived on in an atmosphere of deprivation.

From the age of ten Richard had good tutoring in remedial reading and some individual psychotherapy for over three years. Then, after a year of good adjustment, he stole an automobile in order to get to his mother who was in trouble. He was sent to a reform school for two years. No further information was recorded in the clinic record.

This case history seems to be a very confusing one from the standpoint of reading disability. It is replete with emotional traumata, deprivation and poverty of all sorts. No history of infantile experiences related to scoptophilia or to the inhibition of taking in knowledge through seeing could be ascertained, even in psychotherapy, but it may have been there. On the other hand, it is difficult to see how all these catastrophic events, or any one or two of them, would have singled out reading as a focus for inhibition of development.

Harvey F., aged seven years and three months, was referred to a school psychologist at the end of his first year in school because he was failing in all of his subjects. He was negative at home and at school, and he could not get along with other children.

On the Stanford-Binet Test he registered a mental age of nine years and two months and an I.Q. of 126 in spite of the fact that he was a nonreader. According to the psychologist, "His performance on the Binet revealed considerable scatter of intellectual traits. Vocabulary and knowledge of abstract words were at a superior level, judgment and comprehension were extremely superior and reasoning was excellent." The psychologist considered that his I.Q. might be higher than the test reflected, but found that "reading analysis revealed a reading score of zero. However, of greater importance was the finding that the child has no recognition of letters. There was some evidence of reversals, however the primary defect was lack of visual recognition of letters. . . . There was no evidence or suggestion of an emotional reaction responsible for the child's basic problem."

After the psychological study, Harvey was referred for remedial reading, but no progress could be made because of his extremely negative attitude. He continued in school with "social promotions" up to the fourth grade, when his outspoken rebellious behavior led to expulsion from school and referral to a child guidance clinic for psychotherapy. By this time he had developed such strong resistance to anything resembling school that no attempt was made to give him additional remedial reading for several months. During that time psychotherapy consisted mainly of exploratory walks and games with the boy, during which efforts were made to interpret his disability to him in terms of other disabilities such as color-blindness, tone-deafness and physical awkwardness. Being a bright lad, he quickly became interested in his problem, and when he once understood it he consented to return for remedial reading lessons.

Some months later the reading clinic reported that "Harvey is like a changed boy" and that "he is learning rapidly now and enjoys coming to the reading clinic." He progressed so that individual tutoring was no longer needed and he was in a group. By this time he was almost twelve years old. He continued in the reading clinic and had a teacher for homebound children for the next year. Then he returned to public school, but it was necessary to place him in the fourth grade. At the age of fourteen, when he was in the fifth grade, he got into trouble because he drove his father's car on the public streets. After this he was sent to a very good private school where there were provisions for remedial reading.

Harvey had been adopted at the age of four months by parents in the professional class, and he remained the only child in this home. The parents were somewhat older than average for a baby and they expected a great deal of conformity from the boy. The father had little time to spend with the child, and the mother admitted that she was an overanxious person. Before entering kindergarten the boy had become quite negativistic and had temper tantrums. Also, he was a feeding problem, but this seemed to be part of his negativism. He was told about his adoption before he started school.

It is obvious that there were many unfavorable environmental factors in this case. However, he did have a definite reading disability which, combined with his high general intelligence, complicated his adjustment and disappointed the parents.

In this case, as in some others, the study was not complete from the standpoint of answering several questions. Harvey's neurological and eye examinations showed no evidence of physical defect, but in the psychological study no school achievement tests, no Bender-

Gestalt test and no Rorschach test were given, possibly because of Harvey's poor cooperation or because it was felt that the tests given had revealed enough to go on. Also, no notation was made about confused dominance.

Clem C. was referred to a child guidance clinic when he was eleven years and eight months old because he was not learning in school. He had spent two years in each of the first three grades, and there was doubt about promotion to the fourth grade when he would become twelve years old. Parents, teachers, and others were convinced that the boy was not mentally retarded.

At the time of referral the psychologist did not establish a rating on the Stanford or Wechsler tests, probably because the boy would not cooperate. The Eisonson's Examination was given and showed "errors in reading, reading comprehension, spelling, and arithmetic." The Rorschach revealed widespread evidence of emotional disturbances. It was considered that the boy was prepsychotic and that any additional pressure for school progress might precipitate a psychotic break.

In the intake study no mention was made of the possibility that this boy had a specific reading disability, which may have been of fundamental importance. In the initial interview with the mother she stated that Clem had definite reversal tendencies: saw for was, ton for not, etc. She mentioned that he used inappropriate words: pie for cake, knife for fork, morning for night, etc. Regardless of these suggestive leads indicating dyslexia, it was thought that psychotherapy was most needed. Individual attention was not available at the moment so the boy was started in group psychotherapy in the fall, and he went on into the fourth grade in public school. Remedial reading was not recommended and was not available in the school or clinic, but the mother kept asking for some such tutoring.

The continuing study in the clinic unfolded a variety of facts that were helpful in the understanding of the total problem. Clem was the youngest of three children, and at one point his mother admitted that he was her favorite child. The older brother and sister had progressed in school without difficulty. Clem weighed eight pounds after a normal birth, and he sat up at six months and walked at nine months. In talking he was about average, according to the mother. She claimed that he was a good baby and that there were no difficulties until he entered school and "couldn't learn." More detailed history from the mother revealed no early experiences by the boy that might have led to inhibition of looking in order to gain knowledge.

The father was a mail carrier, even though he had had some college work. The mother went back to work not too long after Clem was born, leaving him in the care of a Negro mother substitute in the daytime. In contrast to her husband, the mother had a rather important secretarial position. The marital relations were described as happy and satisfactory until after Clem was born. Then the father began to drink too much on weekends and entered into some extramarital affairs; the mother gained satisfaction in her career; they drifted apart. A physician referred the couple to a psychiatrist because of the marital discord, but Mr. C. would not consent to see the psychiatrist. In such a family situation there might well have been some elements of emotional deprivation.

Information was obtained from other sources where Clem had had some special study before coming to the child guidance clinic. At the age of eight years and six months while in the second grade, he was examined by a psychologist from the State Board of Welfare. On the Wechsler (WICS) he obtained a verbal I.Q. of 91, a performance I.Q. of 99, and a full-scale I.Q. of 94. A repetition of the same test three years later resulted in almost the same figures, a gain of two points in the performance and full-scale results. No reference to a specific reading disability was made in either report.

A month after the first WICS study, Clem was examined by a pediatric neurologist at a medical school. No evidence of "structural neurological disease" was found, but it was noted that the boy had difficulty with right and left orientation. The EEG was "equivocal," but beyond this there was no information about dominance or the possibility of dyslexia.

During the first year at the clinic Clem was in group psychotherapy and in the fourth grade at the age of twelve, but without remedial reading therapy. He improved in his group adjustment, and some of his school grades went up above the failure level. He received "A" in conduct.

To the writer it appears that Clem probably has a specific reading disability and that his learning difficulty is not due fundamentally to the marital discord in his home or to other emotional factors. That these environmental factors may have aggravated the handicap cannot be denied. But one wonders what the outcome might have been if expert remedial reading could have been started before Clem failed in the first grade. One also wonders what the ultimate outcome might be if Clem could have the benefit of remedial reading at this time.

Boy, seven years and two months, repeating first grade.

Counted orally from 1 to 10 quickly and correctly.

His writing of the same figures is shown at left—going vertically and with the addition of 1 before each figure.

When shown the omission of 6, he counted orally back down to 1.

When shown the omission of 9, he added it with the 9 reversed.

He printed his full name horizontally with correct and readable letters, but could not name any of the letters while looking at his own printing.

While looking at his first name Larry in print, he was asked to spell it orally. The result was "Ldyy."

There was evidence of confused dominance. He appeared to be right-handed but was left-eyed.

FIGURE 2. Vertical writing, reversals, and omissions in number work.

Without giving detailed case histories, some of the characteristics peculiar to dyslexic children are presented in graphic form. For example, the oral spelling and the reading of a nine and a half-year-old girl (I.Q. 91) are shown below:

Oral Spelling		Reading of Words	
boy —	boy	boy —	boy
girl —	gril	girl —	girl
dog —	god	won —	man
book —	bok	book —	look
pen —	pae	now —	two
chair —	char	chair —	cow

Her reading test scored in the low first-grade level, and she appeared to be right-handed, but was definitely left-eyed. An interesting feature of her confusion appeared in telling time. At 1:40 p.m. she said the time was 8:10 (a reversal of the hands on the clock).

In addition, Figures 2 through 4 show the problem of directionality, educational profiles, and family trees respectively.

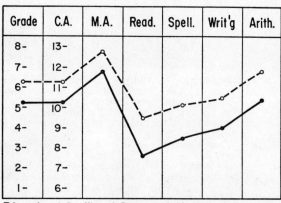

Educational Profile of Boy, aged 10 years & 3 months.

C.A.= Chronological Age
M.A.= Mental Age
——— Original Tests
— — · After on year of
        remedial reading

Educational Profile of Boy, aged 7 years & 4 months

FIGURE 3. Educational profiles of two children before and after remedial reading.

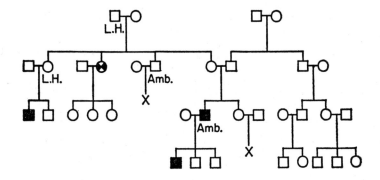

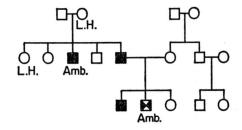

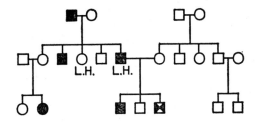

☐= Male   ▨ = Reading Disability   L.H.= Left Handedness
◯= Female   ☒ = Speech Disorder   Amb.= Ambidexterity
                                          X =No Offspring

FIGURE 4. Family trees showing reading and speech disabilities and confused
dominance in three families.

A Borderline Case of Dyslexia

Thomas D., a fourteen-year-old boy who was in the seventh grade,

was referred to a child guidance clinic because of exhibitionism before younger girls and because he wrote a sexually suggestive letter
to a girl. Also, his parents were concerned because, although the boy
seemed to be bright, he made low marks in school.

The psychological report from the clinic gave an estimated I.Q.
of between 115 and 120, but no school achievement tests were done.
However, from the history, the psychiatric evaluation, and other psychological studies there came a "textbook picture" of many of the
factors found in learning inhibition as described in the psychoanalytic
literature. The early conditioning provocative of voyeurism—the seeing of the parents nude, the paradoxical prohibition about looking
or peeping—and other blocks that delayed progression from the
narcissistic level through the oedipal stage and on to good ego development were recorded.

In its interpretation to the parents and the boy, the clinic concentrated on the boy's exhibitionism and paid little attention to his scholastic problem. The clinic recommended rather intensive psychotherapy
for all three, but the parents and the boy did not accept this suggestion.
It reflected too much on the ego of each one, although both parents
were professional people. The parents "shopped around," trying to
find some other answer and hoping that the problem was a transient
one of adolescence.

In this process the writer, although not in clinical practice at the
time, was prevailed upon to see the boy. It was evident that he was
bright and charming. He admitted his socially unacceptable actions,
but cared not to discuss them, saying that such activities would not
happen again. Discussion of other subjects indicated that he had a
feeling of insecurity within the family and at school. He revealed
that because of his poor grades his mother had stopped his boy scout
activities and his athletic team participation at school. Also, social
activities were curtailed and he was "campused" at home to do his
homework and bring up his grades without any specific help.

The boy admitted that he was a slow reader and a poor speller
and that he was failing in history because it required so much reading.
When asked to read an article in *Sports Illustrated* he read word by
word without much fluency. After some ordinary words he stalled
at the word "athlete." With help in pronouncing this word, he con-

tinued to the next line where he encountered the word "athletics" and stalled again. In oral spelling he was correct with short and familiar words, but he spelled chair as "chiar" and table as "tabel." He claimed that he was right-handed but sometimes liked to bat left-handed. Schilder's test for handedness was inconclusive and tests for eyedness showed no particular preference.

In the family history it was found that the only sibling, a brother, was definitely mixed in dominance. He too had a language problem which was revealed in his high school grades and in his college boards.

From the somewhat limited information obtained by the writer, it appears that Thomas had a definite, although mild, language disability. This interpretation met with some acceptance by the parents, and they made a half-hearted effort to provide remedial reading. Consideration was given to placing the boy in a preparatory school where special help would be given, but this was not carried out. In the following four years there was only one more incident of exhibitionism, and this occurred with younger boys, not with girls.

This case, although not studied in detail by the writer, appeared to be one of mild dyslexia. It is possible to interpret the learning inhibition as a symptom of personality disorder stemming from the early experiences that also produced the exhibitionism. On the other hand, it may be that an innate developmental lag produced an increasing frustration for the ego of this pubertal boy. Then with curtailment of other avenues of expression and satisfaction, he reverted to earlier patterns of action.

Acquired Dyslexia in Children

There is no doubt that dyslexia with all of its distortions in reading, spelling, and writing occurs in adults as a result of brain damage. The same distortions occur in children as the result of brain damage, but in the majority of such cases the alleged brain trauma occurred before the child entered school and had an opportunity to demonstrate whether or not he had full capacity in reading, spelling and writing. In other words, consideration must be given to the possibility that the dyslexia found in brain-damaged children may have been present on a constitutional basis. This point is seldom considered, and it is difficult to substantiate.

The following case is recorded in some detail as an illustration of acquired dyslexia, but it will be seen that the diagnosis is open to question.

A nineteen-year-old male was admitted to a psychiatric hospital for study because he had been a chronic behavior problem. The history revealed that the birth, at term, was difficult, requiring the use of instruments, but there was no definite evidence of birth injury. While he was described as a healthy and active child, it was reported that he had convulsions, temper tantrums and enuresis until he entered school. No further information about the convulsions could be obtained, and they never recurred after he was six years old. He walked and talked at an early age and was considered very bright by his parents and neighbors. He had measles, mumps and scarlet fever in childhood, but there were no complications.

He entered school at six years of age and made steady progress without difficulty in any subject until he received a head injury during a football game when he was nine. He was unconscious for twenty-four hours, and a fracture of the skull in the left temporoparietal region was found by X ray. For more than a year after the injury he had periods of somnolence lasting twenty-four hours, and for about two years he complained of blurring of vision.

Following this head trauma, his mother and teachers noted bizarre behavior for the first time. His drowsy periods alternated with periods of overactivity and unexplained and uncontrolled fits of anger. His school achievement dropped markedly, and he had to repeat the sixth grade. He seemed unable to concentrate or to comprehend what he read. Ultimately he completed about two years of high school work, but with poor grades. Starting at about fourteen years of age he began to drink heavily and engage in sexual escapades with prostitutes. At the age of seventeen, he was admitted to the Boston Psychopathic Hospital following his apprehension for the theft of a car. A diagnosis of psychopathic personality was made at that time. A year later he was committed to a state hospital for six months. There he was hyperactive and destructive, used obscene language, and, according to his account, was in wet packs more than once. At this hospital it was considered that he had a psychosis due to some organic brain disturbance.

While he was under the writer's observation at nineteen, his behavior varied markedly, but most of the time he was overactive. His mood varied between depression and irritability. One feature was his constant query as to why he behaved as he did. The physical examination was negative, except for a traumatic cranial asymmetry. Neurological examinations, spinal fluid studies, and other laboratory tests were negative. Encephalography showed symmetrical dilatation of the ventricular system with incomplete and unsatisfactory visualization of the subarachnoid spaces.

During the psychological studies he showed restlessness, fidgetiness, hyperactivity and explosive behavior. On psychological tests his reaction time was quick, and his performance tended to be careless and noncritical. Although he wrote with his right hand, his two hands had approximately equal strength. His speech was stumbling. Visual acuity, balance and fusion showed no defects. Reasoning was confused; sustained, thoughtful, problem-solving was carried out only with great difficulty.

On the Stanford-Binet Test the boy registered an I.Q. of 86. He had poor verbal facility and read badly. Quotients on the Healy tests were widely diverse—66 and 115. School achievement test revealed poor perceptive, apperceptive and comprehension ability. Oral reading was better than reading comprehension. The thinking defect shown in reading and arithmetic computation was similar to that in the intelligence test and pointed to a difficulty in symbolic thinking. His defect appeared to be primarily a central defect in thinking and recognizing the visual symbols that formed the words. On mechanical tests he scored in the upper 10 per cent for adults. On the Bernreuter personality inventory he rated as self-conscious, sensitive, insecure, dependent and sociable.

The psychologist said that marked apperceptive disability was combined with an essential defect in comprehension and in sustained mental elaboration to present a picture of profound organic impairment. These findings, plus the psychiatric observations and the history, made it evident that the patient's handicaps and behavior were due largely to brain pathology. Although he had a reading disability, it was only part of the broad organic picture. With the history of a difficult birth and convulsions during the preschool years, it is possible that some disorder existed before the head injury at the age of nine. However, the history substantiated that he was well-adjusted and showed no scholastic difficulties or behavior disorder during his first three years in school.

Did Oswald Have Dyslexia?

To speculate about the existence of a specific language disability such as developmental dyslexia in a person who has not been studied directly with this in mind may appear to be rather unscientific. However, from the history of an individual and from his writings important data can be obtained which may be strongly suggestive if not finally conclusive that he did have such a handicap. This seems to be true in the case of Lee Harvey Oswald.

On Sunday, November 24, 1963, two days after the assassination of President Kennedy, the newspaper accounts about Oswald's history contained several items suggesting the possibility that he had been handicapped by reading (and spelling) disability. On that day the author started a letter to Dr. Perry Talkington, a psychiatrist in Dallas, bringing this possibility to his attention with the thought that he or a colleague might be called upon to examine Oswald.

In this letter it was said, "Assuming that he had a reading disability with the consequent years of frustration without understanding or help during his school years, 6 to 17, it might have been a fundamental factor in producing hostility and rebellion against society." Just as the letter was being completed, news came by radio that Oswald had been killed. The letter was completed and sent with the statement that now we shall never know for sure about the existence of such a handicap.

However, soon after the letter was mailed further details about Oswald's life appeared in reports of the Associated Press and in news magazines. Some of them caught the writer's attention because they corroborated and rounded out the picture of a specific language disability. From *Time* and *Life,* the *Saturday Evening Post,* newspaper articles, and other sources he collected additional information that seemed to substantiate his thesis. These sources were used to formulate a chronological history of Oswald's school experiences. Some of the quotations are recorded as follows:

His fourth grade teacher, Emma Livingston, remembers him as a child of average intelligence, but low in achievement. He was a poor speller, poor reader, got Ds in arithmetic. On an IQ test when he was 10, he scored 103.

* * *

From the first day he arrived in New York he couldn't get along. . . . In three months he was absent 47 times. The truant officer picked him up and took him to the Bronx Children's Court and in April, 1953, Judge Delaney sent him to the Youth House for Boys.

* * *

For four weeks Oswald underwent examinations by Dr. Renatus Hartogs, the chief psychiatrist, who concluded that unless the boy received treatment he was possibly in for trouble far more serious than skipping school. . . . He found Oswald to have a schizoid personality—an underlying, hidden, almost passive tendency toward aggression. He was, in short, potentially dangerous. (Writer's note: no mention of language difficulty was made in this report.)

About a month after the assassination an article in *Time* (December 20, 1963) quoted excerpts from letters that Oswald had written to his mother while he was in Russia. The article stated that "Oswald was not much on grammar, spelling or punctuation." Among the many errors in these letters, Oswald spelled Gillette (razor) as "Gillet," necessary as "necisary," and science as "scienace." An example of his writing was, "Thats about all. Ha-ha I very much miss sometime to read you should try and get me the pocket novel '1984' by Wells."

Several months later, *Life* (July 10, 1964) published "Oswald's Full Russian Diary." Sample pages from the diary were reproduced on the magazine cover, and they revealed a mixture of printed and longhand writing, difficult to read in many places. The introductory note of the article said that "Oswald's writing is so undecipherable that the editors had to make an educated guess. Other than that the diary is printed exactly as Oswald wrote it, misspellings and all."

Every entry in the diary contained some spelling errors. A few examples are quoted in context:

"I'll have an answerwer soon"
"she is flabbergasses but aggrees to help"
"my fondis dreams"

"a petty offial"
"my dischare papers"
"suspious about me"
"I am stating to reconsider my disire"
"I decived to take my two week vactition"

Additional examples of misspellings were: "guied," "Sovite," "vauge," "wacth," "rarley," "fonud," "yonuge," "leauge," "patroict," "presenec," "foviengress," "continuenec," etc. In one place "from" was used for "to."

The multitude of spelling errors in his diary cannot be explained on the basis of insufficient education because Oswald was in school for about eleven years and he reached the tenth or eleventh grade. The mistakes are not typically those of the mentally retarded; moreover, Oswald scored an I.Q. of 118 on the WICS test. However, the errors are very characteristic of those made by children and adults who have a specific language disability. Reversals in the order of sequence of letters and omissions of letters and syllables are prominent. Also, the same word is spelled in different ways at different times, and longer or more difficult words are often better spelled than shorter common words which normally would have been learned at an earlier age. It is obvious that Oswald spelled 'by ear"—lacking a clear-cut visual memory pattern of words.

The Warren Report contained little additional information that either corroborated the writer's thesis or refuted it. It did quote a statement made by Dr. Hartogs: "This 13 year old well built boy has superior mental resources and functions only slightly below his capacity level in spite of chronic truancy from school which brought him into Youth House. No findings of neurological impairment or psychotic changes could be made."

In *The Warren Report* there was a brief reference to what was called a "reading-spelling" disability. However, no further evidence could be found in the report that this outspoken disability was taken into account.

It appears that Oswald did a great deal of reading, but this fact alone does not disprove the conjecture that he suffered from the ascribed language disability. It is quite possible for children who have a specific language disability to attain a practical reading facility as they grow older. Even without specialized tutoring they often find avenues of approach through recognition of key words and through the use of sensory modalities other than vision so that they become moderately proficient in silent reading. However, difficulty in reading aloud and the characteristic errors in spelling remain as telltale evidence of the handicap.

As for Oswald, along with his good I.Q. he may have been adept in learning by hearing, and some of his knowledge may have been falsely attributed to his reading. At any rate, an Associated Press report said: "He was invited on a television panel show where he described himself as a Marxist, but denied he was a communist. He stumbled all over himself trying to express his beliefs cogently, and never did."

Further substantiation of the thesis presented here comes from Critchley's monograph on *Developmental Dyslexia*: "In the case of the 'cured' dyslexic, defective writing and spelling may continue to appear long into adult life. Where some degree of writing lies within the competency of a dyslexic, the mistakes are of such a nature as often to make it possible to diagnose the reading defect from a mere perusal of the script. The faults are unlike those met with in the case of a dullard, or a poorly educated person."

Assuming that Oswald did have a specific language disability (developmental dyslexia), one wonders what the outcome might have been if the handicap had been recognized when he started his schooling and appropriate remedial reading had been utilized at that time. Similar questioning arises concerning the study at Youth House when Oswald was thirteen years old, because the revealing type of spelling errors would have been found then as they appeared so obviously in "The Russian Diary."

It is not to be denied that factors such as the absence of a father, the particular role his mother played, sibling rivalry, the moving about with school and environmental changes, the low socioeconomic status, and the continuous lack of security were important in his ego development. However, the questing mind must go on and ask: Did he not have the added burden of developmental dyslexia?

Chapter IX

CAPACITIES OF MAN

We hold these truths to be self-evident, that all men are created equal...

DECLARATION OF INDEPENDENCE (1776)

THIS CHAPTER is included with the intention and hope that it may broaden and, at the same time, emphasize a point of view regarding reading abilities and disabilities. Within the boundaries of physiological variation or innate endowment, there are wide latitudes and longitudes in many sensory and motor capacities. Facility or lack of facility may be found within normal limits in such functions as color vision, "ear for music," sense of rhythm, motor coordination, fluency of speech, taste and smell, writing, and even reading.

In the United States Declaration of Independence there is the well-known statement, "We hold these truths to be self-evident, that all men are created equal and are endowed by their Creator with certain inalienable rights." It is possible to understand the viewpoint of the founding fathers, which was essentially a legal one, but at the same time it is also self-evident that no two persons, even identical twins, are created exactly alike. Thomas Jefferson, one of the signers of the Declaration, certainly had special abilities in many fields that other signers did not possess. His facility for expressing thoughts in written and spoken words, his inventiveness and his artistic tastes were equalled by few men of his time. Were his special gifts attributable soley to his environment and experiences in life?

If creation is considered as the moment of birth rather than the moment of conception, many things may happen during pregnancy that influence the child's capacities. More and more evidence is accumulating which indicates that during the prenatal period physical disturbances and emotional stress for the mother may impair the child's abilities in diverse fields. Regardless of prenatal influences, there is substantiated evidence that newborn infants have differences in various functional abilities. Some are strong and robust in physique; others are weak. Some are easily stimulated or excited; others are placid. Some appear to be irritable from the start; others are good natured. Some infants show activity with some facility of movement; others are a "lump of dough." Oral activity with facility in sucking and swallowing may be quite evident in some newborns, but almost lacking in others.

Observations of these inequities at the start of life have been recorded by many scientific studies of newborn infants. Arnold Gesell recorded by picture and word an authentic description of various differences in the neonate. Differences in the thresholds for startle to loud noises and to pain have been adequately documented as have differences in thresholds for joyous responses as well as gloomy or sad ones. What may gratify one neonate may be disturbing to another.

Lois Murphy's observations of newborn babies amplified their variable characteristics:

Their proportions, the effect of sheer body-mass in proportion to energy and muscles, will have something to do with their activity patterns. Many other differences also appear. One baby will make persistent repeated well-oriented efforts to get its thumb into its mouth, succeeding with fewer trials as time goes on, so that by the tenth day she can get it in directly and instantly; other babies struggle more aimlessly, pushing the thumb in the general direction of the mouth but without getting it there. . . . Some babies waken when other babies cry while others never do, but just sleep until inner demands ring an inner alarm clock. Some babies are almost always relaxed, with few movements, while others seem like a bundle of wiggly wires, jerking and shaking in between little catnaps that do not last long. Some suck readily, others with difficulty; some suck steadily and others fall off to sleep with the least satisfaction. Some effectively bat away at uncomfortable blankets and actually push them aside while others make no such efforts to make themselves comfortable. These simple observations point to differences in thresholds for alarm responses, in oral drive, in motor drive, energy, capacity to exert effort, coordination and integration as well as differences in tempo of learning which have been established in experimental studies of newborns by Dorothy Marquis and others.[1]

---

[1] A more recent summary of observations in this field is to be found in the first issue of the *Journal of The American Academy of Child Psychiatry* (January, 1962).

On through the preschool years before reading is encountered in school, Gesell and many others have shown that abilities and disabilities are already in existence, some of them quite outspoken. Because the child speaks long before he reads, any distortion in his speech patterns becomes obvious in the preschool years. In contrast, reading is noticed only when there is an example of precocity in this function. There is evidence that the majority of children can learn to read before they enter the first grade. Also, evidence is accumulating that reading disability may be predicted during the preschool years.

Let us review some of the functions that may have some analogous relation to reading. The eyes—in addition to seeing words, pictures, shapes and forms—also see colors. Some people have exquisite distinction of all shades of color. On the other hand, some are completely color-blind, seeing everything in shades of black and white. Between these extremes are to be found many gradations in the facility to recognize colors and shades of color. At one end of the spectrum are those who see only shades of gray. Short of the latter extreme are the people who can distinguish yellow quite readily, but have difficulty in telling a red light from a green light except by its position in the traffic signal or by the intensity of the light.

The following quotation from Edward N. Willmer's book on ophthalmology (1946) gives some salient points about color-blindness:

> Abnormalities of colour vision are by no means infrequent, particularly among the male population, in which about eight per cent (Nielsen, 1938) are sufficiently different from the normal to be classed as in some degree colour-blind. In addition to these there are many others whose colour discrimination is but poorly developed as compared with that of most people, but who are not sufficiently different to be regarded as definitely colour-blind. At the other end of the scale there are individuals whose colour sense is particularly acute and more highly developed than the average. Moreover, colour sense is in some measure a matter of education, in that it can be markedly improved by training and practice. Colour appears to enter much less into the lives of some people than of others, but this need not necessarily be due to any irregularity in the functioning of the visual mechanism but may simply be the result of failure to educate the "sense."[2]   ➡→

The eyes of the color-blind are normal and healthy except for an anomaly in the cones of the retina which diminishes the reception of certain light waves. Some authorities use the term "lazy cones" to describe the condition. A color-blind person may have some defect in general vision, of course, or he may even have cataracts or glaucoma, but these disturbances are not related to color vision in a causal manner. Rarely does color-blindness result from brain damage; neither does it have any relation to intelligence.

The possibility that color-blindness could be caused by purely emotional factors seems very remote, but such a disability may be augmented secondarily by emotional factors or become the focus of anxiety that stems from other sources. A color-blind child and his parents are often unaware of the deviation until it is revealed by special testing or by some grievous mistake.

If a person with any kind of color-vision disorder had to attend art school or gain recognition through artistic achievement by painting in colors, he would be frustrated, turn against it, and have emotional and perhaps behavior problems, regardless of a good level of general intelligence and other talents. Carrying the analogy further, if he had to learn language, history or geography on the basis of what he saw in colors rather than in words, he would appear to be an imbecile or idiot, depending on what little color vision he had.

In smell and taste similar wide variations are recognized. It is claimed that expert tea tasters, wine testers or perfume smellers are hard to find, regardless of their patient practice and long apprenticeship. Quite a few people obtain little enjoyment from the taste of food "fit for a king" or from the odor of roses. Some people smell practically nothing at all. This may be due to some disorder in the nose, but it may also be that they were born without much sense of smell.

Concerning another of the special senses, namely hearing, the writer immediately thinks of the "musical ear," not forgetting the

---

[2]A recent study of over 10,000 American school children by Thuline (1964) indicated that 6.2 per cent of the boys had a color-vision defect; only 0.55 per cent of the girls had such a defect. Thuline recognized the hereditary aspects, speculated about the unrecognized effect on school work and recommended that color-vision tests be a part of the preschool physical examination.

"word hearing ear," which will be considered later. In music there are the gifted few who have what is called "perfect pitch." At the other end of the continuum are those who "can't carry a tune in a basket," the so-called tone-deaf.[3] The latter are not deaf in the ordinary sense, of course, nor are they unwilling to hear. There are all gradations between perfect pitch and tone-deafness. The same applies to many other aspects of musical accomplishment or requirements for success in music.

Here is a person, well-known to many, who can attend a musical show, come home, sit down at a piano and play with proper harmony most of the songs heard, although unable to read a note of music and never having had a music lesson of any kind. This is performance "by ear" with no conception of what the music looks like.

Rhythm, intensity of sound, timbre, harmony, consonance (melody), motor coordination, memory, emotional expression and depth of feeling are some of the fields in which ability, somewhat above average, is needed for superior musical performance. If a person—cold in temperament, lacking in a sense of pitch and rhythm and with only mediocre motor coordination—had to attend a school of music, he would suffer great frustration. Carrying the analogy further, if a child, devoid of musical aptitudes, had to obtain his education through reading and performing music, he would be a failure and might very well become a behavior problem or a neurotic. Also, he would likely be classified as mentally retarded.

There are many children whose musical accomplishments remain modest in spite of years of good teaching, daily hours of practice, and much parental urging. Often this is ascribed to lack of motivation, but the cause may be found not only in the lack of facility but also in the fact that there may be more ego satisfaction in attainments in sports, academic studies or mechanical interests where the child has much more ability.

---

[3] In a recent conversation with a colleague, he confessed that he was tone-deaf. He said that his wife, who loved music, had tried to train or test him by striking two different notes on the piano, but he was unable to tell which note was the higher in pitch. He attended concerts to be sociable, but was highly bored and never moved by the music because it sounded like just so much noise to him.

There is good evidence that some musical facilities are inherited. According to Hollingworth, "Musical sensitivity is inborn, and probably cannot be increased in any respect by training. If the various elements are not present in amount and combination suitable for a given degree of achievement in music, no course of training will supply the lack. This is not to say that ultimate achievement, for those who do possess capacity, does not depend on training." The Bach and Strauss families appear to illustrate Hollingworth's statement that musical talents are inherited. There are critics who do not share this view and maintain that environmental influences were paramount in producing the geniuses in these families. Either approach may seem inadequate in considering the genius of Mozart. Although there is no evidence that there were outstanding musicians in his family, Mozart was playing and composing masterpieces of music before the age of six. He must have had some unusual innate endowment. Surely his prodigious accomplishments cannot be attributed to some correct method of teaching, to hours of practice, or to any emotional problems (or lack of them) stemming from his relation to his mother, from deprivation, sexual frustration, parental attitudes or social status. Nor would the cause be found in some abnormality of the brain.

The ear hears words as well as music. Here, too, is found another continuum of gradations in facility that must be attributed in part to original endowment, although it is influenced from birth on by what assails the ear and by the emotional conditioning of the meaning of words. An ambivalent attitude toward words heard seems to start very early in life. Some words are good (pleasurable); some words are bad (naughty and not to be used). Many words in the early vocabulary of the child have to do with the body and its functions. Nose, fingers, and penis have a lot in common in what the child sees, but the names of these organs may have diverse emotional connotations when pronounced and heard. The so-called body image, when reduced to words, is full of terms, some of which are acceptable and others forbidden. If this conditioning about words is important in reading, as some authorities believe, surely it would be evident in a child's speech long before he is called upon to read.

Regardless of such early conditioning, it appears that some people have an inborn facility to "learn by hearing" in contrast to others who have a facility to "learn by seeing." Certain people are quick to admit that their large store of quotations from poetry and prose comes from what they have heard rather than what they have read (and vice versa). Charcot, Freud, and others accepted the idea that some people are visual minded while some are auditory minded.

The existence of word-deafness is of importance in connection with the above discussion, but it has been described elsewhere in the text. Before leaving the topics of hearing and seeing, however, attention is called to the fact that there are people who can hear in color. Letters, words, musical tones and even noises bring a distant color sensation into their awareness simultaneously with the reception of the sound. This is called simply "color hearing," but the term "synesthesia" is used whenever a sensory response other than the one externally stimulated appears simultaneously. There may be combinations other than hearing and color, and in varying graduations.[4]

Peter Ostwald (1964) reported his study of a case of color hearing, reviewed the previous literature, and speculated as to the cause. As might be expected, Ostwald revealed that some writers considered it to be an innate physiological variation while others maintained that it results from early childhood experiences, memories of which are repressed. As a paradigm of the opposing approaches to abilities and disabilities in general, Ostwald cited the opinions of Eugen Bleuler, an authority in psychiatry, and Hug-Hellmuth, both of whom studied their own color hearing in detail. While agreeing with Bleuler's emphasis on constitutional factors, Hug-Hellmuth strongly stressed the importance of infantile sexual experience which, by virtue of stirring

---

[4]The drug, lysergic acid diethylamide, commonly called LSD, often produces synesthesia experiences or reactions. An LSD subject in attempting to describe his experience will say that he can smell the music he is listening to, or can hear the sound of color, or can touch the texture of an odor. One subject said, "I hear what I am smelling . . . I think what I am seeing . . . I am climbing music."

The LSD experiments indicate that any given sensory stimulation can find devious pathways to any or all of the central elaborative mechanisms that serve conscious cognition of any specific sensory modality. Perhaps the synesthesias induced by LSD come about just short of supramaximal stimulation (Pavlov) with releases of inhibition before complete inhibition takes over. At any rate, the LSD experiments seem to corroborate the practice of combining sensory impressions in order to strengthen learning processes.

up pleasurable and painful emotions, can heighten synesthesias and cause them to become fixed in memories and fantasies.

Motor coordination exhibits many excellent examples of special abilities and disabilities, from graceful facility to awkward stumbling. Without there being any evidence of organic impairment, variations in this area may be observed from the first year on. Some children, three or four years of age, can skate, swim and toe-dance with grace, ease and rhythm, while others and even adults fall all over themselves when attempting such activities.

In the enjoyment of dancing, the writer has known some beautiful and intelligent females who, in spite of many dancing lessons, had practically no sense of rhythm and very little suppleness of motion. Others, not so beautiful or bright, can dance like a breeze on a cloud with no lessons at all. The same range of skills is found in the male population, but few people, regardless of sex, instruction, practice and motivation can approach the performances of Fred Astaire.

There are some people who, although quite intelligent and without physical disorder, cannot learn to drive an automobile, hit a golf ball or throw and catch a baseball with just modest skill. An example is the Phi Beta Kappa who cannot hit a tennis ball and cannot dance with rhythm or grace. As a consequence, he withdraws from attempts to compete in any field requiring even a modicum of muscle coordination. Naturally, such a person hates the challenge to compete and belittles all such activities, turning to and focusing on intellectual pursuits.

Poor coordination, awkwardness and lack of facility in muscular movements may be due to organic disturbances in the nervous system and elsewhere. Witness the child with cerebral palsy. On the other hand, even in those with excellent coordination there may be lack of motivation because of emotional inhibition. It seems, though, that it must take a fairly large dose of emotional ingredients to inhibit those with good natural facility in motor coordination from participating in sports, while the lack of facility creates its own emotional block.[5]

The game of chess does not call for motor coordination, but it does

---

[5]Abnormal clumsiness (called dyspraxia or apraxia, sometimes with a prefix of developmental or congenital) has been discussed by Orton (1932), Langford

require the possession of special ability. The fundamentals of chess are not difficult to learn, but mastery of the game requires some unique unexplainable talent that does not seem to come from the environment. At the age of seven, prodigies such as Capablanca and Reshevsky could easily defeat experienced adults who had been playing the game for years. These and a few other masters of chess who, blindfolded, can defeat twenty or more good players at a time must have some unusual innate special ability involving abstract reasoning and visualization.

Only a few real masters of chess appear in each generation. Since these masters spend most of their hours absorbed in the game, history tells us little about their capacities in other fields or about their emotional problems. History does reveal that some years ago the chess team at Cambridge University in England engaged in a correspondence tournament with the nearby asylum known as Bedlam. Bedlam, with a team of thoroughly "disabled" players, won.

Chess, well played, calls for some kind of abstract reasoning, and this topic leads to consideration of mathematics. There are a few people who can glance at a great column of figures, running ten or more columns both vertically and horizontally, and give with little hesitation the answers to any combination of additions, subtractions, and divisions as suggested by onlookers while the onlookers are dumbfounded by the quick and correct answers.

Mathematical geniuses appear sporadically in each generation in contrast to the multitude of very intelligent people who fumble through ordinary bank accounts and income tax returns, making mistakes in spite of their exertions. There is some evidence that males have more mathematical ability than females, but this may be due to practice and motivation.

John von Neumann was one of the world's foremost mathematicians. By the age of eight years he had mastered calculus. At the same age he could memorize at sight a column in a telephone book and repeat all names, addresses, and telephone numbers. It was von

---

(1955), and others. Also, Orton (1937) described cases of special writing disability (developmental agraphia). The relationship of these special disabilities to other disabilities has been covered by Orton.

Neumann who built the machine called MANIAC (mathematical analyzer, numerical integrater and computer). His discoveries speeded up the making of the atomic bomb. Of course, there are several other examples of such gifted persons—Pythagoras, Euclid, Descartes, Newton, Gauss, Cantor, and Einstein. All of them seem to illustrate the claim that such marvelous talent is not based on emotional experiences but grows out of original endowment of some kind. The same explanation may hold for those who are lacking in mathematical agility.

The following is a quotation from Hollingworth (1926): "Jacques Inaudi (b. 1867) was studied by Binet. Inaudi showed a passion for numbers at six years of age. He could multiply five-place numbers by five-place numbers 'in his head.' His memory for digits given orally was 42. He must hear them, the span being considerably reduced if he only saw them. Binet concluded that he had no particular ability except the gift for calculation and was not generally superior."

Ability or disability in any field is often attributed to the general intelligence of the individual concerned. Educators and others in professional work with children place some degree of confidence in an I.Q. figure as a measure of general intellectual capacity. At the same time, it is recognized that the I.Q. is only a rough measure of many abilities and disabilities, although some professionals and parents do not always see it in such light.

Here is the *idiot savant* who, with an I.Q. of 50, can solve mechanical puzzles that baffle the board members of his school for the feebleminded. On the other hand, a ten-year-old boy with an I.Q. of 140 may have little mechanical sense, or he may be tone-deaf or wordblind (in other words, a nonreader).

At the 1964 annual meeting of the American Psychiatric Association a study was presented by W. A. Horwitz, *et al.* on identical male twins who had been classified as *idiots savants*. They were twenty-four years old and for fifteen years had been at Letchworth Village, a New York State school for mentally retarded children. Their reading level was commensurate with an I.Q. of 60-70. However, either one could instantly identify the day of the week for any given date in any year. Their calculation span extended before and after any known perpetual calendar. Although unable to do simple problems in addition and subtraction, they were able to name the day of the week for dates up to and beyond 3500 *A.D.* They correctly said that George Washington was born in 1732 and died in 1799; that he was 67 years old when he died; and that he would be 232 years old if he had lived until 1964. Many other prodigious feats of a similar kind were recorded for these identical twins.

All the psychologists and psychiatrists who had studied these boys could not explain this almost unbelievable facility, nor could the twins tell how they did it. Surely it was not the result of emotional experiences in early life, which might have inhibited all other learning processes and left this single facility to run rampant. Studies of the chromosomes are being carried out on the assumption that some unusual genetic complication may be found.

In the field of general intelligence the ever-intriguing question of heredity *versus* environment goes on and on. It appears that no other item in this controversy has been more studied and frequently exploited and misrepresented than the tests resulting in an I.Q. At the present time it is generally agreed that the I.Q. figure is not exact at the time the test is given and that it may change to some extent with the passage of time and be influenced by various factors. However, an extremely high I.Q. figure of 140 and above or a low I.Q. figure of 80 or below may be directly related to the size of the brain and the number of brain cells.

But the I.Q. under normal circumstances is a gross measure, and within it or beside it there are many abilities and disabilities that call for special consideration and measurement. Several capacities are measured by the Stanford-Binet tests, and, more directly, verbal and performance abilities are measured by the Wechsler-Bellevue scales.[6]

It is well-recognized that intelligence is not a single trait, but is

---

[6]Rabinovitch (1959) pointed out that "the most significant finding in the primary case (of reading disability), using the Wechsler Intelligence Tests, is marked discrepancy between performance and verbal I.Q. The mean discrepancy is more than 20 points, with the verbal I.Q. lower than the performance by more than 40 points in some cases. There is a general verbal incapacity relative to intellectual potential which is much less marked in secondary retardation, regardless of the child's reading level." (Rabinovitch's term "primary" refers to innate or constitutional causes, while the term "secondary" is reserved for emotional causes.)

constituted of a number of characteristics. Abilities and disabilities may be found in verbal comprehension, sight perception, word fluency, visualization of objects in space, kinesthetic sensitivity, induction and deduction, reasoning, abstract thought, perception in general. Some people may be high in one area and low in others. Rarely does a person have distinct ability in more than three or four of the above categories, and even then definite disability in one or two of the other fields may be present.

It is possible to carry this discussion of exceptionalities into other and even broader areas of personality characteristics, such as physique or body build, impulse drive, temperament, and character. In the consideration of these personality characteristics, the same points of view would apply.

In fact, the same points of view hold for the entire animal kingdom. It is well-known that bloodhounds have a special acuity in the sense of smell that surpasses all other dogs; and dogs can smell and hear better than humans. Homer or carrier pigeons inherit a faculty for finding their way home which humans seem not to possess. Birds, particularly hawks, can see far better from a distance than humans, but birds cannot read. A few birds can speak, but, compared to humans, they have a disability of speech which is neither organic aphasia nor an emotional learning inhibition. Various animals are bred to bring out distinctive abilities or qualities and to avoid disabilities in the breed.

To return to the topic of reading, many people do not grasp the idea that reading facility presents a broad spectrum, more or less analogous to the variations just under discussion. For such people, either you read or you don't, and if you can't learn to read very well, then you must be quite dim if not outright mentally deficient.

Well-documented in many reports are instances of very superior reading ability. Reference has just been made to von Neumann who could memorize at sight a column in a telephone book and repeat all names, addresses, and telephone numbers. Earlier there is a quotation from Strachey regarding Lord Bowen who could read down the seven columns of the *Times* (London) by merely moving his eyes slowly from the top of the page to the bottom.

The writer recalls a college student who was brought before the student council and charged with cheating on an examination because his answers appeared to be "right out of the textbook." This student asked for any book that happened to be handy; after looking through a chapter very briefly, he handed the book back and repeated almost word for word the entire contents of the chapter. He was found not guilty, but in spite of the evidence before their eyes some members of the council remained dubious. Similar situations have come to light in other colleges.

People like von Neumann, Lord Bowen and the college student are said to have eidetic imagery and photographic memory. At times, though, such a gift or talent may turn out to be a handicap. Quite a few students so "afflicted" get by without much effort by repeating almost exactly what is in the textbook or in their own notebook. They do not have to dig for or reason out the fundamentals of a subject because they can make a good grade without much effort. Sooner or later, this method of learning may become a stumbling block for them because they are not practiced in other ways of learning and reasoning things out for themselves.

Concerning the relation between reading facility and I.Q., Hollingworth said, "Terman has supplied numerous instances of children who learned to read in the third or fourth year of life, all of them of more than 130 I.Q." Terman also supplied the instance of a girl who at the age of two could read fluently from an ordinary primer, reading what a typical six-year-old child could read. On the basis of reading alone, this child would have an I.Q. of 300. Later Terman tested the general intelligence of this child and obtained an I.Q. rating of 150. Usually, precocious reading is associated with a high general level of intelligence, but prodigious reading ability may be definitely above the high general ability.

On the other hand, some children with low I.Q.'s read with startling ability. An Associated Press story from Louisville, Kentucky, dated March 20, 1962, gave an example of a ten-year-old boy who had been in a school for the mentally retarded for five years. Even so, he could read English, French, Latin, German, Spanish and Turkish. He began reading at age three or four and at the age of nine displayed the reading ability of a ninth grader (usually fourteen or fifteen years old). It was stated that the boy may have suffered brain damage at birth, which might have caused the retardation, but such brain injury could not account for his special ability in reading.

In the biographical studies of some very prominent and accomplished people it has been recorded that they were precocious and voracious readers, and many of them exhibited a photographic memory. On the other hand, there is good evidence that some people of great accomplishment did have some degree of reading disability and other language problems. Some of this evidence has come from a study entitled *Cradles of Eminence* by Victor and Mildred Goertzel. This was a study of the parentage, early environment, education and childhood experiences of over 400 eminent men and women of the twentieth century. The subjects were selected according to the frequency of their appearance in biographical volumes.

The Goertzels stated:

> Many of the children of the past who were to become eminent, like the intellectually gifted children of today, tended to possess superior ability in reasoning and in recognizing relationships. They showed intellectual curiosity, had a wide range of interests, did effective work independently They showed their greatest superiority in reading ability; many read at the age of four. Almost all were early readers of good books. They were original thinkers and had scant patience with drill and routine. They were likely to be rejected by their playmates and had parents who valued learning. The majority of them came from middle-class business and professional homes. Their brothers and sisters were capable. Most of those children who became eminent would probably have tested high on today's intelligence tests.

Concerning language ability, the Goertzels found a few who appeared to have some disability which was overcome or compensated for as they grew older:

> Harvey Cushing, eminent brain surgeon, was a very poor speller in his youth—also as an adult, but then it did not matter. His letters home from Yale and Harvard reveal such boners as: priviledge, definate, sacarafice, pharsical, cronicling, and amatures. When he was in grammar school, his mother, who was never one to let time hang on her hands, drove this youngest of her ten children back to school after his noonday lunch. During the half hour in which the horse ambled and Harvey chafed to play ball,

she taught him spelling. When he was in high school, she helped him with his Latin and Greek.

* * *

Woodrow Wilson did not learn his letters until he was nine, or learn to read until he was eleven, because his father read to him. He could not wait for Woodrow to learn to read the books he himself enjoyed and wanted his son to enjoy. The brilliant and verbal minister kept the boy home, read to him, explained the meaning of what he read, then asked Woodrow's reaction to the ideas of the book.

* * *

George Patton III, a California rancher and lawyer, did not believe in teaching children to read until they were adolescent and could read history books for themselves. George Patton III kept George Patton IV home on their isolated ranch and read to him. When father went to work, the mother and an aunt took over the storybook. They read nursery jingles, graduated him to stories of witches, to animals that speak, to goblins, to legends. When George Patton IV went away to boarding school at twelve to be tutored for West Point, he was an authority on epics, he could write script, but he could not read print. To say that he was unhappy at school is an understatement.

At twelve George could not read for himself. . . . At West Point he gained favor with his instructors by a punctilious keeping of the rules. He never learned too read well, although his memory was extraordinary. He got through West Point by memorizing whole lectures and texts and parroting them verbatim.

In the Goertzel study there was evidence that other eminent people probably had some degree of language disability in reading, spelling and writing as well as in speech. The writer has examined the biographies of several such people and has found corroborating evidence not only for those mentioned above but also for men of eminence such as Thomas A. Edison, Auguste Rodin, Paul Ehrlich, Gamal Nasser and others. Thanks to their superior ability in general, these people did learn to read and write, though it was later than most children do. The telltale spelling errors that characterize dyslexia remained with them for life.

In discussion of the gifted reader and the disabled reader, some observations about the reading development of the average child should be mentioned for comparison. Arnold Gesell (1946) said that the rudiments of reading for the average child are to be found when the two-year-old names pictures in a book; the three-year-old identifies four printed geometric forms; the four-year-old recognizes salient capital letters; and the five to six-year-old recognizes salient printed words. Even more specifically, he said that the average six-year-old "recognizes words and phrases, and perhaps sentences" and the seven-year-old "can read sentences." As noted elsewhere, in connection with the work of Moore and Delacato, there is evidence that the average child can learn to read during his fourth and fifth years of life.

Another authority on child development, Jean Piaget, while not directly interested in reading ability, made some pertinent observations that are related to learning to read. Piaget contended that the child's approach to handling his communication with the environment changes at about the age of seven or seven and one-half. Abstract thinking has already been developing, but at about this time the cognitive processes gain dominance over perceptual development. A child with perceptual disturbances can therefore begin to solve perceptual problems cognitively. For example, to find whether a four-sided figure is a square or a rectangle, he can now measure the sides. Many similiar crutches will help him to compensate for his perceptual limitations. Also, according to Piaget, the age at which a child normally begins to read with facility is coincident with the age at which he turns from being an egocentric individual to being a more socially oriented person. Since reading helps in this evolution toward externalization, a dyslexic child may continue for some time at his stage of autism. On the other hand, the urge to socialize may help him to find ways to circumvent and overcome his language impediment.

In quite recent years speed reading has become a topic of considerable importance. Special classes in speed reading are springing up in colleges, in high schools and in private enterprises. Executives of big business corporations and officials high in government are taking such courses. Practically everyone can increase reading speed to some degree with help and with diligent practice, but there is a speed limit for the ordinary reader if comprehension, retention and enjoyment of reading count for anything. Specially gifted and prodigious readers do exist, as mentioned elsewhere, but they are about one in a few hundred thousand. It may happen that such a person is not aware of this special gift, only to have it revealed in a course of instruction on speed reading.

In the not-so-scientific literature we read about people who have increased their rate of reading from a good average of about 200 to 300 words per minute to 2,000 or 3,000 words per minute. Recently, *Time* magazine told of a college girl who "chewed up" a sociology textbook at the rate of 14,000 words per minute. Also, in a letter to *Time* a man claimed that he read both Testaments of the Bible and several other lengthy volumes in one evening just before retiring for sleep. You just can't turn pages that fast!

Chapter X

SUMMARY AND SUGGESTIONS

"Half the World Can't Read." This startling statement is the title of a report on reading published by UNESCO. Of course there are many nations in which no effort is made to teach reading to the masses, but in the United States, where we have compulsory education to the age of sixteen, 11 per cent of the adult citizens are functionally illiterate, i.e., unable to read up to a fourth-grade level. In less than 2 per cent of the adult population can illiteracy be attributed to general mental retardation.

Among school children in this country (six to seventeen years of age), over 10 per cent of those not mentally retarded are more than two years retarded in reading according to their mental age ability. Several authorities consider this to be a very conservative estimate.

Rarely does difficulty in reading stand alone as the only learning impediment in the field of language. Almost invariably difficulties in spelling and writing, in speech and even in the proper hearing of words can be found as components of language disturbances. Because speech defects are obvious to all, they receive recognition without debate as to their existence, but often without awareness of their relation to the total language disorder. However, in this book direct discussion of speech defects has been omitted.

Reading disability with its accompanying disturbances in other language functions has been labeled under a variety of terms such as word-blindness, congenital word-blindness, strephosymbolia, specific reading disability, developmental dyslexia, reading retardation and even aphasia. The disparate terminology reflects the numerous conceptions concerning the causes of reading disability.

During the past seventy years many writers have suggested several causal factors, most of which have been considered in the text. At the present time, however, there is general agreement that the causes can be classified under three groupings:

1. Organic damage to the brain as it occurs in adults through

strokes, head injury, or the like; or in children through birth injury, encephalitis or head trauma.

2. Environmental or social-emotional influences, such as deprivation of developmental stimulation and/or conditioning against learning. Lack of opportunity, poor teaching or poor teaching techniques, over-crowded classrooms and poverty may contribute to poor reading ability, but these conditions are rarely fundamental in causation.

3. Innate or constitutional endowment with some evidence of hereditary predisposition. It is here that the concept of a developmental lag is most applicable, although a similar lag may accompany the first two groups.

For most laymen and even some professional people the "differential diagnosis" lies between (1) and (2). Many intelligent people make no differentiation at all and believe that if a child cannot read he must be feebleminded. If some, although slight, evidence of acquired brain damage can be found either in the history, in some deviation in the neurological or psychological examinations, or in the EEG (elec-troencephalogram), there is a strong tendency to ascribe language disturbance to organic brain damage. In some of the so-called organic cases, it is possible that preceding the organic insult the child may have been "born that way," i.e., destined to have a language dis-ability. The damage may have directly or indirectly augmented the predisposition to language inaptitude.

There is a strong all-or-none attitude which says, "If no evidence of (1) organic damage can be established, then the language dis-ability must be due to (2) environmental and emotional causes." Af-ter the differentiation is argued and a stand taken, there may come an admission that these two causes are sometimes related and maybe intertwined so that they cannot be unravelled. Finally, the debate of one side against the other (1) *versus* (2) may be disrupted by calling attention to (3) innate or constitutional endowment with the concept of development lag. For those people who recognize only (1) and (2), this third issue confuses their understanding of reading difficul-ties. These same people seem to have a definite resistance to accepting this third causal factor as one of any importance.

The organicists (neurologists and some psychiatrists) have been cognizant of the importance of innate endowment in their studies of language dysfunction, but their views often leave the impression that there is some deficit or damage in the central nervous system in such disturbances. At the same time, they take pains to point out the emotional problems and the personality deviations that follow. Orton, a psychiatrist and neuropathologist; Hermann, a neurologist; and Bender, a child psychiatrist—all outstanding in the field of language disorders—were aware of the emotional problems accompanying language handicaps, but they did not postulate a deficit or damage in the brain.

The environmentalists (many psychoanalysts, educators and psychologists) have recognized individual differences in innate endowment, but have placed emphasis on the environmental experiences of the child in accounting for reading disability. Several of their theories and many alleged environmental causes were reviewed in this book. Here and there the writer questioned how emotional experiences in infancy and early childhood, or the poverty of the child's milieu, could produce all the symptoms of developmental dyslexia with its accompanying word-blindness, reversals in spelling, lack of clear-cut directionality, confusion of dominance and the family histories of language disturbances.

There may be some positive answer to the above question in the accumulating evidence concerning the effects of deprivation at the start of life in producing developmental lag on a neurophysiological basis. Nielsen and others have produced evidence to show that either side of the brain can take over dominance and language functions in the first two years of life, but after that or after spech is established the right hemisphere in right-handed children cannot readily do so because of "deprivation of use." Also, evidence is accumulating that social-emotional immaturity due to deprivation and emotional trauma may be so widespread as to include delay of language functions and establishment of dominance within the framework of gross or generalized immaturity. However, that deprivation and emotional trauma could pick out reading and spelling alone seems incredible. Where such appears to be the case, there must have been a specially prepared physiological soil, or, to use Freud's expression, some somatic compliance.

From some professional sources claims are made that reading dis-

ability is only one of several symptoms of a general emotional immaturity problem and, therefore, the only solution lies in an intensive
psychotherapy of the child and his parents. While such psychotherapy
is valuable and often vitally needed after a child has suffered three or
four years of frustration in school, it is not available to any appreciable
extent. In North Carolina, for example, psychotherapy of this kind is
available for not over one hundred cases a year for the estimated
100,000 children with reading disability. Even the best psychotherapy
cannot give optimum results in most cases unless it is combined with
the services of specially trained remedial reading teachers.

Obversely, thousands of children with specific reading disability
have been greatly benefitted by remedial reading without psychotherapy, although such treatment might have been salutary. Whether
it is recognized or not, the remedial reading teacher uses some elements
of psychotherapy.

From other professional sources claims are made that the method
of teaching is the chief cause of reading disability. Some believe that
the look-say method is at fault, and others believe that the phonic
techniques are not needed. Three out of four children readily learn
to read by the look-say method, but the other one in four cannot. Attention is called to the fact that specific reading disability existed before the look-say method was introduced and that it exists where the
phonic method is used. In the latter situation, though, the reading
disability may not become so blatant or outspoken, because the
method is part of the approach in overcoming the handicap.

Irrespective of the cause of reading disability, we cannot expect
child guidance or mental health clinics to meet the needs of dyslexic
children because of the large numbers involved and because such
clinics are not equipped to meet the total problem. Clinics can give
valuable diagnostic help in difficult cases, but must turn most of the
"treatment" back to the schools. It becomes obvious, then, that the
problem of reading disability must be met almost entirely by our public schools as they are attempting to meet the problems of mental retardation, speech disorders, hearing and vision handicaps, and even
the needs of the gifted child. Many schools do have programs for the
various deviations mentioned above, but relatively few have such pro-

grams for dyslexic children even though they outnumber any of the groups.

In meeting the needs of dyslexic children, all public schools should have kindergartens. This statement may seem to be irrelevant since children are rarely taught reading, spelling and writing until they are in the first grade. Also, in many areas it is taken for granted that all children are enrolled in kindergartens, but according to the report of the Bureau of the Census for 1963, only about 54 per cent of the five-year-olds are enrolled in kindergartens.

The principal function of the kindergarten is not to teach the rudiments of the three R's, but rather to promote social-emotional development and give early experience in "learning to learn." However, evidence is accumulating which indicates that the average child can make a good start with the three R's before the age of six.

Perhaps most important is the opportunity that kindergartens provide for the screening of all children with regard to their abilities and disabilities before they enter the first grade. Along with the preschool physical and dental examinations, psychological studies should be carried out for all children in order to have a broad-gauge estimate of their general intellectual capacity and some leads or intimations about special abilities and disabilities. Group testing by teachers and, where indicated, individual studies by psychologists properly fall within the public school domain. Incapacities in speech, hearing and vision (including color vision) should be diagnosed through the preschool physical examination. The more subtle, yet serious, incapacities in visual and/or auditory perception—not due to eye or ear disorder but producing language disabilities—should be recognized or predicted during the kindergarten year.

Lauretta Bender was one of the first to claim that reading disability could be predicted before the child starts to learn to read. In recording observations in the preschool nursery at Bellevue Hospital in 1941, she wrote, "Some of our problem preschool children whose hyperkinesis and infantile asocial behavior had no other explanation have since proved to be reading disabilities. They showed slight motor retardation with a motility disorder, almost unclassifiable, often but not always associated with left-handedness. . . . In the 1920's and

1930's these symptoms were mistaken for postencephalitic conditions." Later Bender pointed out that her test (the Bender-Gestalt Test) was useful when applied to preschool children in revealing some of the developmental lag characteristic of specific reading disability.

Arnold Gesell (1949) stated that "in the preschool years a discerning teacher (nursery or kindergarten) may detect evidences more or less predictive of potential reading disabilities . . . specific weakness in drawing and in form perception, ill-defined handedness, reduced acuity, atypical directionality in movement patterns, and so on." Katrina de Hirsch (1954) added to Gesell's observations:

> Clinical observation shows that it is possible to predict future dyslexias in a fairly large percentage of three-, four-, and five-year olds who are originally referred on account of motor-speech delays, developmental word-deafness and severe dyslalia. Examination of motor, perceptual and emotional performance has shown a number of basic and specific dysfunctions which seem to underlie a variety of language disturbances. . . . They frequently have difficulty in finer muscular control; some of them show a degree of apraxia. Many are late in establishing cerebral dominance and have trouble with right-left progression. Bender-Gestalt tests show striking immaturity in visuo-motor functioning. Body image is usually very primitive. These children show disturbances in figure-background relationships, they are often hyperactive and have difficulty with patterning of motor and behavioral responses. They have, in fact, trouble at every level of integration.

Beth H. Slingerland's Screening Tests for Identifying Children with Specific Language Disability can be used for preschool children. "From these tests," Slingerland says, "the normal to highly intelligent children identified as showing extreme to marginal degrees of SLD (specific language disability) have been placed in self-contained classrooms with a trained or in-training teacher using an adaptation for classroom use of the Orton-Gillingham technique."

Marianne Frostig's Developmental Test of Visual Perception measures (1) eye-hand coordination, (2) figure-ground perception, (3) perception of form constancy, (4) perception of position in space, and (5) perception of spatial relationship. The assessment of perceptual disability in these areas is important for remedial reading, but equally important for predicting reading disability is the fact that the test proved to be valid when used with kindergarten children.

From a different approach, Cohen (1963) reported on a study concerned with "Prediction of Underachievement in Kindergarten Children." In this study an effort was made to predict which kindergarten children would not learn up to their I.Q. potential as they passed through the first grade. In his summary Cohen said, "Using observations of behavior, a team of teacher, psychologist and psychiatrist was able to predict this learning problem."

Frances Triggs formulated tests of reading readiness skills that are applicable at the kindergarten level. Although she recognized the fundamental causes of reading disability, she thought that early adequate teaching methods would prevent reading failure in most instances. She said, "Research has shown us that the most important purpose of testing is not prediction, but evaluation. But evaluation is empty unless it is followed by diagnoses of the causes of poor achievement and by corrective measures—measures which will prevent failure, not merely predict."

The contributions of several other authorities on reading disability, including Marion Monroe and Anna Gillingham, could be cited to bear out the claim that specific language disability can be diagnosed or at least predicted in children before they are six years old. However, little is to be gained by even the most precise prediction unless the schools are prepared to deal with the problem in the first grades and thereby obviate failure.

Other considerations about the curriculum in kindergartens should be mentioned at this point. As stated above, children with average capabilities can make progress in learning to read, write, spell, and even compute while still of kindergarten age. The studies and demonstrations of Omar Kahyyam Moore and Carl H. Delacato are noteworthy in this respect.

During the latter half of the 1950's Moore carried out basic studies and experimentation that resulted in the production of the "talking typewriter." This machine is a combination of a special electric typewriter, a screen that exhibits letters, words and pictures, and a tape recorder that can be programmed to talk. The child sits by himself before this machine and operates only the typewriter keyboard. It is claimed that by using this machine, a three-year-old can learn the alphabet and then progress to the recognition of words and sentences with the production of stories before he is six. It is apparent that with this device vision, hearing, vocalization, movement and touch are combined in a synchronized, yet flexible, manner. It is claimed that all children thoroughly enjoy using the machine and ask for more. No reference could be found regarding what happens when a dyslexic child confronts or is confronted by this "friendly" yet impersonal instrument. There seems to be a tacit implication that the method circumvents specific language disability, and perhaps it does to a certain extent, but study of its application to dyslexics is called for.

Delacato and his associates, the Domans, have produced instructions and equipment designed for parents to use in teaching preschool children to read. Their methodology came from their broad experience in dealing with developmental therapy in cases of brain-damaged children. The writer has no first-hand knowledge concerning the efficacy of the Doman-Delacato Reading Development Program for preschool children. Here, again, is the tacit implication that the method prevents reading retardation regardless of specific disability.

At any rate, the writer is inclined to agree with educators and some parents who say that sporadic teaching of reading at home or in kindergartens is not advisable. The few privileged children so taught have to stand by in the first grade, waiting for others to catch up, feeling bored, and making others feel inferior. However, it is predicted that when we have public school kindergartens for *all* children the three R's will be included in the kindergarten curriculum.

Also with reference to kindergartens, attention is called to the fact that the educational theories and practices which Dr. Maria Montessori introduced in her *Casa dei Bambini* in 1906 are enjoying a remarkable resurgence throughout the United States. On the theory that "things are the best teachers," she provided practical play objects such as blocks with letters in sandpaper. It is thought that the child's experimentation with the play material subtly develops his ability to discriminate the shapes of various objects through vision and touch. It is claimed that the performance of play with the available objects prepares the child for reading, writing and computation. Of course,

there are many other facets in the Montesorri method which in..
that the total program might be helpful for a dyslexic child.

If kindergartens and/or the above-outlined preschool psychological studies are not available before the child enters the first grade, then such studies should be carried out immediately. Knowing the general capacity, the emotional maturity, the reading readiness, and other characteristics of each child is highly desirable right from the start. This procedure is recommended in the interest of all children and not just those with some disability.

The methods of teaching reading from the first grade on have been discussed in the text with details about the battle between the exponents of the look-say method and the exponents of the phonic method. Out of this controversy comes the conclusion that, from the start of reading tuition, the phonic approach with emphasis on the alphabet, the sound of letters and their combinations, the syllables of words and other detailed characteristics of the printed word should receive basic attention. The good points of the look-say method should be retained, but in addition to the mere seeing of words and pictures, the auditory, tactile and other sensory modalities should be brought into the teaching of reading. This generalized approach is suggested not only for children whose visual perception is below par, but also for those gifted in quick visual perception in order to enhance their understanding and use of the English language. Also, it gives them a tool that enables them to approach words they have not seen before.

It is recognized that the phonic method of teaching reading will not do away with all reading problems. It may alleviate some of the borderline instances of reading lag, but there will remain a large number of reading disabilities where more specialized techniques are required, particularly remedial reading methods. Trained remedial reading teachers are needed in schools to a greater extent than speech therapists or the trained teachers for the mentally retarded.

In remedial reading an important basic principle is the use of sensory modalities or avenues of perception other than visual. Hearing and saying the letters or words, together with the muscular feel produced while writing in the right direction, are combined with the visual impression—all acting simultaneously and one reinforcing the others. In this associational manner and with considerable repetition, the correct engrams finally become established. Of course, remedial reading must be individualized according to the needs of the child and his emotional problems. Also, the teacher-pupil relationship is important and the teacher should recognize her psychotherapeutic role. Further details about remedial reading are to be found in the writings of Orton, Monroe, Gillingham, Norrie and others. For a more detailed description of remedial reading techniques, the reader is referred to a recent article by Childs which appeared in *Dyslexia in Special Education,* a monograph published by The Orton Society.

Other modalities of sensory impression are being used experimentally in remedial reading. *Time* (June 12, 1964) reported about an ingenious system of color-coding sounds introduced by Caleb Gattegno. He used rainbow-hued cards for vowel sounds and less distinct colors for consonants. He was quoted as saying, "Color serves as an extra dimension to help the learner associate the image of the letters with sound until he has mastered it. It makes nonphonetic English a phonetic language without changing the traditional spellings." This method, called "Words in Color," is being tried in several schools in the United States. It is presumed, of course, that the children are tested for color vision before they attempt to read by this method.

The touch or tactile sense, used by the blind in reading Braille, has not been specifically employed in remedial reading. The writer knows that an electronic device has been perfected which, by code, can transmit information through touch. The simple code is easily learned and is received through a small mechanism that can be attached to the arm or any part of the body. Originally the instrument was devised to give the blind a more expedient reading method, but it may be of use in other ways. The device has been used in the case of a child with reading disability with apparent benefit.

The use of color and touch to augment avenues of approach in remedial reading suggests that other sensory impressions might be utilized. Perhaps musical tones, using single tones for vowels and combined tones for consonants would be as valuable as "Words in Color." This idea may have been tested or experimented with; if so, the writer does not know of it.

Another method in the teaching of reading has made use of the Initial Teaching Alphabet (I.T.A.) which was developed by Sir

James Pitman, grandson of the originator of the Pitman shorthand method. This method may prove to be a valuable adjunct in the teaching of remedial reading. In the I.T.A., a forty-four-symbol alphabet, each symbol or letter has only one possible sound. It was devised for use with children who are just learning to read. It was first tried in 1961 with English children of kindergarten age. Because the results were encouraging, the method is now being employed both in England and in the United States. It is claimed that the children who have learned to read by this method have no difficulty transferring to the regular twenty-six-letter alphabet and reading English as ordinarily written. It is reported that I.T.A. has been tested with a small group of retarded readers in a third grade; all of them pulled up to grade level within five months. Sir James and other proponents of I.T.A. say that it is only a tool and not a "system" of reading instruction. One wonders if a dyslexic child could learn this phonic alphabet and make the transfer without considerable difficulty.

Only a few school systems have a supervisor skilled in remedial reading who is on a level with supervisors of speech, music, art and special education. In some of the larger cities there are several remedial reading teachers who go from school to school, helping the grade teachers but having little time for group classes or for individual tutoring in reading. In addition, Slingerland and others have demonstrated the advantages of having special classes for reading retardates.

While the programs mentioned above meet the problem to a certain extent, they do not meet it completely. It is suggested that a more comprehensive program would consist of ungraded classes in the first three years of elementary school combined with team teaching. In such a program children between six and nine years of age would progress with special help according to their abilities; specialized teachers would deal with different subjects; each pupil would have several teachers and move from room to room for different subjects just as high school students do.

Because approximately 50 per cent of the child's school time in the first three years is given over to language arts, the most important teacher would be the one dealing with reading, spelling and writing. This teacher would be highly trained in the recognition of special disabilities and in all remedial techniques used in the language field outside of speech. At the same time she would be conversant with the relation of speech disorders to her particular field. Under her would be assistant teachers with special training in language arts. These teachers would have several classes each day graduated according to language learning ability, and they would have time for individual remedial reading lessons.

The stumbling block for all remedial reading programs is the dearth of qualified teachers. Few universities or teachers' colleges offer well-rounded training in this field. Much more prominent and numerous are courses pertaining to speech disorders, mental retardation, and other handicaps. The National Council of Teachers of English made a survey of teacher qualification at the elementary level. Of the 7,417 secondary teachers of English from large and small schools in all sections of the country who participated in the survey, only 50.5 per cent earned college majors in English. Two-thirds of them do not consider themselves well-prepared to teach composition and oral skills; 90 per cent do not consider themselves well-prepared to teach reading. In proposing steps to overcome these inadequacies, the Council placed emphasis on English in general but with little attention to reading *per se*.

An item in the *Journal of the American Medical Association* (June 8, 1964) said that "the HEW Department granted more than $1.3 million to 71 colleges and universities to train teachers of children who have serious speech and hearing defects." Congress has appropriated even larger sums for the training of teachers for the mentally retarded. Apparently the President, Congress, HEW, and even the Children's Bureau are not aware of the need to train remedial reading specialists.

Concerning the viewpoint of educators, it is interesting to note that the Council for Exceptional Children of the National Education Association at its Forty-Second Annual Convention in 1964 recognized for the first time Specific Language Disability (SLD) as an area of exceptionality. The papers presented in the Section on Special Language Disability have been published as a monograph by The Orton Society.

The evidence just cited showing the lack of awareness concerning dyslexia at the national level can be duplicated at state and local levels. The subtlety of the handicap[1] can be held to account in large measure for this oversight, but the prevalence of the problem calls for more organized action along several fronts. The methods used in attacking other health and handicap problems should be helpful in planning programs for dyslexia.

Outstanding programs designed to combat and prevent mental retardation, epilepsy, cerebral palsy, speech and hearing disorders, visual impairment, and specific diseases such as polio and cancer, are in existence at all levels from the grass roots to the top national echelons. All of these programs have had the guidance and backing of the professions concerned, but fundamental in the success of each effort has been the intense interest and beneficence of lay people, many of whom were parents of or otherwise related to a disabled person. Often a handicapped person has instigated or led the organization which represents his type of disability. What Franklin Roosevelt did for polio, what Helen Keller did for the blind, and what Clifford W. Beers did for the mentally ill will never be forgotten.

Before World War II some broadminded and enlightened parents of children with epilepsy opened their secret doors, found other families with the same secret, and with professional guidance established the American League against Epilepsy—now known as the Epilepsy Foundation. Although cerebral palsy was being treated through retraining methods earlier in this century, it was not until after World War II that the parents of birth-injured children became brave enough to face the public in an organized and forthright manner. Now we have the United Cerebral Palsy Association.

In the early 1950's parents who had mentally retarded children had

---

[1]In *The Pediatric Patient 1964* it was stated that "the University of Oklahoma Child Study Center recently reported that nearly half (373) of 800 children referred by physicians and other professionals because of presumed retardation had normal or near-normal intelligence. About 45% of the intellectually normal had specific perceptual disorders, most of them remediable. . . ."

In psychiatric consultation work with public schools, the writer has found more than one dyslexic child of average intelligence assigned to a special education class for the mentally retarded. Also, surveys show that about one child in ten is so emotionally disturbed that he cannot profit by or fit into regular class work. Here, too, it is the writer's surmise that almost one-half of these emotionally disturbed children are dyslexics whose fundamental need is the proper kind of remedial reading tuition.

the courage to form their own local societies and bring the problem before the public. Rather quickly the National Association for Retarded Children came into being. Partly because of the activities of this organization and partly because of the advances in our knowledge about retardation, the National Institute of Mental Health and the National Institute of Neurological Diseases and Blindness began to take a more active interest in mental retardation. Active educational, service, training and research programs are now in existence at all levels. President Kennedy and his family added their support to the movement. The role that President Kennedy played in furthering the mental retardation movement was not unlike that played by President Roosevelt in the battle against polio. One wonders what would happen if we had a President with a dyslexic child.

Although developmental dyslexia is three times as prevalent as mental retardation, there is a lag in public and even professional interest in reading disability. In many places this lag amounts to a vacuum. The Orton Society, a national organization, is the outspoken exception to this statement. Year by year since its inception in 1947, it has made great contributions to knowledge in the field of dyslexia. The organization is made up of lay and professional people, but remains relatively small and struggles for financial support. Perhaps The Orton Society will be expanded to include state and local chapters and become more like the National Association for Mental Health or the National Association for Retarded Children.

At the national level the Secretary of Health, Education, and Welfare should be fully enlightened about developmental dyslexia. The departments under his jurisdiction, particularly the national health institutes and the Department of Education, should have specific research, training and educational programs in this field.

At the state level the departments of education should encompass the needs of dyslexic children and provide for them as they have for retarded, crippled and other handicapped children. State departments of health and mental health can and should contribute to a statewide program for dyslexic children. State colleges and universities should train an adequate number of teachers qualified in remedial reading.

At the local level the public schools should have special and adequate provisions for all children who have reading disability. Perhaps help will have to come from state and national sources, but the local schools should take the initiative and not wait for the programs to be forced upon them from above. Locally, too, the parents of children with reading disability should recognize the problem and band together in order to instigate action on behalf of the dyslexic children in the schools and clinics. Following the example of the parents of retarded children, local parent groups may be able to extend their influence to other communities and to higher echelons.

Another suggestion for local action derives from the organization known as Alcoholics Anonymous in which one person who has overcome the handicap of alcoholism aids another who is going through the experience. If older people who have surmounted a language disability could bring themselves to form a group called Dyslexics Anonymous, or the DA's, and give help to youngsters who are faced with the same problem, they would add a viable dimension to remedial reading. They could say to the child, "Look, I know what you are up against. I had the same trouble myself. Here are some of the ways in which I got around it." Although in some communities college students are volunteering to help with reading instruction in elementary schools, it would be more effective to have ex-dyslexics do the job until the schools can meet the need with proper programs in remedial reading. Even then, the DA's would be helpful and able to perform other educational and promotional functions.

As a final summarizing statement, the writer acknowledges that there are important emotional and socioeconomic influences in the causation of underachievement in the process of learning. Also, outspoken or minimal brain damage may account for difficulties in various aspects of language learning. However, it is claimed that in the majority of children with reading, spelling and writing disabilities there is an innate or constitutional predisposition based on hereditary factors. This is not a pessimistic point of view. On the contrary, it is optimistic because it brings in the concept of a developmental lag. When this concept is recognized by all concerned—parents, teachers, diagnosticians, and even the children themselves—good progress in overcoming the handicap can be made by appropriate remedial reading measures, especially if the problem is dealt with early in the life of the child.

BIBLIOGRAPHY

ABRAHAM, W., ED., 1956: *A New Look at Reading*. Boston, Porter Sargent.

AJURIAGUERRA, J. DE, 1957: Les Troubles de la lecture. *Psychiatria, Basel, 134*:97-129.

AJURIAGUERRA, J. DE, HÉCAEN, H., AND MASSONNET, J., 1951: Les Troubles visuo-constructifs par lesion parieto-occipitale droite. *Encéphale, 40*:122-179.

ANDERSON, I. H., AND DEARBORN, W. F., 1952: *The Psychology of Teaching Reading*. New York, Ronald Press.

AUSTIN, M. C., *et al.*, 1961: *The Torch Lighters: Tomorrow's Teachers of Reading*. Cambridge, Harvard Univ. Press.

BACHMANN, F., 1927: Ueber kongenitale Wortblindheit (angeborene Leseschwäche). *Abhandl. Neur. Psych. Psychol. Grenzbeg., 40*:1-27.

BAILEY, PERCIVAL, 1963: Review of La cécité psychique by H. Hécaen and R. Angelerques. *Arch. Gen. Psychiat. (Chicago), 9*:304-305.

BAKWIN, H., 1950: Psychiatric aspects of pediatrics: lateral dominance, right- and left-handedness. *J. Pediat., 36*:385-391.

BAKWIN, H., AND BAKWIN, R. M., 1960: *Clinical Management of Behavior Disorders*. Philadelphia, Saunders.

BARGER, W. C., 1953: An experimental approach to aphasic and non-reading children. *Amer. J. Orthopsychiat., 23*:158-169.

BARGER, W. C., 1959: Late reading in children. *Cerebral Palsy Bull., 7*: 20-26.

BARGER, W. C., *et al.*, 1957: Constitutional aspects in psychiatry of poor readers. *Dis. Nerv. Syst., 18*:289-294.

BASTIAN, H. C., 1882: *The Brain as an Organ of Mind*. London, Kegan Paul, French.

BASTIAN, H. C., 1898: *A Treatise on Aphasia and Other Speech Defects*. London, H. K. Lewis.

BATEMAN, B., 1965: An overview of specific language disabilities. *Bull. Orton Soc., 15*:1-12.

BENDA, C. E., *et al.*, 1964: The relationship between intellectual inadequacy and emotional and sociocultural deprivation. *Compr. Psychiat., 5*:294-313.

BENDER, LAURETTA, 1938: A Visual Motor Gestalt Test and Its Clinical Use. Research Monograph No. 3. American Orthopsychiatric Association. New York, Amer. Orthopsychiat. Assoc. Inc.

[171]

BENDER, L., 1946: Organic brain disorders producing behavior disorders in children. In: *Recent Trends in Child Psychiatry.* N. D. C. Lewis and B. Pacella, Eds. New York, Grune and Stratton, pp. 155-192.

BENDER, L., 1954: *A Dynamic Psychopathology of Childhood.* Springfield, Thomas.

BENDER, L., 1956: Research studies from Bellevue Hospital on specific reading disability. *Bull. Orton Soc., 6*:1-3.

BENDER, L., 1956: *Psychopathology of Children with Organic Brain Disorders.* Springfield, Thomas.

BENDER, L., 1957: Specific reading disability as a maturational lag. *Bull. Orton Soc., 7*:9-18.

BENDER, L., 1958: Problems in conceptualization and communication in children with developmental alexia. In: *Psychopathology of Communication.* New York, Grune and Stratton, p.p. 155-176.

BENDER, L., 1960: Genetic data in evaluation and management of disordered behavior in children. *Dis. Nerv. Syst., 21*:57-64.

BENDER, L., 1961: The brain and child behavior. *Arch. Gen. Psychiat. (Chicago), 4*:531-547.

BENDER, L., AND SCHILDER, P., 1951: Graphic art as a special ability in reading disabilities in children. *J. Clin. Exp. Psychopath., 12*:147-156.

BENTON, A. L., 1958: Significance of systemic reversal in right-left discrimination. *Acta Psychiat. Scand., 33*:129-137.

BENTON, A. L., 1962: Dyslexia in relation to form perception and directional sense. In: *Reading Disability: Progress and Research Needs in Dyslexia.* J. Money, Ed. Baltimore, Johns Hopkins Press, pp. 81-102.

BENTON, A. L., AND BIRD, J. W., 1963: The EEG and reading disability. *Amer. J. Orthopsychiat., 33*:529-536.

BENTON, A. L., AND JOYNT, R. L., 1960: Early descriptions of aphasia. *Arch. Neurol. (Chicago), 3*:205-221.

BENTON, A. L., AND KEMBLE, J. D., 1960: Right-left orientation and reading disability. *Psychiat. Neur., 139*:49-60.

BETTS, E. A., 1936: *The Prevention and Correction of Reading Difficulties.* Evanston, Row, Peterson.

BETTS, E. A.,1957: *Foundations of Reading Instruction.* New York, American Book.

BETTS, E. A., AND BETTS, T. M., 1945: *An Index to Professional Literature on Reading and Related Topics.* New York, American Book.

BINGLEY, T., 1958: Mental symptoms in temporal lobe epilepsy and temporal lobe gliomas. *Acta Psychiat. Scand., 33* Suppl. 120.

BIRCH, H. G., 1962: Dyslexia and maturation of visual function. In: *Reading Disability: Progress and Research Needs in Dyslexia.* J. Money, Ed. Baltimore, Johns Hopkins Press, pp. 161-169.

BIRCH, H. G., AND BELMONT, L., 1964: Auditory-visual integration in normal and retarded readers. *Amer. J. Orthopsychiat., 34*:852-861.

BLANCHARD, P., 1928: Reading disabilities in relation to maladjustment. *Ment. Hyg., 12*:772-793.

BLANCHARD, P., 1929: Attitudes and educational disabilities. *Ment. Hyg., 13*:550-563.

BLANCHARD, P., 1935: Psychogenic factors in some cases of reading disability. *Amer. J. Orthopsychiat., 5*:361-374.

BLANCHARD, P., 1936: Reading disabilities in relation to difficulties of personality and emotional development. *Ment. Hyg., 20*:384-413.

BLANCHARD, P., 1946: Psychoanalytic contributions to the problem of reading disabilities. In: *The Psychoanalytic Study of the Child.* New York, International Universities Press, Vol. II, pp. 163-187.

BLAU, A., 1949: *The Master Hand.* Research Monograph No. 5. American Orthopsychiatric Association. New York, Amer. Orthopsychiat. Assoc. Inc.

BOSHES, B., AND MYKLEBUST, H. R., 1964: A neurological and behavioral study of children with learning disorders. *Neurology, 14*:1-12.

BRAIN, W. R., 1941: Visual object-agnosia with special reference to the Gestalt theory. *Brain, 64*:43-62.

BRAIN, W. R., 1941: Visual disorientation. *Brain, 64*:244-272.

BRAIN, W. R., 1945: Speech and handedness. *Lancet, 2*:837-841.

BRAIN, W. R., 1955: Aphasia, apraxia and agnosia. In: K. Wilson: *Neurology.* London, Butterworth, Vol. III, pp. 1413-1483.

BRAIN, W. R., 1965: *Speech Disorders.* 2nd Edition, Washington, D. C., Butterworths.

BRAZELTON, T. B., 1961: Psychophysiologic reactions in the neonate. *J. Pediat., 58*:508-518.

BRONNER, A. F., 1917: *The Psychology of Special Abilities and Disabilities.* Boston, Little, Brown.

BRYANT, N. D., 1964: Some conclusions concerning impaired motor development among reading disability cases. *Bull. Orton Soc., 14*:16-17.

CASTNER, B. M., 1935: Prediction of reading disability prior to first grade entrance. *Amer. J. Orthopsychiat., 5*:375-387.

CHARTERS, W. W., 1941: Reading. *Educ. Research Bull., 20*:145-146.

CHILDS, S. B., 1959: The teaching of reading abroad. *Bull. Orton Soc., 9*:19-25.

CHILDS, S. B., 1965: Teaching the dyslexic child. In: *Dyslexia in Special Education.* Monograph—Vol. I. Pomfret, Conn., The Orton Society, pp. 35-53.

CHILDS, S. B., AND CHILDS, R., 1962: *Sound Phonics.* Cambridge, Mass., Educators Publishing Service.

CHRISTINE, D., AND CHRISTINE, C., 1964: The relationship of auditory discrimination to articulation defects and reading retardation. *Elem. School J., 65*:97-100.

CLAIBORNE, J. H., 1906: Types of congenital amblyopia. *JAMA, 47*: 1813-1816.

CLEMENS, R. L., 1961: Minimal brain damage in children: an inter-disciplinary problem, medical, paramedical and educational. *Children, 8*:179-183.

CLEMENS, R. L., 1964: Obscure causes of school failure—a pediatric viewpoint. *Bull. Orton Soc., 14*:32-39.

CLEMENTS, S. D., AND PETERS, J. S., 1962: Minimal brain dysfunction in the school age child. *Arch. Gen. Psychiat. (Chicago), 6*:185-197.

COHEN, T. B., 1963: Prediction of underachievement in kindergarten children. *Arch. Gen. Psychiat. (Chicago), 9*:444-450.

COHN, R., 1961: Delayed acquisition of reading and writing abilities in children: a neurological study. *Arch. Neurol. (Chicago), 4*:153-164.

COLE, E. M., 1938: Disabilities in speaking and reading. *Med. Clin. N. Amer., 22*:607-616.

COLE, E. M., 1942: The neurological aspects of defects in speech and reading. *New Eng. J. Med., 226*:977-980.

COLE, E. M., 1945: Correction of speech and reading difficulties. *Rhode Island Med. J., 28*:94-97 & 131-133.

COLE, E. M., AND WALKER, L., 1964: Reading and speech problems as expressions of a specific language disability. In: *Disorders of Communication*. Baltimore, Williams & Wilkins. Vol. XLII, pp. 171-189.

CONANT, J. B., 1959: *The American High School Today.* New York, McGraw-Hill.

CONANT, J. B., 1961: *Learning to Read.* Princeton, N. J., Educational Testing Service.

CRITCHLEY, M., 1927: Some defects in reading and writing in children. *J. State Med., 35*:217-223.

CRITCHLEY, M., 1953: *The Parietal Lobes.* Baltimore, Williams & Wilkins.

CRITCHLEY, M., 1959: *The Study of Language-Disorder: Past, Present and Future.* The Centennial Lectures. New York, G. P. Putnam's Sons.

CRITCHLEY, M., 1963: The problem of developmental dyslexia. *Proc. Roy. Soc. Med., 56*:209-212.

CRITCHLEY, M., 1964: *Developmental Dyslexia.* London, William Heinemann Medical Books.

DALY, W. C., AND LEE, R. H., 1960: Reading disabilities in a group of M-R children. *The Training School Bull., 57*:85-93.

DEARBORN, W. F., 1931: Ocular and manual dominance in dyslexia. *Psychol. Bull., 28*:704-715.

DEARBORN, W. F., 1933: Structural factors which condition special disability in reading. *Proc. Amer. Ass. for Mental Deficiency, 38*:266-283.

DEARBORN, W. F., 1939: The nature and causation of disability in reading. In: *Recent Trends in Reading.* Suppl. Educ. Mon. No. 49. W. S. Gray, Ed. Chicago, Univ. Chicago Press.

DEARBORN, W. F., AND LEVERETT, H. M., 1945: Visual defects and reading. *J. Exp. Educ., 13*:111-124.

DELACATO, C. H., 1959: *The Treatment and Prevention of Reading Problems.* Springfield, Thomas.

DELACATO, C. H., 1965: *The Diagnosis and Treatment of Speech and Reading Problems.* Springfield, Thomas.

DIACK, H., 1960: *Reading and the Psychology of Perception.* Nottingham, Peter Skinner.

DORIS, J., AND SOLNIT, A. J., 1963: Treatment of children with brain damage and associated school problems. *J. Amer. Acad. Child Psychiat., 2*:618-635.

DOZIER, P., 1940: Specific reading disability. *Journal-Lancet, 60*:202-204.

DOZIER, P., 1953: The neurological background of word deafness. *Bull. Orton Soc., 3*:6-10.

DREIFUSS, F. E., 1963: Delayed development of hemispheric dominance. *Arch. Neurol. (Chicago), 8*:510-515.

DREW, A. L., 1956: A neurological appraisal of familial word-blindness. *Brain, 79*:440-460.

DRILLIEN, C. M., 1964: *The Growth and Development of the Prematurely Born Infant.* Baltimore, Williams & Wilkins.

DUCKER, S., AND NALLY, T., 1956: *The Truth about Your Child's Reading.* New York, Crown Publishing Co.

DUNCAN, J., 1953: *Backwardness in Reading: Remedies and Prevention.* London, Harrap.

DURBROW, H. C., 1952: Teaching the strephosymbolic. I. At the primary level. *Bull. Orton Soc., 2*:7-9.

DURRELL, D. D., 1956: *Improving Reading Instruction.* Yonkers-on-Hudson, N. Y., World Book.

EAMES, T. H., 1932: A comparison of the ocular characteristics of unselected and reading disability groups. *J. Educ. Res., 25*:211-215.

EAMES, T. H., 1934: Anatomical basis of lateral dominance anomalies. *Amer. J. Orthopsychiat.*, *4*:524-528.

EAMES, T. H., 1935: A frequency study of physical handicaps in reading disability and unselected groups. *J. Educ. Res.*, *29*:1-5.

EAMES, T. H., 1938: The ocular conditions of 350 poor readers. *J. Educ. Res.*, *32*:10-16.

EAMES, T. H., 1944: Amblyopia in cases of reading failure. *Amer. J. Ophthal.*, *27*:1374-1375.

EAMES, T. H., 1945: Comparison of children of premature and full-term birth who fail in reading. *J. Educ. Res.*, *38*:506-508.

EAMES, T. H., 1948: Incidence of diseases among reading failures and non-failures. *J. Pediat.*, *33*:614-617.

EAMES, T. H., 1948: Comparison of eye conditions among 1,000 reading failures, 500 ophthalmic patients, and 150 unselected children. *Amer. J. Ophthal.*, *31*:713-717.

EAMES, T. H., 1950: The relationship of reading and speech difficulties. *J. Educ. Psychol.*, *41*:51-55.

EAMES, T. H., 1955: The relationship of birth weight, the speeds of object and word perception, and visual acuity. *J. Pediat.*, *47*:603-606.

EAMES, T. H., 1957: Frequency of cerebral lateral dominance variations among school children of premature and full-term birth. *J. Pediat.*, *51*:300-302.

EDGREN, J. G., 1894: Amusie (musikalische aphasia). *Deutsch Z. Nervenheilk, 6*:1-65.

EISENBERG, L., 1959: Office evaluation of specific reading disability in children. *Pediatrics, 23*:997-1003.

EISENBERG, L., 1962: Introduction. In: *Reading Disability: Progress and Research Needs in Dyslexia.* J. Money, Ed. Baltimore, Johns Hopkins Press, pp. 3-7.

EISENSON, J., 1958: Aphasia and dyslexia in children. *Bull. Orton Soc., 8*:3-8.

EPHRON, B. H., 1953: *Emotional Difficulties in Reading.* New York, Julian Press.

ETTLINGER, G., AND JACKSON, C. V., 1955: Organic factors in developmental dyslexia. *Proc. Roy. Soc. Med., 48*:998-1000.

ETTLINGER, G., JACKSON, C. V., AND ZANGWILL, O. L., 1956: Cerebral dominance in sinistrals. *Brain, 79*:569-588.

ETTLINGER, G., WARRINGTON, E., AND ZANGWILL, O. L., 1957: A further study of visual-spatial agnosia. *Brain, 80*:335-361.

EUSTIS, R. S., 1947: The primary etiology of the specific language disabilities. *J. Pediat., 31*:448-455.

EUSTIS, R. S., 1947: Specific reading disability. *New Eng. J. Med., 237*: 243-249.

EUSTIS, R. S., 1949: Right- or left-handedness. A practical problem. *New Eng. J. Med., 240*:249-253.

FABIAN, A. A., 1945: Vertical rotation in visual-motor performance; its relation to reading reversals. *J. Educ. Psychol., 36*:129-145.

FABIAN, A. A., 1951: Clinical and experimental studies of school children who are retarded in reading. *Quart. J. Child Behavior, 3*:15-37.

FABIAN, A. A., 1955: Reading disability: an index of pathology. *Amer. J. Orthopsychiat., 25*:319-326.

FALCK, F. J., AND FALCK, V. T., 1961: Communicative disorders: a multidisciplinary problem. *JAMA 178*:290-295.

FALCK, F. J., AND FALCK, V. T., 1962: Disorders of neurological integrative mechanisms. *Asha, 4*:439-440.

FALEK, A., 1959: Handedness, a family study. *Amer. J. Hum. Genet., 2*:52-62.

FENICHEL, O., 1937: The scoptophilic instinct and identification. *Int. J. Psychoanal., 18*:6-34.

FENICHEL, O., 1945: *The Psychoanalytic Theory of Neurosis.* New York, W. W. Norton.

FERNALD, G. M., 1943: *On Certain Language Disabilities: Nature and Treatment.* Baltimore, Williams & Wilkins.

FERNALD, G. M., 1943: *Remedial Techniques in the Basic School Subjects.* New York, McGraw-Hill.

FERNALD, G. M., AND KELLER, H., 1921: The effect of kinaesthetic factors in the development of word recognition in the case of non-readers. *J. Educ. Res., 4*:355-377.

FILDES, L. G., 1921: A psychological inquiry into the nature of the condition known as congenital word-blindness. *Brain, 44*:286-307.

FISHER, J. H., 1905: A case of congenital word-blindness (inability to learn to read). *Ophthal. Rev., 24*:315-318.

FISHER, J. H., 1910: Congenital word-blindness (inability to learn to read). *Trans. Ophthal. Soc. U. K., 30*:216-225.

FLESCH, R., 1955: *Why Johnny Can't Read—What You Can Do About It.* New York, Harper.

FLOWER, R. M., GOFMAN, H. F., AND LAWSON, L. I., Eds., 1965: *Reading Disorders: A Multidisciplinary Symposium.* Philadelphia, Davis.

FRANKLIN, A. W., Ed., 1962: *Word-blindness or Specific Developmental Dyslexia.* London, Pitman Med.

FREUD, S., 1891: *On Aphasia.* Trans., E. Stengell, 1953. New York, International Universities Press.

Freud, S., 1901: Psychopathology of everyday life. In: *The Standard Edition of the Complete Psychological Works of Sigmund Freud.* London, Hogarth Press. Vol. VI.

Freud, S., 1905: Three essays on sexuality. In: *The Standard Edition of the Complete Psychological Works of Sigmund Freud.* London, Hogarth Press. Vol. VII, pp. 125-243.

Freud, S., 1909: Five lectures on psycho-analysis. In: *The Standard Edition of the Complete Psychological Works of Sigmund Freud.* London, Hogarth Press. Vol. XI, pp. 9-55.

Freud, S., 1910: The psychoanalytic view of psychogenic disturbances of vision. In: *The Standard Edition of the Complete Psychological Works of Sigmund Freud.* London, Hogarth Press. Vol. XI, pp. 209-218.

Frostig, M., 1963: Visual perception in the brain-injured child. *Amer. J. Orthopsychiat., 33*:665-672.

Frostig, M., and Horne, D., 1964: *The Frostig Program for the Development of Visual Perception.* Chicago, Follett.

Frostig, M., Lefever, D. W., and Whittlesey, J. R. B., 1964: *Developmental Test of Visual Perception.* Palo Alto, Consulting Psychologists Press.

Gallagher, J. R., 1950: Specific language disability: cause of scholastic failure. *New Eng. J. Med., 242*:436-440.

Gallagher, J. R., 1958: European research in reading disability. *Bull. Orton Soc., 8*:11-14.

Gallagher, J. R., 1960: Specific language disability: dyslexia. *Bull. Orton Soc., 10*:5-10.

Gallagher, J. R., 1962: Word-blindness (reading-disability; dyslexia): its diagnosis and treatment. In: *Word-blindness or Specific Developmental Dyslexia.* E. W. Franklin, Ed. London, Pitman Med., pp. 6-14.

Gallagher, J. R., 1966: *Medical Care of the Adolescent.* Second Ed. New York, Appleton-Century-Crofts, pp. 122-123.

Gallagher, J. R., and Gallagher, C. D., 1964: Color vision screening of pre-school and first grade children. *Arch. Ophthal. (Chicago), 72*:200-212.

Gann, E., 1945: *Reading Difficulty and Personality Organization.* New York, King's Crown Press, Columbia Univ.

Gates, A. I., 1922: *The Psychology of Reading and Spelling; with Special Reference to Disabilities.* New York, Teachers Coll. Contrib. Educ. No. 129, Columbia Univ.

Gates, A. I., 1937: *Diagnosis and Treatment of Extreme Cases of Reading Disability.* Chicago, Nat. Soc. Study Educ. Yearbook.

GATES, A. I., 1941: The role of personality maladjustment in reading disability. *J. Genet. Psychol., 59*:77-83.

GATES, A. I., 1955: *The Improvement of Reading.* New York, Macmillan.

GERSTMANN, J., 1924: Fingeragnosie. Eine umschreibne Störung der Orientierung am eigenen Körper. *Wien. Klin. Wschr., 37*:1010-1012.

GERSTMANN, J., 1927: Fingeragnosie und isolierte Agraphie. *Z. Ges. Neurol. Psychiat., 108*:152-177.

GERSTMANN, J., 1940: Syndrome of finger agnosia, disorientation for right and left, agraphia and acalculia. *Arch. Neurol. Psychiat. (Chicago), 44*:398-408.

GERSTMANN, J., 1958: Psychological and phenomenological aspects of disorders of the body image. *J. Nerv. Ment. Dis., 126*:499-512.

GESCHWIND, N., 1962: The anatomy of acquired disorders of reading. In: *Reading Disability: .Progress and Research Needs in Dyslexia.* J. Money, Ed. Baltimore, Johns Hopkins Press, pp. 115-129.

GESELL, A., 1925: *The Mental Growth of the Pre-school Child.* New York, Macmillan.

GESELL, A., 1945: *Embryology of Behavior.* New York, Harper.

GESELL, A., AND AMATRUDA, C. S., 1947: *Developmental Diagnosis.* New York, Paul B. Hoeber.

GESELL, A., AND AMES, L. B., 1946: The development of directionality in drawing. *J. Genet. Psychol., 68*:45-61.

GESELL, A., AND AMES, L. B., 1947: Development of handedness. *J. Genet. Psychol., 70*:155-163.

GESELL, A., AND BULLIS, G. E., 1949: *Vision, Its Development in Infant and Child.* New York, Paul B. Hoeber.

GESELL, A., AND ILG, F. L., 1946: *The Child from Five to Ten.* New York, Harper.

GILLINGHAM, A., 1956: The prevention of scholastic failure due to specific language disability. *Bull Orton Soc., 6*:26-31.

GILLINGHAM, A., AND STILLMAN, B. W., 1960: *Remedial Training for Children with Specific Disability in Reading, Spelling, and Penmanship.* Cambridge, Mass., Educators Publishing Service.

GOERTZEL, V., AND GOERTZEL, M. G., 1962: *Cradles of Eminence.* Boston, Little, Brown.

GOLDBERG, H., 1965: Neurological and psychological aspects of reading disabilities. In: *Dyslexia in Special Education.* Monograph—Vol. I. Pomfret, Conn., The Orton Society, pp. 91-95.

GRAY, C. T., 1922: *Deficiencies in Reading Ability; Their Diagnosis and Remedies.* Boston, Little, Brown.

GRAY, C. T., 1940: Reading ability and personality development. *Educational Forum, 4*:133-138.

GRAY, W. S., 1917: *Studies of Elementary School Reading through Standardized Tests.* Suppl. Educational Monographs, Vol. I, No. I. Univ. of Chicago.

GRAY, W. S., 1921: Diagnostic and remedial steps in reading. *J. Educ. Res., 4*:1-15.

GRAY, W. S., 1925: *Summary of Investigations Relating to Reading.* Chicago, Univ. Chicago Press. (Additional summaries published from time to time. Last summary in *J. Educ. Res., 52*:203-221, 1959.)

GRAY, W. S., 1957: *Teaching of Reading and Writing: An International Survey.* Cambridge, Harvard Univ. Press.

GRUNEBAUM, M. G., *et al.*, 1962: Fathers and sons with primary neurotic learning inhibitions. *Amer. J. Orthopsychiat., 32*:462-472.

GUTTMAN, E., 1936: Congenital arithmetic disability and acalculia. *Brit. J. Med. Psychol., 16*:16-35.

GUTTMAN, E., 1942: Aphasia in children. *Brain, 65*:205-219.

HALLGREN, B., 1950: Specific Dyslexia ("congenital word-blindness"): A Clinical and Genetic Study. *Acta Psychiat. Scand. Suppl. 65.*

HARPER, P. A., 1962: *Preventive Pediatrics.* New York, Appleton-Century-Crofts.

HARRIS, A. J., 1957: Lateral dominance, directional confusion, and reading disability. *J. Psychol., 44*:283-294.

HARRIS, A. J., 1960: *How to Increase Reading Ability.* New York, Longmans Green.

HARRIS, A. J., 1962: *Effective Teaching of Reading.* New York, David McKay.

HARRIS, A. J., AND ROSWELL, F. G., 1953: Clinical diagnosis of reading disability. *J. Psychol., 36*:323-340.

HARRIS, I. D., 1961: *Emotional Blocks to Learning.* New York, Crowell-Collier.

HARTMANN, H., 1956: Notes on the reality principle. In: *The Psychoanalytic Study of the Child.* New York, International Universities Press, Vol. XI, pp. 31-53.

HEAD, H., 1920: Aphasia and kindred disorders of speech. *Brain, 43*: 87-165.

HEAD, H., 1920: Aphasia: an historical review. *Brain, 43*:390-450.

HEAD, H., 1926: *Aphasia and Kindred Disorders of Speech.* New York, Macmillan.

HEGGE, T. G., 1937: The significance of special reading disabilities in mentally handicapped problem children. *Amer. J. Psychiat., 94*:77-87.

HELLMAN, I., 1954: Some observations on mothers of children with intellectual inhibitions. In: *The Psychoanalytic Study of the Child.* New York, International Universities Press, Vol. IX, pp. 259-273.

HENSCHEN, S. E., 1926: On the function of the right hemisphere of the brain in relation to the left in speech, music and calculation. *Brain, 49*:110-123.

HERMANN, K., 1949: Alexia-agraphia. A case report (acquired reading and writing disabilities, temporary word-blindness of the congenital type). *Acta Psychiat. Scand. 25*:449-455.

HERMANN, K., 1956: Congenital word-blindness. (Poor reading in the light of Gerstmann's syndrome). *Acta Psychiat. Scand. Suppl. 108*: 177-184.

HERMANN, K., 1959: *Reading Disability: A Medical Study of Word-Blindness and Related Handicaps.* Springfield, Thomas.

HERMANN, K., AND NORRIE, E., 1958: Is congenital word-blindness a hereditary type of Gerstmann's syndrome? *Psychiatria, Basel, 136*: 59-73.

HERMANN, K., AND VOLDBY, H., 1946: The morphology of handwriting in congenital word-blindness. *Acta Psychiat. Scand., 21*:349-363.

HILDRETH, G. H., 1945: A school survey of eye-hand dominance. *J. Appl. Psychol., 29*:83-88.

HILDRETH, G. H., 1946: Speech defects and reading disability. *Elem. School J., 46*:326-332.

HILDRETH, G. H., 1958: *Teaching Reading.* New York, Holt.

HINCKS, E., 1926: *Disability in Reading and its Relation to Personality.* Cambridge, Harvard Univ. Press.

HINSHELWOOD, J., 1895: Word-blindness and visual memory. *Lancet, 2*:1564-1570.

HINSHELWOOD, J., 1896: A case of dyslexia: a peculiar form of word-blindness. *Lancet, 2*:1451-1454.

HINSHELWOOD, J., 1896: The visual memory for words and figures. *Brit. Med. J., 2*:1543-1544.

HINSHELWOOD, J., 1898: A case of "word" without "letter" blindness. *Lancet, 1*:422-425.

HINSHELWOOD, J., 1899: "Letter" without "word" blindness. *Lancet, 1*:83-86.

HINSHELWOOD, J., 1900: Congenital word-blindness. *Lancet, 1*:1506-1508.

HINSHELWOOD, J., 1900: *Letter-, Word- and Mind-blindness.* London, H. K. Lewis.

HINSHELWOOD, J., 1902: Four cases of word-blindness. *Lancet, 1*:358-363.

HINSHELWOOD, J., 1907: Four cases of congenital word-blindness occurring in the same family. *Brit. Med. J., 2*:1229-1232.

HINSHELWOOD, J., 1912: The treatment of word-blindness, acquired and congenital. *Brit. Med. J., 2*:1033-1035.

HINSHELWOOD, J., 1917: *Congenital Word-blindness*. London, H. K. Lewis.

DE HIRSCH, K., 1952: Specific dyslexia or strephosymbolia. *Folia Phoniat., Basel, 4*:231-248.

DE HIRSCH, K., 1954: Gestalt psychology as applied to language disturbances. *J. Nerv. Ment. Dis., 120*:257-261.

DE HIRSCH, K., 1957: Tests designed to discover potential reading difficulties at the 6-year-old level. *Amer. J. Orthopsychiat., 27*:566-576.

DE HIRSCH, K., 1963: Two categories of learning difficulties in adolescents. *Amer. J. Orthopsychiat., 33*:87-91.

DE HIRSCH, K., 1965: Early identification of specific language disabilities as seen by a speech pathologist. In: *Dyslexia in Special Education*. Monograph—Vol. I. Pomfret, Conn., The Orton Society, pp. 73-79.

HOLLINGWORTH, L. S., 1918: *The Psychology of Special Disability in Spelling*. Contributions to Education No. 88. New York, Teachers College.

HOLLINGWORTH, L. S., 1925: *Special Talents and Defects*. New York, Macmillan.

HOLT, L. B., 1964. Reading difficulties. In: *Pediatric Ophthalmology*. Philadelphia, Lee & Febiger, pp. 327-336.

HORWITZ, W. A., *et al.*, 1965: Identical twin—"idiot savants"—calendar calculators. *Amer. J. Psychiat., 121*:1075-1079.

HUEY, E. B., 1898: Preliminary experiments in the physiology and psychology of reading. *Amer. J. Psychol., 9*:575-586.

HUEY, E. B., 1908: *The Psychology and Pedagogy of Reading*. New York, Macmillan.

HUGHES, J., *et al.*, 1949: Electroencephalographic study of specific reading disabilities. *E.E.G. & Clin. Neurophysiol., 1*:377-378.

INGRAM, T. T., 1960: Pediatric aspects of specific developmental dysphasia, dyslexia, and dysgraphia. *Cerebral Palsy Bull., 2*:248-277.

JACKSON, E., 1906: Developmental alexia (congenital word-blindness). *Amer. J. Med. Sci., 131*:843-849.

JACKSON, J. HUGHLINGS, 1931: *Selected Writings of John Hughlings Jackson*. J. Taylor, Ed. London, Hodder and Stoughton.

JARVIS, V., 1958: Clinical observations on the visual problem in reading disability. In: *The Psychoanalytic Study of the Child.* New York, International Universities Press, Vol. XIII, pp. 451-470.

JENSEN, A. R., 1963: Learning ability in retarded, average and gifted children. *Merrill-Palmer Quart., 9*:123-140.

JONES, E., 1923: The child's unconscious. In: *Papers on Psychoanalysis.* London, William Wood.

KANNER, L., 1950: *Child Psychiatry.* Springfield, Thomas, pp. 567-577.

KANNER, L., 1952: Emotional interference with intellectual functioning. *Amer. J. Ment. Defic., 56*:701-707.

KAWI, A. A., AND PASAMANICK, B., 1958: Association of factors of pregnancy with reading disorders of childhood. *JAMA, 166*:1420-1423.

KENNARD, M. A., RABINOVITCH, R. D., AND WEXLER, D., 1952: The abnormal electroencephalogram as related to reading disability in children with disorders of behavior. *Canad. Med. Ass. J., 67*:330-333.

KEPHART, N. C., 1960: *The Slow Learner in the Classroom.* Columbus, Ohio, Charles E. Merrill.

KERR, J., 1897: School hygiene, in its mental, moral and physical aspects. *J. Roy. Statit. Soc., 60*:613-680.

KINSBOURNE, M., AND WARRINGTON, E. K., 1963. The developmental Gerstmann syndrome. *Arch. Neurol. (Chicago), 8*:490-502.

KIRK, S. A., 1962: *Educating Exceptional Children.* Boston, Houghton Mifflin.

KIRK, S. A., AND BATEMAN, B., 1962: Diagnosis and remediation of learning disabilities. *Exceptional Child., 29*:73-98.

KIRK, S. A., AND McCARTHY, J. J., 1961: The Illinois test of psycholinguistic abilities. *Amer. J. Ment. Defic., 66*:399-412.

KLEIN, E., 1949: Psychoanalytic aspects of school problems. In: *The Psychoanalytic Study of the Child.* New York, International Universities Press, Vol. III-IV, pp. 369-390.

KLEIN, M., 1930: Importance of symbol-formation in the development of the ego. *Int. J. Psychoanal., 11*:24-39.

KLEIN, M., 1931: A contribution to the theory of intellectual inhibition. *Int. J. Psychoanal., 12*:206-218.

KNIGHT, E. H., 1952: Spelling disability as a symptom of emotional disorder. *Bull. Menninger Clin., 16*:84-91.

KOLSON, C. J., AND KALUGER, G., 1963: *Clinical Aspects of Remedial Reading.* Springfield, Thomas.

KORNRICH, M., Ed., 1965: *Underachievement.* Springfield, Thomas.

KOTKOV, B., 1965: Emotional syndromes associated with learning failure. *Dis. Nerv. Syst., 26*:48-55.

KUROMARU, S., AND OKADA, S., 1961: On developmental dyslexia in Japan. Paper read at the 7th International Congress of Neurology, Rome.

KUSSMAUL, A., 1877: Disturbances of speech. In: *Clycopaedia of the Practice of Medicine*. H. von Ziemssen, Ed. Trans., J. A. McCreery. New York, William Wood, Vol. XIV, pp. 581-875.

LANGFORD, W. S., 1955: Developmental dyspraxia—abnormal clumsiness. *Bull. Orton Soc., 5*:3-9.

LAUFER, M. W., 1962: Cerebral dysfunction and behavior disorders in adolescents. *Amer. J. Orthopsychiat., 32*:501-506.

LAUNAY, C., 1952: Etude d'ensemble des inaptitudes à la lecture. *Sem. Hôp Paris, 28*:1463-1474.

LEVY, D. M., 1957: Capacity and motivation. *Amer. J. Orthopsychiat., 27*:1-8.

LIPPMAN, H. S., 1962: *Treatment of Children in Emotional Conflict*. New York, McGraw-Hill, pp. 177-191.

LISS, E., 1935: Libidinal fixations as pedagogic determinants. *Amer. J. Orthopsychiat., 5*:126-131.

LISS, E., 1937: Emotional and biological factors involved in learning processes. *Amer. J. Orthopsychiat., 7*:483-489.

LISS, E., 1940: Learning—its sadistic and masochistic manifestations. *Amer. J. Orthopsychiat., 10*:123-129.

LISS, E., 1941: Learning difficulties. *Amer. J. Orthopsychiat., 11*:520-524.

LISS, E., 1949: Psychiatric implications of the failing student. *Amer. J. Orthopsychiat., 19*:501-505.

LISS, E., 1955: Motivations in learning. In: *The Psychoanalytic Study of the Child*. New York, International Universities Press, Vol. X, pp. 100-116.

LORDAT, J., 1843-44: Analyse de la parole pour servir à la théorie de divers cas d'alalie et de paralalie. *J. Soc. Pr., Montpellier 7 and 8*. Paris, Baillière.

McCREADY, E. B., 1910: Congenital word-blindness as a cause of backwardness in school. *Penn. Med. J., 13*:178-187.

McCREADY, E. B., 1910: Biological variation in the higher cerebral centers causing retardation. *Arch. Pediat., 27*:506-513.

McCREADY, E. B., 1926: Defects in the zone of language (word-deafness and word-blindness). *Amer. J. Psychiat., 83*:267-277.

McFIE, J., 1952: Cerebral dominance in cases of reading disability. *J. Neurol. Neurosurg. Psychiat., 15*:194-199.

MAHLER, M. S., 1942: Pseudoimbecility: a magic cap of invisibility. *Psychoanalyt. Quart., 11*:149-164.

MALMQUIST, E., 1958: *Factors Related to Reading Disabilities in the First Grade of the Elementary School.* Stockholm, Almquist and Wiksell.

MARKS, A., AND SAUNDERS, J. C., 1963: Strephosymbolia in children with neuropsychiatric disorders. *Amer. J. Psychiat., 119*:1087-1088.

MARUYAMA, M., 1958: Reading disability: a neurological point of view. *Bull. Orton Soc., 8*:14-16.

MASLAND, R. L., *et al.*, 1959: *Mental Subnormality.* New York, Basic Books.

MEEK, L. M., 1925: *A Study of Learning and Retention in Young Children.* New York, Teachers College, Columbia Univ.

MENNINGER, K. A., 1924: Letters of the alphabet in psychoanalytic formation. *Int. J. Psychoanal., 5*:462-465.

MILLER, A. D., MARGOLIN, J. B., AND YOLLES, B. F., 1957: Epidemiology of reading disabilities. *Amer. J. Public Health, 47*:1250-1256.

MONEY, J., ED., 1962: *Reading Disability: Progress and Research Needs in Dyslexia.* Baltimore, Johns Hopkins Press.

MONROE, M., 1928: *Methods for Diagnosis and Treatment of Cases of Reading Disability.* Genetic Psychology Monographs. Vol. IV, Nos. 4 and 5.

MONROE, M., 1932: *Children Who Cannot Read.* Chicago, Univ. Chicago Press.

MONROE, M., 1937: *Remedial Reading.* Boston, Houghton Mifflin.

MONROE, M., 1951: *Growing into Reading.* New York, Scott Foresman.

MONTESSORI, M., 1917: *The Advanced Montessori Method.* London, Witteinemann.

MORGAN, W. P., 1896: A case of congenital word-blindness. *Brit. Med. J., 2*:1378.

MOUNTCASTLE, V. B., ED., 1962: *Interhemispheric Relations and Cerebral Dominance.* Baltimore, Johns Hopkins Press.

MURPHY, L. B., 1957: Psychoanalysis and child development. *Bull. Menninger Clin., 21*:177-188.

MYKLEBUST, H. R., AND BOSHES, B., 1960: Psychoneurological learning disorders in children. *Arch. Pediat., 77*:247-256.

NAMNUM, A., AND PRELINGER, E., 1961. On the psychology of the reading process. *Amer. J. Orthopsychiat., 31*:820-828.

NETTLESHIP, E., 1901: Cases of congenital word-blindness (inability to learn to read). *Ophthal. Rev., 20*:61-67.

NEWBROUGH, J. R., AND KELLY, J. G., 1962: A Study of Reading Achievement in a Population of School Children. In *Reading Disability: Progress and Research Needs in Dyslexia.* J. Money, Ed. Baltimore, Johns Hopkins Press, pp. 61-72.

NICHOLLS, J. V. V., 1959: The office management of patients with reading difficulties. *Canad. Med. Ass. J., 81*:356-360.

NICHOLLS, J. V. V., 1960: Congenital dyslexia: a problem in aetiology. *Canad. Med. Ass. J., 82*:575-579.

NIELSEN, J. M., 1937: Unilateral cerebral dominance as related to mind blindness. *Arch. Neurol. Psychiat., (Chicago), 38*:108-136.

NIELSEN, J. M., 1941: *Text Book of Clinical Neurology.* New York, Paul B. Hoeber.

NIELSEN, J. M., 1946: *Agnosia, Apraxia, Aphasia. Their Value in Cerebral Localization.* New York, Paul B. Hoeber.

NORRIE, E., 1939: *Om Ordblindhed.* Copenhagen.

NORRIE, E., 1960: Word-blindness in Denmark. *The Independent School Bulletin,* April.

NOYES, A. P., AND KOLB, L. C., 1963: *Modern Clinical Psychiatry.* Philadelphia, Saunders.

NURCOMBE, B., AND PARKER, N., 1964: The idiot savant. *J. Amer. Acad. Child Psychiat., 3*:469-488.

OBERNDORF, C. P., 1939: The feeling of stupidity. *Int. J. Psychoanal., 20*:443-451.

OGLE, W., 1867: Aphasia and agraphia. *St. George's Hosp. Rep., 2*:83-122.

ORTON, J. L., 1957: The Orton story. *Bull. Orton Soc., 7*:5-8.

ORTON, J. L., AND KARNES, L. R., 1965: A history of specific dyslexia in relation to special education. In: *Dyslexia in Special Education.* Monograph—Vol. I, Pomfret, Conn., The Orton Society, pp. 5-22.

ORTON, S. T., 1925: "Word blindness" in school children. *Arch. Neurol. Psychiat., (Chicago), 14*:581-615.

ORTON, S. T., 1926: Neuropathology lectures. *Arch. Neurol. Psychiat., (Chicago), 15*:763-775, and *16*:451-470.

ORTON, S. T., 1928: Specific reading disability—strephosymbolia. *JAMA, 90*:1095-1099.

ORTON, S. T., 1928: An impediment to learning to read—a neurological explanation of the reading disability. *School and Society,* Vol. XXVIII, No. 715. Sept.

ORTON, S. T., 1928: A physiological theory of reading disability and stuttering in children. *New Eng. J. Med., 199*:1046-1052.

ORTON, S. T., 1929: The three levels of cortical elaboration in relation to certain psychiatric symptoms. *Amer. J. Psychiat., 8*:647-655.

ORTON, S. T., 1929: The "sight reading" method of teaching reading, as a source of reading disability. *J. Educ. Psychol., 20*:135-142.

ORTON, S. T., 1929: The neurological basis of elementary education. *Arch. Neurol. Psychiat., (Chicago), 21*:641-646.

ORTON, S. T., 1929: Certain failures in the acquisition of written language: their bearing on the problem of cerebral dominance. *Arch. Neurol. Psychiat., (Chicago), 22*:841-850.

ORTON, S. T., 1929: Neurological studies of some educational deviates from Iowa schools. *J. Iowa Med. Soc., 19*:155-158.

ORTON, S. T., 1929: The relation of the special educational disabilities to feeblemindedness. In: *Proceedings of the Fifty-Third Annual Session of the American Association for the Study of the Feebleminded.*

ORTON, S. T., 1929: The need of consolidation of psychiatric thought by a broad program of research. (Presidential address). *Amer. J. Psychiat., 9*:1-17.

ORTON, S. T., 1930: Familial occurrence of disorders in acquisition of language. *Eugenics,* Vol. III, No. 4, April.

ORTON, S. T., 1931: Special disability in spelling. *Bull. Neurol. Inst. New York, 1*:159-192.

ORTON, S. T., 1932: Some studies in language function. In: *Localization of Function in the Cerebral Cortex.* Baltimore, Williams & Wilkins. Vol. XIII, pp. 614-633.

ORTON, S. T., 1937: *Reading, Writing and Speech Problems in Children.* (The Salmon Memorial Lectures). New York, W. W. Norton.

ORTON, S. T., 1939: A neurological explanation of the reading disability. *Educ. Rec.* (Suppl. No. 12), *20*:58-68.

ORTON, S. T., 1942: Discussion of a paper by Dr. J. G. Lynn. *Arch. Neurol. Psychiat., (Chicago), 47*:1064.

ORTON, S. T., 1943: Visual functions in strephosymbolia. *Arch. Ophthal., (Chicago), 30*:707-713.

ORTON, S. T., AND GILLINGHAM, A., 1933: Special disability in writing. *Bull. Neurol. Inst. New York, 3*:1-32.

ORTON, S. T., AND TRAVIS, L. E., 1929: Studies in stuttering. *Arch. Neurol. Psychiat., (Chicago), 21*:61-68.

OSTWALD, P. F., 1964: Color hearing. *Arch. Gen. Psychiat. (Chicago), 11*:40-48.

PARK, G. E., 1948: Reading difficulty (dyslexia) from the ophthalmic point of view. *Amer. J. Ophthal., 31*:28-34.

PAVENSTEDT, E., *et al.,* 1962: Symposium on research in infancy and early childhood. *J. Amer. Acad. Child Psychiat., 1*:5-107.

PEARSON, G. H. J., 1952: A survey of learning difficulties in children. In: *The Psychoanalytic Study of the Child.* New York, International Universities Press, Vol. VII, pp. 324-341.

PEARSON, G. H. J., 1954: *Psychoanalysis and the Education of the Child.* New York, W. W. Norton.

PEARSON, G. H. J., AND ENGLISH, O. S., 1937: *Common Neuroses of Children and Adults.* New York, W. W. Norton.

PENFIELD, W., AND RASMUSSEN, T., 1950: *The Cerebral Cortex of Man.* New York, Macmillan.

PENFIELD, W., AND ROBERTS, L., 1959: *Speech and Brain-Mechanisms.* Princeton, Princeton Univ. Press.

PETERS, A., 1908: Ueber kongenitale Wortblindheit. *München Med. Wschr., 55*:1116 & 1239.

PIAGET, J., 1959: *The Language and Thought of the Child.* New York, Humanities Press.

POLLACK, M. F. W., AND PIEKARZ, J., 1963: *Reading Problems and Problem Readers.* New York, David McKay.

PRENTICE, N. M., AND SPERRY, B. M., 1965: Therapeutically oriented tutoring of children with primary neurotic learning inhibitions. *Amer. J. Orthopsychiat., 35*:521-531.

PRECHTL, H. F. R., 1962: Reading difficulties as a neurological problem in childhood. In: *Reading Disability: Progress and Research Needs in Dyslexia.* J. Money, Ed. Baltimore, Johns Hopkins Press, pp. 187-193.

RABINOVITCH, R. D., 1959: Reading and Learning Disabilities. In: *American Handbook of Psychiatry.* S. Arieta, Ed. New York, Basic Books, pp. 857-869.

RABINOVITCH, R. D., 1962: Dyslexia: Psychiatric Considerations. In: *Reading Disability: Progress and Research Needs in Dyslexia.* J. Money, Ed. Baltimore, Johns Hopkins Press, pp. 73-81.

RABINOVITCH, R. D., *et al.,* 1954: A research approach to reading retardation. In: *Neurology and Psychiatry of Childhood.* Baltimore, Williams & Wilkins, 363-396.

REED, J. C. AND AULD, F., JR., 1963: Learning and reading disturbances. In: *The Enclyclopedia of Mental Health.* A. Deutsch, Ed. New York, Franklin Watts, Vol. III, pp. 930-949.

REINHOLD, M., 1954: An analysis of agnosia. *Neurology, 4*:128-136.

REINHOLD, M., 1963: The effect of laterality on reading and writing. *Proc. Roy. Soc. Med., 56*:203-206.

Report of the San Francisco Curriculum Survey Committee. April 1, 1960. Prepared for the Board of Education.

RIESE, W., 1954: Auto-observation of aphasia. (*re* Lordat). *Bull. Hist. Med., 28*:237-242.

RIFE, D. C., 1951: Heredity and handedness. *Sci. Mon., 73*:188.

RIFE, D. C., 1955: Hand prints and handedness. *Amer. J. Hum. Genet., 7*:170-179.

ROBERTS, L., 1955: Handedness and cerebral dominance. *Trans. Amer. Neurol. Ass., 80*:143-160.

ROBINSON, H. M., 1956: *Why Pupils Fail in Reading.* Chicago, Univ. Chicago Press.

ROBINSON, H. M., 1964: Summary of investigations relating to reading. *The Reading Teacher, 17*:326-394.

ROSEN, V. H., 1955: Strephosymbolia: an intrasystemic disturbance of the synthetic function of the ego. In: *The Psychoanalytic Study of the Child.* New York, International Universities Press, Vol. X, pp. 83-99.

ROSWELL, F. G., 1954: Observations on causation and treatment of learning disabilities. *Amer. J. Orthopsychiat., 24*:784-788.

ROSWELL, F. G., AND NATCHEZ, G., 1964: *Reading Disability: Diagnosis and Treatment.* New York, Basic Books.

RUBENSTEIN, B. O., et al., 1959: Learning impotence: a suggested diagnotic category. *Amer. J. Orthopsychiat., 29*:315-323.

SAUNDERS, R. E., 1961: Psychotherapy with remedial reading. *Bull. Orton Soc., 11*:46.

SAUNDERS, R. E., 1962: Dyslexia: its phenomenology. In: *Reading Disability: Progress and Research Needs in Dyslexia.* J. Money, Ed. Baltimore, Johns Hopkins Press, pp. 35-45.

SAUNDERS, R. E., 1962: Emotional growth and reading growth. *Bull. Orton Soc., 12*:7-13.

SAUNDERS, R. E., 1965: Dyslexia: more than reading retardation. In: *Dyslexia in Special Education.* Monograph—Vol. I. Pomfret, Conn., The Orton Society, pp. 25-35.

SCHAPRINGER, A., 1906: Congenital wordblindness in pupils of the public schools. Paper read before the Section on Ophthalmology of the New York Academy of Medicine, February 19, 1906.

SCHIFFMAN, G., 1964: Early identification of reading disabilities: the responsibility of the public schools. *Bull. Orton Soc., 14*:42-44.

SCHILDER, P., 1944: Congenital alexia and its relation to optic perception. *J. Genet. Psychol., 65*:67-88.

SCHILDER, P., 1950: *Image and Appearance of the Human Body.* New York, International Universities Press.

SCHILDER, P., 1964: *Contributions to Developmental Neuropsychiatry.* L. Bender, Ed. New York, International Universities Press.

SCHMITT, C., 1918: Congenital word blindness or inability to read. *Elem. School J., 18*:680-700 & 757-769.

SCHREIBER, D., 1962: The school dropout—fugitive from failure. *Bull. Nat. Ass. Sec. School Prin., 46*:233-241.

SCHROCK, R., 1915: Uber kongenitale Wortblindheit. *Klin. Mbl. Augenheilk, 54*:167-184.

SHARPE, P., 1956: Teaching the strephosymbolic at the high school level. *Bull. Orton Soc., 6*:20-22.

SILVER, A. A., 1961: Diagnostic considerations in children with reading disability. *Bull. Orton Soc., 11*:5-11.

SILVER, A. A., AND HAGIN, R. A., 1960: Specific reading disability: delineation of the syndrome and relation to cerebral dominance. *Compr. Psychiat., 1*:126-134.

SILVER, A. A., AND HAGIN, R. A., 1964: Specific reading disability. *Amer. J. Orthopsychiat., 34*:95-102.

SILVER, A. A., AND HAGIN, R. A., 1965: Developmental language disability simulating mental retardation. *J. Amer. Acad. Child Psychiat., 4*:485-495.

SILVERMAN, J. S., *et al.*, 1959: Clinical findings in reading disability children. *Amer. J. Orthopsychiat., 29*:298-314.

SKYDSGAARD, H. B., 1942: *Den Konstitutionelle Dyslexi*. Copenhagen, Arnold Busck.

SLINGERLAND, B. H., 1964: *Screening Tests for Identifying Children with Specific Language Disability*. Cambridge, Mass., Educators Pubblishing Service.

SLINGERLAND, B. H., 1965: A public school program of prevention for young children with specific language disability. In: *Dyslexia in Special Education*. Monograph—Vol. I. Pomfret, Conn., The Orton Society, pp. 53-65.

SMITH, D. E. P., AND CARRIGAN, P. M., 1959: *The Nature of Reading Disability*. New York, Harcourt, Brace.

SOLMS, H., 1948: Beitrag zur Lehre von der sog, kongenitalen Wortblindheit. *Mschr. Psychiat. Neurol., 115*:1-54.

SOLOMAN, P., *et al.*, 1961: *Sensory Deprivation*. Cambridge, Harvard Univ. Press.

SPEARMAN, C. E., 1927: *The Abilities of Man*. London, Macmillan.

SPEARMAN, C. E., AND JONES, L. W., 1951: *Human Ability*. London, Macmillan.

SPERRY, B. M., *et al.*, 1952: Destructive fantasies in certain learning difficulties. *Amer. J. Orthopsychiat., 22*:356-365.

SPERRY, B. M., *et al.*, 1958: Renunciation and denial in learning difficulties. *Amer. J. Orthopsychiat., 28*:98-111.

SPERRY, B. M., *et al.*, 1959: The relation of motility to boys' learning problems. *Amer. J. Orthopsychiat., 28*:640-646.

SPERRY, R. W., 1961: Cerebral organization and behavior. *Science, 133*:1749-1757.

SPERRY, R. W., 1964: The great cerebral commissure. *Sci. Amer., 210*: 42-52.

STANGER, M. A., AND DONOHUE, E. K., 1937: *Prediction and Prevention of Reading Difficulties.* New York, Oxford Univ. Press.

STATTEN, T., 1953: Behavior patterns, reading disabilities, and EEG findings. *Amer. J. Psychiat., 110*:205-206.

STEPHENSON, S., 1904: Congenital word-blindness. *Lancet, 2*:827-828.

STEPHENSON, S., 1907: Six cases of congenital word-blindness affecting three generations of one family. *The Ophthalmoscope, 5*:482-484.

STERBA, E., 1943: On spelling. *Psychoanalyt. Rev., 30*:273-276.

STEWART, R. S., 1950: Personality maladjustment and reading achievement. *Amer. J. Orthopsychiat., 20*:410-417.

STRACHEY, J., 1930: Some unconscious factors in reading. *Int. J. Psychoanal., 11*:322-332.

STRAUSS, A. A., AND KEPHART, N. C., 1955: *Psychopathology and Education of the Brain-Injured Child.* New York, Grune and Stratton.

STUART, M., 1963: *Neurological Insights into Teaching.* Palo Alto, Pacific Books.

SUBIRANA, A., 1964: The problem of cerebral dominance: the relationship between handedness and language function. *Bull. Orton Soc., 14*:45-66.

SYLVESTER, E., AND KUNST, M. S., 1943: Psychodynamic aspects of the reading problem. *Amer. J. Orthopsychiat., 13*:69-76.

TERMAN, L. M., 1925: *Mental and Physical Traits of a Thousand Gifted Children, Genetic Studies of Genius.* Stanford, Stanford Univ. Press.

TERMAN, S., AND WALCUTT, C. C., 1958: *Reading: Chaos and Cure.* New York, McGraw-Hill.

THOMAS, C. J., 1905: Congenital word-blindness and its treatment. *The Ophthalmoscope, 3*:380-385.

THOMAS, C. J., 1908: The aphasias of childhood and educational hygiene. *Public Health, London, 21*:90-100.

THOMPSON, L. J., 1947: Special disabilities in children with organic brain pathology. *N. Carolina Med. J., 8*:224-228.

THOMPSON, L. J., 1956: Specific reading disability— strephosymbolia. *Bull. Orton Soc., 6*:3-9.

THOMPSON, L. J., 1964: Did Lee Harvey Oswald have a specific language disability? *Bull. Orton Soc., 14*:89-90.

THULINE, H. C., 1964: Color-vision defects in American school children. *JAMA, 188*:514-518.

TIEN, H. C., 1960: Organic integrity test (OIT). *Arch. Gen. Psychiat. (Chicago), 3*:43-52.

Tien, H. C., and Williams, M. W., 1965: Organic integrity test (OIT) in children. *Arch. Gen. Psychiat. (Chicago), 12*:159-165.

Tjossem, T. D., *et al.*, 1962: An investigation of reading difficulty in young children. *Amer. J. Psychiat., 118*:1104-1113.

Tolor, A., and Schulberg, H. C., 1963: *An Evaluation of the Bender-Gestalt Test.* Springfield, Thomas.

Tomkins, C., 1963: The last skill acquired. *The New Yorker Magazine, 39*:127-157.

Town, C. H., 1911: Congenital asphasia. *The Psychological Clinic,* November 15, 1911.

Traxler, A. E., 1941: Ten years of research in reading. *Educ. Rec. Bull.,* No. 32. New York, Educational Records Bureau. Also, as above, No. 46, 1946, No. 64, 1955, and No. 75, 1961.

Triggs, F. O., 1960: *Reading.* Privately printed by the author, Kingscote, Apt. 3G, 419 W. 119 St., New York City.

Tulchin, S. H., 1935: Emotional factors in reading disabilities in school children. *J. Educ. Psychol., 26*:443-454.

Van Riper, C., 1964: The speech pathologist looks at reading. *The Reading Teacher, 17*:505-510.

Vernon, M. D., 1957: *Backwardness in Reading.* Cambridge, Cambridge Univ. Press.

Vorhaus, P., 1952: Rorschach configurations associated with reading disability. *J. Proj. Tech., 16*:3-13.

Wagenheim, L., 1959: Learning problems associated with childhood diseases contracted at age two. *Amer. J. Orthopsychiat., 29*:102-110.

Walcutt, C. C., Ed., 1961: *Tomorrow's Illiterates.* Boston, Little, Brown.

Walker, L., and Cole, E. M., 1965: Familial patterns of expression of specific reading disability in a population sample. *Bull. Orton Soc., 15*:12-24.

Walters, R. H., *et al.*, 1961: A study of reading disability. *J. Consult. Psychol., 25*:277-283.

Walton, J. N., *et al.*, 1962: Clumsy children: developmental apraxia and agnosia. *Brain, 85*:603-612.

Washburn, R. W., 1929: A study of the smiling and laughing of infants in the first year of life. *Gen. Psychol. Monogr., 6*:403-537.

Wepman, J. M., 1958: *The Auditory Discrimination Test.* Chicago, Language Research Associates.

Wepman, J. M., 1960: Auditory discrimination, speech and reading. *Elem. School J., 60*:325-333.

Wepman, J. M., 1961: The interrelationship of hearing, speech and reading. *The Reading Teacher, 14*:245-247.

WEPMAN, J. M., 1962: Dyslexia: its relationship to language acquisition and concept formation. In: *Reading Disability: Progress and Research Needs in Dyslexia.* J. Money, Ed. Baltimore, Johns Hopkins Press, pp. 179-187.

WEPMAN, J. M., *et al.*, 1960: Studies in aphasia: background and theoretical formulations. *J. Speech and Hearing Disorders, 25*:324-331.

WERNICKE, C., 1874: *Die aphasische Symptomencomplex.* Breslau, Taschen.

WILBUR, H. B., 1867: Aphasia. *Amer. J. Insanity, 24*:1-28.

WILGUS, S., 1922: Alexia (cortical word-blindness) with agraphia in a child. *Illinois Med. J., 42*:291-295.

WILLMER, E. N., 1946: *Retinal Structure and Colour Vision.* Cambridge, Cambridge Univ. Press.

WITKIN, H. A., 1954: *Personality through Perception.* New York, Harper.

WITKIN, H. A., 1962: *Psychological Differentiation; Studies of Development.* New York, John Wiley.

WITTY, P. A., 1947: Reading retardation in the secondary school. *J. Exper. Educ., 15*:314-317.

WITTY, P. A., AND KOPEL, D., 1936: Factors associated with the etiology of reading disability. *J. Educ. Psychol., 27*:222-230.

WOOD, N. E., 1960: *Language Disorders in Children.* Monograph, Soc. Res. Child Devel., Vol. XXV, No. 3, Lafayette, Ind., Purdue Univ.

X. (ANONYMOUS), 1936: Experiences of a sufferer from word-blindness. *Brit. J. Ophth., 20*:73-76.

YOUNG, R. A., 1938: Case studies in reading disability. *Amer. J. Orthopsychiat., 8*:230-254.

ZANGWILL, O. L., 1960: *Cerebral Dominance and its Relation to Psychological Function.* Edinburgh, Oliver & Boyd.

ZANGWILL, O. L., 1962: Dyslexia in relation to cerebral dominance. In: *Reading Disability: Progress and Research Needs in Dyslexia.* Baltimore, Johns Hopkins Press, pp. 103-115.

ZANGWILL, O. L., 1964: The current status of cerebral dominance. In: *Disorders of Communication.* Baltimore, Williams & Wilkins, pp. 103-119.

AUTHOR INDEX

[195]

Saunders, R. E., xiv, 117
Schapringer, A., 17
Schilder, P., 41, 45, 82
Schmitt, C., 24
Schreiber, D., 98
Schulberg, H. C., 39
Silver, A. A., 44, 45, 54
Silverman, J. S., 77-79
Skydsgaard, H., 47
Slingerland, B. H., 160
Solms, H., 47
Solnit, A. J., 83
Sperry, B. M., 80, 84
Sperry, R. W., 108
Staver, N., 80
Stengel, E., 11
Stephenson, S., 16
Sterba, E., 55
Strachey, J., 66
Subirana, A., 87
Sylvester, E., 72

Terman, L. M., 150
Thomas, C. J., 16
Thuline, H. C., 141
Tolor, A., 39
Triggs, F. O., 161

Ulrich, D., 80

Van Loan, M., 85
Velie, L., 97

Wagenheim, L., 111
Walcutt, C. C., xiv, 89
Walker, L., 45
Walters, R. H., 85
Walton, J. N., 58
Warrington, E. K., 50
Wernicke, C., 8
Wexler, D., 110
Wilbur, H. B., 13
Willmer, E. N., 140
Witty, P. A., xiv

X. (anonymous), 112-115

Zangwill, O. L., 107

SUBJECT INDEX

A

Abilities, special, 13, 24, 55, 67,
139, 143, 146, 149
Adult cases, 112, 116, 117-121
Agenesis, 14, 16, 24, 28, 32, 100,
110
Aggression, 68, 72, 79
Agnosia, 33, 101
Alexia, 3, 10, 17, 33, 103
Ambidexterity, 34, 37, 107
Ambilaterality, 106, 107
Amblyopia, 17
Angular gyrus, 29, 102, 104
Aphasia, vii (see Chapter I)
Apraxia, 32, 33 (see also
Dyspraxia)
Autobiographies, 112-116

B

Bender-Gestalt test, 38
Biochemical considerations, 109
Body image, 32, 39, 40, 82, 102,
143
Brain damage, viii, 3 ,43, 52, 83,
109, 111, 155
Broca's era, 6

C

Castration, 65, 68, 71, 74, 77
Chess, 146
Childhood schizophrenia, 42
Classification of reading disability,
xvii, 52, 155
Color hearing, 144
Color vision, 140, 141
Corpus Callosum, 102, 108

D

Delinquency, vii, 44
Dominance, xi, 30, 32, 35, 37, 40,
44, 54, 103, 105-109
Dropouts, vii, 98

Dyscalculia, 49, 50
Dyslexia, acquired, 131
Dyslexia, developmental
classification, xvii, 52, 155
clinical manifestations, xii
(see also Chapter VIII)
definition of, vii, x
etiology of, xi, 21, 71, 86
incidence of, ix, xii-xvi
prediction of, 44, 159-161
Dyspraxia, 53, 57, 58, 145

E

Edipal (oedipal) factors, 71, 76,
77, 80, 84
Educational profiles, 128
Ego development, 68, 75, 82, 83
Eidetic imagery, 25
Electroencephalograms (EEG),
42, 110, 156
Emotional factors, xi, xviii, 34, 43,
57, 157 (see also Chapter V)
Environmental factors, xi (see also
Chapter VI)
Exhibitionism, 64, 73
Extension test, 45, 54

F

Foreign languages, viii, 16, 47, 87
Freud's concepts, 9-11, 61-64

G

Gerstmann's syndrome, 49, 53, 102
Gestalt psychology, 38, 53, 90
Gifted, 13, 149, 151

H

Handedness, 34, 35, 37, 54, 106
Heredity, xvii, 28, 29, 34, 37, 44,
48, 49, 53, 129
Heterophasia, 117